MARK M. FAGAN

UPBUILDERS

BY

LINCOLN STEFFENS

Introduction by Earl Pomeroy

UNIVERSITY OF WASHINGTON PRESS

SEATTLE AND LONDON

TO MY FATHER

JOSEPH STEFFENS, SACRAMENTO, CALIFORNIA

FOREWORD

Is IT hope that is wanted? Wide-eyed optimism? Here it is, in this book. And faith?
Faith in democracy? It is here. And a hint
as to what one man can do? Here it is. Here
are faith in the many men; hope for all; and,
for the few who think they would like to lead,
encouragement, the inspiration of humble
examples, and some notion of how to proceed.
This book contains five straight, true stories,
each telling what one straight, true man has done
with democracy, and through them all shines
forth at last one truth upon which, as a foundation, Man can build with and for Mankind:

*Wherever the people have found a leader who
was loyal to them; brave; and not too far ahead,
there they have followed him, and there has been
begun the solution of our common problem; the
problem of the cities, states, and nations — the
problem of civilized living in human communities.*

It has not mattered much who the leader was,
or what. His religion has made no difference,
nor his social status; nor his financial condition;
nor his party. Mark Fagan — first in my heart,

as he is in my book — Mark is an Irish Catholic
Republican undertaker, but he carried Democratic Jersey City three times running. Everett
Colby who turned upside down Essex, the county
next to Mayor Fagan's — Senator Colby was a
Wall Street broker; the heir of a rich railroad
builder; a college graduate; and he looks his
part. But to the voters of Essex the boy looked
sincere, and they helped him to beat his boss,
and theirs. Ben Lindsey was a Democratic
politician and a County Judge, when he began
to do justice to children, and when, at the last
Denver election (1908), both the old parties
and the "best" people, both men and women
(who vote in Colorado), and some of the larg-
est churches, all "went back" on the "kids'
judge."—

"I went to the people," he wrote me. "I went
into the shops and the workers received me
with open arms. . . . It was a glorious
victory! . . . The Mary Murphys in the
mills, the men there, and the kids in the street
— the people won it."

W. S. U'Ren was a blacksmith in Colorado,
before he became, while a visitor in Oregon, a
lobbyist there, the people's lobbyist; and, as
such, began to hammer out legislative tools for
the use of democracy everywhere. This strange,

great legislator does not run for office, so there is no way of proving that the voters of Oregon appreciate his service, but they elect his laws, and that's all he asks. He leads and the people follow his leadership.

But the most amazing example of the democracy of democracy is the case of Rudolph Spreckels. A capitalist, the president of the First National Bank of San Francisco, and a millionaire in his own right, this young man is a member of the rich, aggressive, unpopular Spreckels family of California, and, personally autocratic, unbending, hard, it did seem impossible that he should be able to lead the fight against the low vice and the high financial corruption of the so-called Labour administration of his city. And most of his own kind of people opposed, and they still doubt him, but the common people, the rank and file of the uneducated, anonymous mob — they followed him. They, too, jeered at first, and he never replied or explained. Francis J. Heney did; the prosecutor told the people everything. But Spreckels did his work in his private, business-like, undemocratic way; and the people watched him from afar. And, making thus at long range their quiet study of the man, they were able to penetrate class and party prejudice and a cloud of evidence as thick as a Pacific fog —

somehow, the people perceived that this Spreckels was "all right."

The people are pretty wise. They are ignorant, and they can be and often are, corrupted, but not many educated individuals are as wise as the mass of men when individuals haven't tampered with them.

"Give me a jury of thieves," said a well-known district attorney, "and, if I can keep them apart from any influence excepting that of the law and the evidence in court, they will convict a guilty thief of theft."

The world's wise doubt the world's wisdom, and they have reason to; they differ very, very often; and, of course, the wise individual decides, and he tells the mute masses, that he is right. But, Euripides observed long ago in wise old Greece, that

" The world's wise are not wise."

And history and observation bear out the poet and the district attorney. Juries are juster than judges; they feel through the facts for the human story and through the letter of the law for the spirit thereof. The public is fairer than the press; the readers allow for the bias of the newspaper. An audience is more open-minded than the critics. "Have I had a good time?" the playgoer asks and the

question is more fundamental than the critics'
criterion of art. And all the world knows that
the world has welcomed, since Euripides, not
only other artists (Wagner, for example), but
prophets (Jesus, for example), and scientific
discoverers (Darwin, for example), who were
opposed by the authorities in art, church, state,
and science.

Uninformed and misinformed; pauperized or
over-worked; misled or betrayed by their leaders
— financial, industrial, political and ecclesias-
tical, the people are suspicious, weary, and very,
very busy, but they are, none the less, the first,
last, and best appeal in all great human cases.
Certainly the first rule for the political reformer
is: Go to the voters. And the reason seems to
be, not that the people are better than their
betters, but that they are more disinterested;
they are not possessed by possessions; they have
not so many "things" and "friends." They
can afford, they are free to be fair. And, though
each individual in the great crowd lacks some
virtues, they all together have what no individual has, a combination of all the virtues.

Mercy, for example, and forgiveness. It's
wonderful how the people will pardon error.
Mistakes don't count for very much in the
long run and the people, who make so many

themselves, they seem to know that better than the wise men who should know why it is so.

Everett Colby had served the boss of Essex (and the bosses of the boss) faithfully, ignorantly and, therefore, innocently, during three sessions of the legislature, till he saw the evil thereof, and appealed to the people to beat the system. He went, as Mark Fagan advised, and as we have just seen Judge Lindsey go, to the shops. The workers, aware of his antecedents, heard him coldly. But when he had finished his first speech one of his audience asked a question. This worker wanted to know if Mr. Colby "hadn't voted in the assembly" for a certain notoriously bad bill.

"Yes," Mr. Colby answered, quick and straight. "And not only for that bill," he said. "I think, if you will look up my record that you will find me introducing, voting or speaking for nearly every bad measure of that sort which came up in my time. But, as I have been trying to explain, I didn't understand those things. I've only just come to understand them. But I do think I understand them now."

That was enough. The word was passed "down the line" that this young rich fellow was "on the level," and that was all the voters of Essex wanted to know. They elected him.

They forgave his transgressions as they would
have theirs forgiven them. They gave Colby
another chance, just as they will a drunkard or a
thief or a captain of industry. Indeed, there is
reason for thinking that Colby was helped by
his bad record of errors. The people suspect
(and very wisely, too) all superiority, and Colby's
candid, free confession of ignorance and guilt,
made him a fit representative of his neighbours
in Essex County, New Jersey, U. S. A.

Senator Colby has been retired since; and Mark
Fagan was beaten; and Lindsey may be, and
Spreckels. "Republics are ungrateful," Mr.
Dooley quotes, and he adds: "That's why they
are Republics." The people are not constant.
And the forces of corruption are. In Jersey
the "interests" became alarmed at the issues
the Colby-Fagan "New Idea" movement was
raising: taxation; representative government; the
direct election of the United States Senators;
home rule; etc., so they threw into the situation
a "moral issue," the liquor traffic. This is an
important question, but it is so important that
to drop it into a reform movement with other
issues up, is to break up that other movement,
and — fail to solve the liquor question. If I
were a political boss, in danger of losing my
crown, I would get the church to come out

against the saloon. That would save me, and it would not cost the saloons very much.

The liquor issue in Jersey checked, but it did not stop reform in that state. Mr. Colby has quit, for awhile, but Mark Fagan and most of the other Jersey leaders, have gone on fighting. As I am writing these lines, Mark is preparing to run again for Mayor of Jersey City. And Mr. Heney says Spreckels can't quit; and I say Ben Lindsey can't; and W. S. U'Ren —impossible!

It's hard labour; it's the hardest work in the world; and the least steady, and the most never-ending; but there's a fascination about the service of the public which holds men. It takes courage, and self-sacrifice; patience and eternal vigilance; faith and hope and human understanding; and it costs pain and disappointment and sorrow. I have seen strong men break down and weep like children because, forsooth, I had said, out of kindness and only half-believing it then, that some day, after they were dead, men would acknowledge and, ceasing to suspect their motives, might appreciate their devotion to men. It's an un-grateful career, politics is. But — and here's some more optimism for the optimists that are not mere cheerful idiots: here's a truth I would like to shout so that it might be heard some 1909 years away:

The happiest men I know in all this unhappy life of ours, are those leaders who, brave, loyal, and sometimes in tears, are serving their fellow-men.

And who are their fellow-men that accept their service? We are, you and I; we are the people who beat, but who also elect these leaders of ours. And what are we? Well, if I listen to my own thoughts, and my own conscience, and to my own heart, and yours; and if you hearken only to yours, and mine, we may not recognize the voice of God. But, if we heed, as Mark Fagan must, and Ben Lindsey, and Rudolph Spreckels, the proud; if we should have to hear and abide by the votes of the great, mixed, smelly mass of us, then we, too, should both be and obey the voice of humanity. And that is divinity enough for Man, and for the little leaders of men.

LINCOLN STEFFENS.

Boston, May 15, 1909.

CONTENTS

ILLUSTRATIONS

INTRODUCTION

WHEN Lincoln Steffens wrote the articles that went into *Upbuilders*, 1905-8,[1] he was probably better known than he would be until he published his *Autobiography* a quarter of a century later (1931). Norman Hapgood later remembered him as the "best general reporter" in New York City in the 1890's. Shortly after Steffens joined *McClure's* in 1901, he began the series of articles on municipal corruption that went into *The Shame of the Cities* (1904) and *The Struggle for Self-Government* (1906). Steffens later referred to the first of them, on "Tweed Days in St. Louis," as "the first muckraking article."[2]

[1] "A Servant of God and the People" [Mark Fagan], *McClure's Magazine*, XXVI (January, 1906), 297-308; "The Gentleman from Essex" [Everett Colby], *ibid.* (February, 1906), 420-33; "Ben B. Lindsey: The Just Judge," *ibid.*, XXVII (October, 1906), 563-82, XXVIII (November, December, 1906), 74-88, 162-76; "Rudolph Spreckels," *American Magazine*, LXV (February, 1908), 390-402; "U'Ren, The Law Giver," *ibid.*, LXV (March, 1908), 527-40.

[2] Norman Hapgood, *The Changing Years: Reminiscences...* (New York, 1930), pp. 107-9; *The Autobiography of Lincoln Steffens* (New York, 1931), p. 373.

McClure's was already popular; with Steffens, Ida M. Tarbell, Ray Stannard Baker, and others, it gained new influence. They stood, *Current Literature* said, for "a new kind of journalism, which deals with the burning issues of the day with as much vigor as the daily newspaper, but with a thoroughness which makes its record a part of our permanent political literature." Steffens' articles had "done more to awaken the American conscience to civic duty than anything else that has been written in many years." The new journalism continued popular despite the impatience with the more sensational literature of exposure that Theodore Roosevelt expressed when he denounced the muckrakers in March, 1906. Steffens and his associates on *McClure's* felt confident enough of public favor to buy the *American Magazine* later that same year. Steffens himself became as newsworthy as the bosses he exposed, and much in demand as a lecturer. Although a series of syndicated articles on Congress that he wrote was a flat failure, the common complaint of editors was not that they were too sensational or censorious but rather that they lacked the color and personal detail that the public expected of him.[3]

[3] *Current Literature,* XXXVI (June, 1904), 610-11; *Autobiography,* pp. 357-73, 581. Complaints appear in the Steffens Papers (MSS in the Columbia University Library, New York).

Steffens did not significantly revise the seven articles on the five reformers of *Upbuilders:*[4] they appeared in the book almost unchanged except for paragraphing. And each has remained a standard source, probably the most commonly cited single source, on each of the reformers. Of the five, apparently only Everett Colby complained of inaccuracy to Steffens, and he referred only to a brief statement in the foreword, that Colby had "quit, for awhile" (*Upbuilders,* p. xiv), rather than to the

[4] The publisher's announcement referred to five "upbuilders" —men who "have fought for the rest of us"—but listed six names, including that of William Randolph Hearst. Hearst was candidate for mayor of New York City in 1909; he had been a member of Congress (1903-7) and candidate for governor when Steffens wrote an article on him in 1906. Apparently, at one stage Steffens planned to substitute La Follette for Hearst. *Publisher's Weekly,* No. 1968 (October 16, 1909), p. 1075; Steffens, "Hearst, The Man of Mystery," *American Magazine,* LXIII (November, 1906), 3-22; Steffens Papers, Henry M. Lanier to Steffens, March 31, April 28, 1909 (unless otherwise described, all letters to or from Steffens are from the Steffens Papers). The title of the book was Lanier's suggestion. Like the article on Spreckels (see below, pp. 244-84), the article on Hearst shows Steffens' interest in undemocratic qualities. In *The Industrial Republic: A Study of the America of Ten Years Hence* (New York, 1907), pp. 199-200, Steffens' friend, Upton Sinclair, compared Hearst with Abraham Lincoln and described him as "the man of the coming hour," the most likely and most interesting prospect for the Democratic presidential nomination in 1912. Sinclair later admitted, "I have never reprinted this book, because of the embarrassing fact that I had prophesied Hearst as a radical president of the United States. He really looked like a radical then...." Sinclair, *American Outpost: A Book of Reminiscences* (New York, 1932), p. 185.

article itself, for which he had specifically sent his thanks.[5] The historian of the progressive movement in New Jersey drew on Steffens and found his accounts consistent with other evidence, including interviews with Colby and Mark Fagan.[6]

The articles also reveal significant stages in Steffens' own intellectual development. In his *Autobiography*, he delighted in describing the complexities of his travels along what Granville Hicks called "a strictly American path to Communist conclusions," but also sometimes remembered less than happened. Ever an artistic raconteur, sometimes he also remembered more. Paul C. Smith asked him how it was that in his conversational duels with the great, recalled verbatim, " '*you* always come out on top.' He smiled and said, 'Well, damn it, I'm a reporter. *I* always did!' "[7]

[5] Everett Colby to Steffens, January 27, 1906, September 20, 24, 1909. According to Ransom E. Noble, who interviewed Colby in 1935, Colby said that Steffens' article was accurate but that Colby "had [a] row with Steffens" for referring to Percy Rockefeller (*Upbuilders,* p. 57), feeling that since Rockefeller was "wholly innocent," his name should not appear.

[6] Ransom E. Noble, *New Jersey Progressivism Before Wilson* (Princeton, N.J., 1946) ; Arthur S. Link, *Woodrow Wilson: The Road to the White House* (Princeton, N.J., 1947), pp. 135-36. According to Noble in 1966, Fagan said in 1935 that the article was probably accurate, that Steffens had a keen mind and saw how things really were. Noble recalled feeling "that after months of painstaking research I was coming up with essentially the same picture of New Jersey politics that Lincoln Steffens had drawn some 30 years before."

Steffens' associates commonly described his early work as essentially factual, as impartial as Miss Tarbell's *History of the Standard Oil Company*. Reviewing *The Shame of the Cities*, William Allen White said that Steffens had made "an important step in the scientific study of government in America. . . . And the best thing about it is that . . . it merely presents facts, without trying to form theories about them . . ., with no reforms to promise or suggest. . . ." Steffens himself sometimes insisted on his detachment as a journalist. He indignantly refused to give to President Roosevelt evidence of misconduct in the government of the United States before he published it: "I must report to my readers, the public, and not to anyone else. . . ." Hutchins Hapgood thought that Steffens kept himself aloof not so much because of journalistic ethics as because of his own ego, because he enjoyed being both close to events and above them: he was "unconsciously too self-preservative to commit himself intensely to any feeling that took from his fully conscious ambitions."[8]

---

[7] Granville Hicks, "Lincoln Steffens: He Covered the Future: The Prototype of a Fellow-Traveler," *Commentary*, XIII (February, 1952), 147; Paul C. Smith, *Personal File* (New York, 1964), p. 149; on the conversations, cf. Brand Whitlock to Julian Street, January 4, 1933, in Whitlock, *Letters and Journal* . . ., ed. Allan Nevins (New York, 1936), I, 538.

[8] White in *McClure's*, XXIII (June, 1904), 221; Steffens

According to the story of his lifelong search for truth that is the theme of the *Autobiography,* Steffens had concluded by about 1904 or 1905 that political corruption was a consequence not of men or character but of pressure. "But I did not, I could not, write that yet. I still believed . . . that there were some kinds of men that would neither buy nor sell and that the job was to get such men into power" (p. 469). In fact, Steffens had already written of the futility of electing good men, the inexorability of the "boss system," which he called "the result of the commercial development of the country," before he joined *McClure's,*[9] and S. S. McClure was complaining soon after the series of articles on cities began, "he makes every fact bend to this notion."[10] Theodore Roosevelt protested that Steffens ignored the overriding importance of morality, that he distorted details to fit them into an "impressionistic picture," and that in speaking of "the system" he lapsed into the single-minded religious enthusiasm of the Fifth Monarchy men of Oliver Cromwell's time.[11]

---

to Roosevelt, March 6, 1908; Hutchins Hapgood, *A Victorian in the Modern World* (New York, 1939), pp. 277, 583-84.

[9] "Great Types of Modern Business, VI—Politics," *Ainslee's Magazine,* VIII (October, 1901), 217, 219, 220.

[10] S. S. McClure to John S. Phillips, March 20, 1903, quoted in Peter Lyon, *Success Story: The Life and Times of S. S. McClure* (New York, 1963), p. 219.

[11] Theodore Roosevelt to Steffens, November 4, 1907 and June 5, 1908, in Roosevelt, *Letters . . .* (Cambridge, Mass.,

It is difficult to read the articles and Steffens' correspondence without concluding that he had committed himself to reform and reformers more than he remembered in later years. His enthusiasms continued for a few years unembarrassedly to embrace both determinism and reform, and to leave little room for cold science. "I am not a scientist," he said in the foreword to *The Shame of the Cities* (1904). "My purpose was ... to see if the shameful facts ... would not burn through our civic shamefulness and set fire to American pride" (pp. 17-18). At that stage he emphasized the power of "the system." In later articles, including those in *Upbuilders,* he concentrated on those who challenged it. *Upbuilders* was, according to B. O. Flower, "a missionary for civic righteousness and democratic advance." Steffens "writes of all with contagious enthusiasm," said *Living Age.*[12]

Steffens had always established close relationships with people in the news, whether simply for the information they might give him or for his personal satisfaction. "He cultivated the 'big fellows' and always knew what was going on," Upton Sinclair recalled.[13] During his muckraking days, he became

1951-54), V, 829-30, VI, 1052.

[12] B. O. Flower, in *Twentieth Century,* I (December, 1909), 260; *Living Age,* CCLXIII (November 6, 1909), 379.

[13] Upton Sinclair, *My Lifetime in Letters* (Columbia, Mo., 1960), p. 50.

especially close to some of the reformers he reported on, well beyond the call of professional duty.

In his relations with Fagan and Colby, Steffens was more the impartial reporter than with any of the other five reformers of *Upbuilders*. He lost touch with them first, and he strangely ignored their later careers when he mentioned them in his *Autobiography* (p. 500). At the time of the articles, Colby thanked Steffens with more than ordinary appreciation for accurate publicity: "I am sure it will help and make me feel more than ever the responsibility of our movement. We will not disappoint you and your many readers but will keep up the fight until the end." Colby joined Steffens in drawing Robert M. La Follette into George Record's campaign for the Senate in 1906. When Fagan failed to win re-election in 1909, Steffens referred to him among "my friends who ... were beaten this year. ..."[14]

Steffens had stronger ties with some of the westerners, and especially with Ben Lindsey, La Fol-

[14] Colby to Steffens, January 27, 1906; and cf. *ibid.,* October 20, 1905. "The help you are giving us is beyond calculation," wrote an associate. "The picture of Colby ... is most cleverly calculated to spur him on." Alden Freeman to Steffens, January 28, 1906. Belle C. and Fola La Follette, *Robert M. La Follette* ... (New York, 1953), I, 215; Steffens to Joseph Steffens, November 13, 1909, *Letters of Lincoln Steffens* (New York, 1938), I, 230.

lette, Tom Johnson, and Brand Whitlock and other associates of Johnson in Ohio. He later told how, as a guest in the La Follettes' home in 1904, he had met Mrs. La Follette's friendliness coldly because he wanted to write an article out of nothing but what La Follette's enemies were giving him: "... any friendly intimacy between me and the La Follettes might spoil the effect I wished to get" (*Autobiography*, p. 457). Likewise, in Ohio he was at first the impartial investigator, "exact, painstaking, unflinchingly accurate," Frederic C. Howe recalled. But "Steffens changed after that. ... Under the influence of Tom Johnson he came to believe in the single tax." He became a warm friend and ally of La Follette, helping him to raise money for his campaign for re-election to the Senate in 1910, conferring in the inner circle of his supporters for the presidency in 1912. And as a single taxer he became a member of the Joseph Fels Fund Commission in 1909, with Johnson and Howe. "We were a humorous group who did not take very seriously what we were doing," Steffens recalled in his *Autobiography* (p. 642); but he remembered more detachment than his associates noted at the time. "Lincoln Steffens is as convinced a Single Taxer as you will find anywhere in this country," said Louis F. Post in 1910, when Steffens served on both the Publicity Bureau and the Lecture Department. The single tax was a link to Colby and other reformers in New Jersey of whom he wrote, and to William S. U'Ren, as well as to Whitlock, Howe, and Johnson.[15]

He had in fact become influential as a reformer, and not merely a reporter of reform; and his fame extended beyond the more sophisticated centers of metropolitan journalism. "Wherever he goes it is expected that his mission is to dig up corruption in politics and government," observed the Oregon City *Enterprise* when Steffens arrived to visit U'Ren early in 1907, "and by the aid of the publicity which his forceful pen can give, to help remedy the evils." Soon after he arrived at Denver to write on Ben Lindsey in 1906, he had entered into reform politics in Colorado. Edward P. Costigan (later senator) and others advised Steffens what to say in the interests of the cause—and expressed dismay when he encouraged Lindsey to disregard them and set out on his own course. Steffens' first article on Lindsey, which he had sent to Lindsey for corrections,

[15] Frederic C. Howe, *Confessions of a Reformer* (New York, 1925), pp. 182-84; La Follette, *Robert M. La Follette*, I, 220, 299, 389-91; Mary Fels, *Joseph Fels: His Life-Work* (New York, 1916), p. 186. In his *Autobiography* (pp. 641-44), Steffens discusses the single tax only as a project that Fels asked Steffens to help him to promote, not as an idea to which he and Johnson and Howe committed themselves. *Single Tax Conference Held in New York City November 19 and 20, 1910* ... (Cincinnati, 1911), pp. 11, 29; Arthur N. Young, *The Single Tax Movement in the United States* (Princeton, N.J., 1916), p. 243.

became campaign material in Lindsey's race for the governorship: he ordered ten thousand copies. In his enthusiasm Steffens went so far as to try to persuade E. W. Scripps to endow Lindsey with an income that would free him to pursue his political plans.[16]

Steffens described himself as more of a central figure in the progressive movement of California than he was in Colorado or on the Fels Fund Commission. Again he recalled both influence and amused detachment: "They were fun, those meetings of that board of strategy.... I labored humorously, and I think pleasantly, for the exposure in San Francisco of the universal state of business corruption to show What was hurting us, not Who." Meanwhile, at the offices of the *American Magazine*, John Phillips, the editor, worried over Steffens' partisanship and reminded him that it was not his job to help Francis Heney to work out his problems in San Francisco.[17] Ultimately Steffens be-

[16] Oregon City *Enterprise*, March 15, 1907; Costigan to Steffens, July 4, 1906; J. H. Carsey to Steffens, September 29, 1906; Lindsey to Steffens, December 20, 1909; E. W. Scripps, *I Protest: Selected Disquisitions of E. W. Scripps,* ed. Oliver Knight (Madison, Wis., 1966), pp. 481-82.

[17] *Autobiography*, p. 557. Writing to his sister, Laura, he said, "It's interesting to see these political conversions of men like Spreckels; they are something like religious conversions.... But I don't know. I'm only watching and learning." November 13, 1910, in *Letters*, I, 254; Irving G. Cheslaw, "An Intellectual

came a public figure in the trials of the brothers McNamara and of Clarence Darrow.

Yet it was in California, his boyhood home, that Steffens most signally lost touch with reform and reformers. He associated himself with those who ended on the periphery of power. His principal articles on graft in San Francisco featured Heney and his associate in the prosecution, William J. Burns, the detective. He was never close to Hiram Johnson, who became the leading figure when a bullet removed Heney from the courtroom. Rudolph Spreckels, whom he cited in the foreword to *Upbuilders* as "the most amazing example of the democracy of democracy" (p. ix), soon fell out with other reformers in the state and went on to new interests. Steffens continued to correspond with Heney, Fremont Older, and others of Spreckels' friends for a while—as late as 1910 he was carrying messages to Roosevelt for the California progressives[18]—but without influence in either Sacramento or Oyster Bay he was miscast for liaison. Then his involvement in the trials in Los Angeles in 1911-12 cut drastically into his reputation as either a reformer or an impartial reporter of reform. "Having identified myself with a 'cause,'" he wrote later, "my

Biography of Lincoln Steffens" (unpublished Ph.D. thesis, Columbia University, 1952), p. 83.

[18] Meyer Lissner to Steffens, June 13, 1910.

name suggested propaganda, labor propaganda to capitalists and treason, interference, folly to labor" (*Autobiography*, p. 690).

Steffens' work ceased to interest editors, as he said, at about the same time that he lost contact with the main currents of American politics, and interest in them. After Los Angeles he went from Mexico in 1914, to Russia in 1917, and then to Italy. He had hoped to republish some of his other magazine articles, such as the two on Heney, but he never did. His next book, *Moses in Red* (1926), marked his movement well beyond reform.

Each of Steffens' five subjects was near the height of his success or fame as a reformer; each but one (U'Ren) was in his thirties when Steffens wrote on him, and younger than Steffens himself. Curiously, it is the article on Spreckels, who did least in politics, that came closest to anticipating Steffens' later turn of mind—the fascination that he found in Benito Mussolini and other dictators: Steffens dwells on his "autocratic, unbending, hard, ... undemocratic" ways (p. ix) as a potential boss rather than as a democrat.[19]

Mark M. Fagan (1869-1955) had been mayor of Jersey City since 1902. "In New Jersey," Roose-

---

[19] Steffens was interested in similar qualities in Hearst. Cf. note 4, above.

velt greeted the news of his re-election in 1905, "it
looks as if there had been a genuine triumph of the
right kind of Republicanism within the party itself."
The next year, with Everett Colby and George L.
Record, Fagan failed in his attempt to nominate
reform (New Idea) candidates for the legislature,
and then, after declaring for municipal ownership,
he lost to the Democratic candidate (1907). He
lost again in 1909. In 1912 he refused to join Record in supporting Roosevelt for the presidency, instead endorsing Governor Woodrow Wilson, who
had appointed him to the Hudson County Board
for the Equalization of Taxes in 1911. He won a
four-year term as president-mayor and director of
public affairs of Jersey City in 1913, despite the
refusal of Joseph Tumulty, Wilson's secretary, to
help him and Record, but lost in 1917 to a ticket
organized by Frank Hague, who profited by the
Roman Catholic church's opposition to Fagan's
program of building public schools. (In his *Autobiography*, Steffens quoted Fagan as saying, "Why,
it was my Church that finally beat me" [p. 500].)
A bipartisan reform group asked him to run against
Hague in 1929, but he remained out of politics, con-
tinuing in business as a funeral director until 1945.[20]

[20] Roosevelt to Henry Cabot Lodge, November 8, 1905, in
Letters, V, 70; Link, *Woodrow Wilson*, pp. 135-38, 271, 468;
John Blum, *Joe Tumulty and the Wilson Era* (Boston, 1951),

Everett Colby (1874-1943), state senator from Essex County, New Jersey (1906-9), refused to run for governor in 1907, in large part because he distrusted Record. He was one of the group who in January, 1912, drafted the letter of six governors inviting Roosevelt to seek the presidential nomination; he was the Progressive candidate for governor in 1913. He served on the Republican National Committee in 1916, as one of six Progressives, and on the platform committee in 1920, but bolted again in 1924, supporting John W. Davis. He served in the Food Administration and in the Army during the First World War; after the war he advocated joining the League of Nations and the World Court, and recognizing the Soviet Union. He served on the New Jersey Republican State Committee, 1934-38.[21]

Benjamin B. Lindsey (1869-1943) was judge of the juvenile court of Denver from 1900 to 1927. Failing to get the Democratic nomination, he ran unsuccessfully as an independent candidate for governor of Colorado in 1906. He served on the national committee of the Progressive party in 1912,

---

p. 77; *New York Times*, November 28, 1915; Dayton B. McKean, *The Boss: The Hague Machine in Action* (Boston, 1940), pp. 41-43; *New York Times,* May 9, 1917, March 24, 1929, May 15, 1929, July 17, 1955.

[21] He lost his seat in the election of 1908. Noble, *New Jersey Progressivism,* pp. 27-120; La Follette, *Robert M. La Follette,* I, 385; *New York Times,* June 20, 1943.

but supported Wilson in 1916. He went to Europe on Henry Ford's "peace ship" in 1915. He lost his judgeship when the state supreme court declared (1927) that his last election had been invalid; two years later the court disbarred him on the charge of practicing law while holding judicial office. In 1934 he was elected judge of the Los Angeles County Superior Court, serving until his death.[22]

Rudolph Spreckels (1872-1958), the financier of reform in San Francisco, supported Robert M. La Follette for the Republican presidential nomination in 1912 and Wilson in the general election, financing La Follette's campaign in California and heading the Wilson National Progressive Republican League. He refused appointment as ambassador to Germany in 1913; he opposed preparedness in 1916. He helped in La Follette's campaign for re-election to the Senate in 1916; and he was western regional director in La Follette's presidential campaign in 1924; but thereafter he stood apart from progressive politics. The papers reported that in 1934 he lost his fortune, estimated at thirty million dollars; that same year he told an old friend from progressive days that he had joined Father Charles E.

[22] *New York Times,* July 1, 1927; *Survey,* LVII (February 15, 1927), 623; Lindsey and Rube Borough, *The Dangerous Life* (New York, 1931), pp. 399-411; *New York Times,* March 27, 1943.

Coughlin's National Union for Social Justice.[23]

William S. U'Ren (1859-1949), author of the Oregon System, held no public office after his one term as a Populist in the state legislature of 1897 (which never convened, for want of a quorum), although he ran for governor of Oregon as an independent in 1914 and for the legislature as a Republican in 1932 and 1934. In 1909 he became vice president of the Short Ballot Association, of which Wilson was the first president and Lindsey a member. Wilson credited U'Ren with persuading him that direct legislation would work; and it was Wilson who gave national currency to the saying that Oregon had "two legislatures, one at the capital and the other under W. S. U'Ren's hat." Long an advocate of the single tax, and secretary of the Oregon Single Tax League, 1908-17, U'Ren became, with Steffens, a member of the national committee of the National Single Tax League in 1917. "I read 'Progress and Poverty' in 1882," he said at a Single Tax Conference in 1910, "and I went just as crazy over the Single Tax idea as any one else ever did. . . . All the work we have done for Direct Legislation has been done with the Single Tax in view. . . ." In

[23] La Follette, *Robert M. La Follette,* I, 423, 433, 580, II, 1122; *New York Times,* October 5, 1958; William E. Leuchtenburg, *Franklin D. Roosevelt and the New Deal* (New York, 1963), p. 103.

1920, in association with leaders of the Non Partisan League and the State Federation of Labor, he proposed a constitutional amendment to represent occupational groups in the legislature. He voted for Franklin D. Roosevelt in 1932, but soon reproached him for attacking his critics and for offering doles rather than fundamental reform; he proposed colonies for the unemployed and a system of vesting in every person the right to a job.[24]

Upbuilders sold slowly—by August, 1910, almost 10 months after publication, 684 copies. Even if Steffens reached most of his readers through *McClure's,* as is probable,[25] this was a poor showing. In 1931-37 the *Autobiography* appeared in six American editions, two of which were still in print thirty years later. Yet the student of Steffens and the Progressive era and the history of journalism

[24] Link, *Woodrow Wilson,* pp. 124-25; Portland *Oregon Daily Journal,* May 19, 1911; Robert C. Woodward, "W. S. U'Ren and the Single Tax in Oregon," *Oregon Historical Quarterly,* LXI (March, 1960), 46-63; *Single Tax Conference,* pp. 21-23; *Oregon Voter,* XXI (June 5, 1920), 561-81; Robert C. Woodward, "William Simon U'Ren: In an Age of Protest" (M.A. thesis, University of Oregon, 1956), pp. 156-58; Portland *Oregonian,* March 11, 1934; Otis L. Graham, Jr., *An Encore for Reform: The Old Progressives and the New Deal* (New York, 1967), p. 68.

[25] *The Shame of the Cities* had sold around three thousand copies, *The Struggle for Self-Government* under one thousand. Henry M. Lanier to Steffens, March 31, 1909.

should know Steffens' early books as well as the *Autobiography*, just as the student of Henry Adams should know Adams' *History* as well as the *Education*—a book much like the *Autobiography*, as the two authors were much alike. Steffens told his father, to whom he dedicated *Upbuilders*, "It contains about all of the foundation of my philosophy and is written about as well as I can write."[26] It deserves further circulation.

EARL POMEROY

Eugene, Oregon
September, 1967

---

[26] Steffens to Joseph Steffens, August 7, 1909, *Letters,* I, 23.

UPBUILDERS

UPBUILDERS

MARK FAGAN, MAYOR

"You saw go up and down Valladolid,
A man of mark, to know next time you saw."
ROBERT BROWNING.

THAT Jersey City should have produced Mark
Fagan is strange enough. But that Mark
Fagan, grave, kind, and very brave, should have
been able, as Mayor, to make Jersey City what it
is: a beginning of better things all over this land
of ours, that is stranger still. And no man there
pretends to understand it. Yet it is a simple
story.

Mark — as they call him — the men, the
women, and the children — was born September
29, 1869, in the fifth ward where he lives now.
His parents were poor Irish, very poor. They
moved over to New York when Mark was a child,
and the father died. Mark sold newspapers.
The newsboy dreamed dreams and fought fights.
He claimed a corner, Twelfth Street and Avenue
A, developed a good trade, and when competition
came, appealed to the man in the store to say

3

if he was n't there first. The man in the store wouldn't decide; he told the boys they must fight it out among themselves, so they laid down their papers and they fought it out. Mark held his corner. "Life is one long fight for right," he says now, this very gentle man, who fights and — holds his corner.

The newsboy's dreams, like his fights, were very simple affairs. When I pried into them, I expected to hear of driving a locomotive or the Presidency, at least. But no, it seems that some men said roughly that they didn't want to buy a paper, others said it kindly. Mark made up his mind that when he became a man he would be like the kind men. Sometimes the nights were cold and the newsboy felt hungry and lonely; passing houses where the family sat in the basement room, all lighted up and warm, with plenty of smoking hot food before them, Mark stopped to look in and he dreamed that when he grew up, he also would have a home. He couldn't go to school; he had only six months of it all told. But he didn't like school; it was indoors, and he has dreamed that he would like to have, in Jersey City, schools on large plots of ground, so that part of the teaching might be done in the open. But this dream came later.

When he was twelve or fourteen Mark became

a helper on a wagon. Then he learned the trade of a frame-gilder with William B. Short, a Scotchman who made a deep impression on the boy. Short was a "genuine man." He was a Republican in politics. The boy was a Democrat by birth, breeding, and environment. But the man pointed out to the little Tammany Democrat on election days the Tammany line-up of men from the street into the saloon and out again, with foam on their lips and something in their hands, to the ballot-box. Mark had a painful time, talking to people on both sides, but what he saw with his own staring eyes, with the honest gilder pointing at the living facts, made the Democrat a Republican.

The next period made the boy a man. His uncle, an undertaker in Jersey City, offered Mark a job, and he moved with his mother and sister back there to take it. Now this business often has a demoralizing effect upon men. They see dreadful sights, and they harden or take to drink. Mark saw dreadful sights; you can see that he sees them now when he recalls those days, but they softened, they sweetened Mark Fagan. He saw homes where the dead mother left nothing but a helpless child -- nothing, you understand, but the child. He saw that the poor suffered greatly from the wrongs of others, not alone of those above, but of those also that were about them, and yet, the poor were great in charity for the poor.

"I came," he says, in his quiet, level tone, "I came to have pity for the poor and — admiration."

You hear that Mark, the undertaker, cared for the living child as well as the dead mother; he stayed with his job after the funeral, and by and by people came to the undertaker with the business of life. His explanation is that he "could write and fix up insurance and things like that." Others could write and fix up insurance; the point was that they trusted Mark to do it, all his neighbors, all nationalities, all ages; and he did it. One of the odd branches of this odd undertaking business was to fix up marriages. It seems that, among the poor also, there comes a time soon after the wedding when husband and wife fall out; love turns to what looks like hate, and sometimes becomes hate. In Jersey City, young married people used, when the crisis arrived, to go to Mark; they'd "tell him on each other"; and he would listen and seem to judge. But what he really did was to get everything said and done with, and then when they were tired and satisfied, and sorry, he "fixed 'em up."

So far there is nothing so very extraordinary

about Mark Fagan. He is a type of the men who, winning the faith and affection of their neighbours, become political leaders. "Popularity" makes them "available" as candidates or "ward bosses." Nothing was further from Mark's mind, but it was inevitable that he should go into politics, and the way he went in was natural and commonplace. One Sunday morning as he was leaving church several young fellows stopped him to propose that he run for the board of freeholders. He was "not adapted," he said; why didn't one of them run? They explained that "Bob" Davis, the Democratic boss, wouldn't let them run; wouldn't let anybody run in their party who wouldn't knuckle under to him. But Mark was a Republican. The ward, like the city and county, was heavily Democratic, and since there was so little chance of winning, the Republican ring would let anybody have the nomination. If Mark would let them, they would arrange it, fight with him, and he might be elected. They couldn't persuade Mark himself, but they knew how to get him. They went to his mother. They explained it to her, and she bade Mark run. He asked her if she understood it all, and she said she didn't, except that it seemed to be a chance to do some good in the ward.

Thus Mark Fagan was started in politics. When he took the Republican nomination and his popularity showed, the fellows that got him into the fight got out. They had to; they were called off by the bosses who ran the two parties as one. That made Mark fight the harder. Left high and dry by "the organization," he went to the people of his district.

"I was bound to win," he says, "and I felt that if I was beaten it would be because I wasn't known to enough of the voters. And, anyhow, I wanted to know my people in my ward."

So he started at 5.45 one morning at one corner of his ward, and he went systematically through it, knocking at every door, seeing every man, woman, and child; he climbed 3,700 flights of stairs in seventeen nights; and he promised to "serve the people of his ward faithfully and honestly." Mark was elected, and dirty Jersey City was amazed.

Now comes the first remarkable thing about this remarkable man. The corruption, political and financial, of the United States is built up on the betrayal of the people by the leaders, big and little, whom they trust, and the treason begins in the ward. The ward leader, having the full, fine, personal faith of his neighbours, takes their confidence and their votes, and he delivers these

things and his own soul to the party bosses who
sell out the interests of the city, state, and nation
to the business leaders, who — as we know now —
use the money we entrust to them to rob us and
corrupt our political, commercial and our higher
life. When Mark Fagan had taken his oath,
the other, older freeholders came to him, and
they invited him into "the combine." There
was no mystery about it. There was a combine and there was graft; of course a man wants
his share of the graft, and though Fagan was a
Republican, party made no difference; both parties were in on it, and Fagan had a right to what
was coming to him. Something — the man
doesn't know exactly what it was — something
which he thinks is religious, made him decline
to go in. He is a quiet man, and he made no
outcry. He didn't perfectly understand anyhow, then, just what it all meant. It simply
"didn't look right" to Mark, so he did not sell
out the people of his ward who trusted him to
serve them. And the worst of it was, he couldn't
serve them. If he wouldn't "stand in," the combine wouldn't let him have anything for his
ward, not even the needed, rightful improve-
ments. All he got were three political jobs,
and they were a gift to him. The combine
having distributed all the offices, had three left

over. Since these were not enough to go around
again, they wrangled till somebody, to save the
combine, suggested giving them all to Mark.
They "kind o' liked" Mark, so this bit of patronage went to him with a whoop.

Mark was not reëlected freeholder. He says
that his inability to do things for the ward did
not hurt him with his people; more of them
voted for him than ever before. But the state
and city rings had had a gerrymander about that
time, and they so arranged the lines of Mark's
ward that he was beaten. He served his neighbours privately till the next year the Republicans
nominated him for the state senate. Hopeless,
anyway, the candidacy fell upon a presidential
year, Bryan's first, and the Democratic County
of Hudson was wild with party enthusiasm.
But the moment Mark was nominated he left
the convention and, fifty feet from the door,
began his campaign; he met two men; he told them
he had just been nominated, that if he was elected
he would serve them "honestly and faithfully,"
and they promised to vote for him. In this
fashion, man to man, he canvassed his county and,
though it went against him, he ran way ahead
of his ticket. And he carried the city.

A Republican who can carry a Democratic
city is the "logical" candidate of his party for

Mayor, and, in 1901, Mark Fagan was nominated. Some of the little bosses warned the big bosses that they couldn't handle him, but the big bosses pooh-poohed the fears of the little bosses. In the first place he wouldn't be elected. The railroads, the public service companies, and some of the greatest corporations in the world have offices and properties in Jersey City, and their agents there had used money so extensively that they ruled absolutely a people supposed to be utterly corrupted. Bribery at the polls, election frauds, ballot-box stuffing — all sorts of gross political crimes had made this home of "common people" and corporations notorious. "Bob" Davis was the Democratic boss, politically speaking; but Mr. E. F. C. Young, banker, leading citizen, public utility magnate, was the business boss who, backing Davis, was the real power. Colonel Sam Dickinson, the Republican boss, was a corporation man, and one might expect that his party, which was in power in the state, would help him. But no. General Sewell, U. S. Senator, Pennsylvania railroad official, and Republican state boss, dispensed Republican patronage in Hudson County, through the Democratic boss, Mr. E. F. C. Young. Sewell was dead now, but the custom survived him, and in 1901 the Democrats nominated against Fagan,

George T. Smith, Young's son-in-law, an employee of the Pennsylvania. So Fagan had against him the money, the "best citizens," the "solid, conservative business interests" of the state and city, and — both rings. Hence, the certainty that Fagan would be defeated. But even if he should win the big bosses believed they could "handle him." They had sized up the man. And if you could size up Mark Fagan — feel his humility and see the pleading, almost dependent look of his honest, trustful eyes — you would understand how ridiculous to the big bosses the worry of the little bosses must have seemed.

An astonished city elected Mark. His quiet campaign from house to house, his earnest, simple promise to "serve you honestly and faithfully," had beaten bribery. His kind of people believed Mark Fagan, and so, though the Republican ticket as a whole was beaten, Mark was Mayor. Being Mayor, Mark assumed that he was the head of the city government. He didn't understand that his election meant simply that his boss had come into his own. He saw Governor Murphy appoint Colonel Dickinson secretary of state, and he heard that the Colonel was to have some of the local patronage of the Republican state government. Mark might have assumed that he had "made" Dickinson. But he was told that it was the other way around. They walked in upon Mark — the Colonel who "made" him; the editor of the paper that "elected" him; and General Wanser who was ready to help "unmake" him, — these and the other big Republican bosses who expected, as a matter of course, to give Jersey City a "good business government," called on the Mayor-elect. Mark, who has no humour, tried to tell me how he felt when they came and took charge of him and his office. Putting one fist to his forehead, and pressing the other hand on the back of his head (a characteristic gesture), he said that he looked up to those men; he felt his own deficiencies of education and experience; he had a heavy sense of his tremendous responsibility; and he wanted help and advice, for he wished to do right. But, you see, he was Mayor. The people looked to him. He might make mistakes; but since he must answer for them to those people, man to man, you understand, and man by man, when he knocked again at their doors, why, Mark Fagan thought he ought to listen to "his party," yes, and be "true to it," yes; but after all, the whole people would expect him to decide all questions — all.

Mayor Fagan didn't realize, at that time, that our constitutional governments were changed, that this was a business nation and that the government represented not the people, but business; not men, but business men. So he sat silent, apart, and perplexed — not indignant, mind you, not quarreling and arguing; no, the others did that; the Mayor only listened perplexed while Colonel Dickinson and General Wanser and the rest discussed "his" policy and "his" appointments; discussed them and disagreed, quarreled, all among themselves, but finally agreed among themselves. And then, when they had settled it all and turned to him, a party in harmony, he "got off something about being Mayor and reserving the right to change some items of the slate and policy." It was their turn to be perplexed. Perplexed? They left him in a rage to "go to the devil."

The Mayor, abandoned, proceeded with a quiet study he was making all by himself of the city. He went about, visiting the departments, meeting officials, and asking questions. People wrote complaints to him, and some of them were as perplexed as the bosses when Mayor Fagan answered their letters in person, looked into their troubles, and went off to "fix 'em up." There were lots of things for a Mayor to do: Parents couldn't get their children into school; no room. Families couldn't get water above the second floor; no force. Cellars were flooded; pipes leaked. Jersey City, corrupt, neglected, robbed, needed everything. And Mayor Fagan took its needs seriously. He must have more schools, more and better sewers, more water; and he did want to add a public bath and parks and music in the parks. "I wanted," he says, "to make Jersey City a pleasant place to live in; I'd like to make it pretty." Jersey City pretty! Were you ever in Jersey City? I suppose when your train was coming through Jersey City you were gathering up your things and being brushed by the porter; you probably never looked out of the window. Well, look next time and you will see that what the railroad attorneys say is true:

"It's nothing but a railroad terminal. They talk about the railroads owning it; the railroads ought to own it. It's the terminal of the traffic of a continent."

Nevertheless, Mark Fagan, who lived there and who knew personally so many families that lived and must always live there, he, their Mayor, dreamed of making it a pleasant city to live in. How? Money, lots of money, was needed, and how was money to be raised for such a purpose? When he had broached his idea to the bosses it seemed to fill them with disgust, and now that they were gone, he didn't know what to do.   He needed help, and help came.

Among the appointments recommended to him by Colonel Dickinson was that of George L. Record, to be corporation counsel.   Record, an able lawyer, had been the principal orator in the campaign, and the Mayor "took to him." But it was whispered that Record was interested in a contracting company which was building waterworks for the city, and the Mayor, suspicious by this time of everybody, hesitated.   Record was resentful, but he had had dreams of his own once.   He had read Henry George and his dreams were of economic reforms — taxation. But he had fought the bosses in vain, and was about ready to give up when, reflecting upon the rock they all had struck at the bottom of this mild Mayor's character, he saw that "by Jove, here was an honest man who could make people believe in his honesty."   He went to see him.   The water business was explained; Record had been engaged only as a broker, and he was out of it.   He was free to take Mark's pledge to be "loyal to the Mayor and the people of Jersey City."   They had a long, warm talk.   The Mayor's mind ran to the betterment of the physical conditions of life; Record's to more fundamental reforms, but taxation was the way to raise money to make the city pleasant.

They outlined a policy. They took in others to form a cabinet: Edgar B. Bacon, Frank J. Higgins, Edward Fry, and Robert Carey — all these, and Record and Fagan, are Mark Fagan. They discuss questions as they arise, and the Mayor decides; they agree, but Mark is the Mayor. Some people say Record is the boss, but he laughs.

"The big grafters know better," he says. "They failed to handle Mark, and when they found that I was 'next' they asked me to sell him out. I didn't tell them that I wouldn't; I told them I couldn't. And I can't, and they know I can't. I can advise, I can instruct, and the man will try, actually try hard to see things as I do. For he trusts me, and he wants to be shown. He wants to know. But he decides; and there's something in him — I don't know what it is — something that tells him what is right. No. I've been a help, a great help, to him, but so have the others of us, and we have helped him to decide to do things no one of us alone would have had the nerve to do. And there's where he is great. It all comes down to this: We all agree on the right thing to do, and we do it; but when the howl goes up and the pull begins to draw, we put it all up to Mark. 'Blame him,' we say; 'we can't help it,' and they blame him. But that eases us, and, you see, Mark prefers it that way. He wants to stand for everything; everything. Oh, he should, yes, but you see, he wants to."

The policy the Mayor and his corporation counsel outlined was to equalize taxation. They couldn't raise the rates; the city was overburdened with taxes already, but the corporations probably dodged their share. Record didn't know that they did; the Mayor was to see, and while he went about with the tax lists and an expert, Record had a talk with the boss, Dickinson. The Mayor had consented to let the Colonel have most of the patronage if "the party" would let him carry out his policy, and Record argued with Dickinson, that having made all the money he needed, it was time for him to play the big game of straight politics, take his ease and the credit of a good administration. Dickinson liked the idea.

The Mayor and his expert reported that the poor paid taxes on about 70 per cent. of the value of their property; privileged persons on about 50 per cent.; the corporations on all the way from 30 per cent. to nothing. Mark Fagan had a new purpose in life. The others laughed at the old, old story; it was new to Mark,

and he raised rates on the tax dodgers. There
was an awful clamour, of course, and there were
pulls, but all complaints were referred to the little
Mayor, who, seeing complex business problems
in a simple way, was a rock.

Then there were the trolleys. These were
valuable privileges. Why shouldn't they pay a fair
tax? There was a reason why they shouldn't:
Republican, as well as Democratic, bosses were
in on them. This didn't deter the Mayor, and
when Record sounded Colonel Dickinson, the
Republican boss winked the other eye. He
wasn't in trolleys, and he had had a bit of a row
with E. F. C. Young, the Democratic boss who
was. As for the other Republican bosses who
were in with Young, they might "see the Mayor"
for themselves. They did. When it was noised
about that the sacred private property of the street
car company in the middle of the public streets
was to be assessed somewhat as ordinary property,
General Wanser, for instance, called on the Mayor.

"What's this I hear you are going to do with the
trolleys, Mark?" he asked.

"Whatever is right," said Mark. "I understand they are undervalued; if they are, we will
raise them."

"Well, now, I'm a good friend of yours, Mark,
and I don't want you to do anything of that sort."

"If you are a good friend of mine," said Mark, "you shouldn't ask me to do anything wrong."

"Don't you know," said Wanser, "that every dollar I have in the world is in this thing?"

Mark Fagan couldn't see the relevancy of this; he talked about other people having every dollar that they had in houses and lots, and yet paying taxes. As General Wanser remarked when he left in high dudgeon, Mark Fagan had "damn queer ideas about things."

He had, and he has. One of his queer ideas is what may be called a sense of public property. All men know that private property is sacred; for centuries that sense has been borne in upon us till even thieves know it is wrong to steal private property. But highly civilized men lack all sense of the sacredness of public property; from timber lands to city streets that is a private graft. And when one day the Mayor received an anonymous note advising him to have the underlying franchise of the trolley company looked up, he was interested. He had the note copied in typewriting, then he scrupulously destroyed the original. The copy he gave to Corporation Counsel Record. Mr. Record discovered to his amazement that the franchise had expired. We need not go into details. The Mayor and his cabinet decided to take the matter into the courts; if the court

decided that the franchise belonged to the city, the
Mayor meant to take it.   To some of the Mayor's
advisers this looked like a dreadful step to take;
they thought of the "widows and orphans" and
other innocent holders of the stock.   It didn't
look so bad to Colonel Dickinson; he thought
only of his rival boss, E. F. C. Young, whom he
had seen grabbing up the street railways under
his nose.   And it didn't look bad to Mayor Fagan;
he thought of the "widows and orphans" who
held no stock except in Jersey City, which —
so it seemed to Mark — had as much right as an
individual or a private corporation to whatever
belonged to it.

Unbeknown to the cabinet, however, while they
were deliberating on their discovery, the great Public Service Corporation was being formed.   The
big men in the Prudential Life and its Fidelity
Trust Company had gone in with the U. G. I.
(United Gas Improvement Co.) of Philadelphia
and the Pennsylvania Railroad crowd to buy up
practically all the trolleys, electric light, and
other available public utility companies of New
Jersey.   Among these purchases were the Jersey
City lines and, also, an electric light company
in which Colonel Dickinson was an employee.
This was embarrassing to Dickinson; E. F. C.
Young was out and Dickinson and his friends were

in. Record told Fagan all about it, but, as he says, "Mark didn't care; he wasn't even interested." He made public his plan to test the franchise, the stock fell and there was a great ado. The Public Service Corporation had walked straight into politics. Tom McCarter, the Attorney-general, was made president of the company and his brother, Robert, was made Attorney-general of the state. As we all know, the new crowd acquired such a heritage of corrupt power that they were able to send the president of the Prudential, John F. Dryden, to the United States Senate. This power, and the power of the U. G. I. (the same that drove Philadelphia to revolt) came down upon Dickinson and Record. The grafters didn't want to see the Mayor, but Dickinson and Record told them they must, so Dryden gave a yachting party up the Hudson. Dryden, Randall Morgan, and Tom McCarter went and Dickinson, Record, and the Mayor's cabinet — all but the Mayor. The party was fog-bound off Hoboken, so they had no sail, and, though they talked, they did no business. They had to see Fagan.

They saw Fagan. The U. G. I. has rooms at Sherry's for such business, and there one afternoon was held a conference which has passed into the traditions of New Jersey. The more important persons present were Mayor Fagan, Record,

Bacon, Carey, and Dickinson representing Jersey City; Tom McCarter, of the Public Service Corporation; and Randall Morgan of the U. G. I. The rooms were luxurious, the entertainment was good, and the conversation friendly and pleasant. When they got down to business, everybody felt as if they ought to be able to agree — everybody but Mark Fagan. He sat apart, cold and still. He says now that he felt at the time that he shouldn't have gone there at all, but that all the way over on the boat and during the conversation he was conning over just what he would say; that it was "not his business, but the city's, and that the case must go to the courts to decide." Tom McCarter spoke for the trolley, Carey for the city, and they got nowhere. Randall Morgan was talking tactfully to the Mayor in a corner, when suddenly McCarter turned upon Mark and said:

"Well, Mr. Mayor, what is your decision?"

The Mayor was ready. He had no decision to give, he said. Jersey City was going to take the case into court, and the courts would decide.

McCarter always loses his temper when opposed by an honest government. "You may be an honest man," he shouted at the Mayor, "but you act like a blackmailer. And you, George Record, I'll never forgive you for letting me put my good money into this trolley company without telling me what you knew about it." He insulted them all, one by one, in turn, including Sam Dickinson, and then he made a famous threat to the whole party:

"To all of you I say, you can't bring your suit without the consent of the Attorney-general, and the Attorney-general is my brother."

No matter what an honest man in office tries to do, if he persists, he comes sooner or later upon the corrupt business back of corrupt politics. And no matter what kind of reform it undertakes, an honest city administration, if it proceeds logically, has to appeal sooner or later to the corrupt state government back of the corrupt city government. Mark Fagan had come, as we have seen, upon the trolley business, and when Tom McCarter pointed to his brother Robert at Trenton, he was showing the Mayor of Jersey City where he must go next. And Mayor Fagan went where Tom McCarter pointed, and what Tom McCarter predicted happened. When Jersey City asked Attorney-general McCarter to take its expired franchise into court, Tom's brother, Robert, refused.

Thus Mark Fagan learned that the trolley was king of his state. And he was to learn that the railroad was queen.

During this, his first administration, the Mayor

had been able, by simply catching tax dodgers and "equalizing" the taxes of privileged individuals and corrupt corporations, to buy a site for a new high school; begin one school, finish another; put up eleven temporary schools, thus providing seats for all the children in the city; and make needed repairs in all the schools. He had built a free bath; established free dispensaries; extended one park, bought another, improved two more, and given free concerts in them all. He improved the fire, street-cleaning, and health departments, and he repaired and extended the sewerage system. But he wanted to do more, and he needed more money. How could he get it?

In the course of his investigations he discovered, what well-informed persons long had known, that railroad property was taxed separately in New Jersey. We needn't go into figures. The point was, the railroads were taxed by a state board which they controlled, and which enabled them to fix their own valuation. Not only that, their tax-rate, as fixed by law, was lower than the local rate on ordinary property. All localities suffered more or less, but in Jersey City, where the railroads needed much and the most valuable ground (water front), every time they bought property for railroad use, they not only paid less taxes on it than the private owner had paid, but they took it off the city list. The obvious effect was that the most valuable taxable property in the city constantly decreased and the tax on the rest as steadily increased and must forever increase.

It was a matter of life and death to Jersey City, to have this system changed, but the city was helpless alone. Mark Fagan, renominated, had to promise to go to Trenton with this business and with the trolley trouble. It was an exciting campaign. The railroads, the public service companies, the taxed corporations — all the corrupt and privileged interests set about beating Mark Fagan, but the Mayor, going from house to house, and making, man to man, his simple promise to be "honest and true" — defeated the system.

Elected, he and his cabinet went to the legislature, and they had their bills introduced. Nothing came of a bill against Robert McCarter. A franchise tax measure was still-born. Their equal tax bill was crude, so the Democrats substituted a better one which the Jersey City Republicans accepted and supported. Referred to a committee, there were hearings on the bill, but it was buried there. The silent power of the king and the queen of the state would not let it come out.

Mark Fagan, with his staring eyes, saw that the government of his state, the control of his own party was in the hands of the most favoured men in and out of the state, those that corrupted it to get and keep privileges. And he wanted to say so. As the session drew to a close, he felt he must do something, but what? He must appeal from the state to the people of the state. How? Somebody suggested a letter to Governor Murphy, and they drew up one which described what Mark Fagan saw. The Mayor wanted to publish it right away. Record objected that he "couldn't see the end of it." The Mayor said it was true; it was his duty to say it; and he wanted to "let the consequences go." Record suggested showing it to Dickinson. The Mayor said "no"; it is characteristic of him to avoid consulting those of his advisers who, he thinks, will oppose an act he believes to be right. Record did show it to Dickinson, however, and to his surprise the boss was for it. The Public Service crowd from Essex had beaten some political legislation of his, so the Colonel, a vindictive man, was for revenge. Record advised one more appeal to Governor Murphy, and he thought that was agreed upon. And Governor Murphy, understanding that the letter was to be withheld, had a luncheon with the other leaders, who decided to do "anything you want." Meanwhile, however, Fagan and Dickinson had handed to the reporters Fagan's famous letter to the Hon. Franklin Murphy, Governor of New Jersey:

March 24, 1904.

"MY DEAR SIR: As Mayor of Jersey City and also a member of the Republican party, I venture to address to you this public communication in the hope of averting a possible calamity to Jersey City and almost certain disaster to the Republican party of New Jersey. The present session of the legislature is drawing to a close. Its record, on the whole, is bad and in some respects is disgraceful. Its control by corporation interests, in the assembly at least, has been absolute. For this condition the Republican party is responsible.

"The bills for equal taxation demanded by a practically unanimous public sentiment, in all New Jersey at least, have been buried in committee at the command of the railroad corporations, and every attempt to move them has been resisted by a solid Republican vote upon the test motions. The Republican majority has made no attempt to defend this action, and has thereby admitted that it cannot be defended. . . .

"Bills affecting Jersey City, notably several

bills to empower the city to sell its surplus water to neighbouring communities, which it has supplied for twenty years, and which desire to renew contracts with us, have been buried in committee.

"A bill to ratify a water contract recently made between Jersey City and East Newark was introduced early in the session, and referred to the committee on boroughs, which committee still holds it. The bill was afterward introduced under another number, and re-referred to the committee on municipal corporations, where it still reposes.

"A bill to allow Jersey City to test the right to a trolley franchise, which we are advised by counsel has expired, has met a similar fate. Our most determined efforts to get these committees to act have been unavailing, because of the Republican members thereof, but we can get no satisfactory reason for, nor explanation of, this action. . . .

"What is the meaning of all this? The answer is plain. A Republican legislature is controlled by the railroad, trolley, and water corporations. And the interests of the people are being betrayed.

"While I charge no man with personal corruption, I do not hesitate to say that this is a condition of affairs which is essentially corrupt, and which, if unchecked, means the virtual control of our state and our party by corporations.

"As a citizen I say that this condition is dangerous and demoralizing. As a public official I protest against this injustice done to Jersey City. As a member of the Republican party I deplore its subserviency to corporate greed and injustice. No political party can long receive the support of the people with such a record as this Republican legislature is making. . . . "

Whatever form the issue takes upon which an honest man in politics makes his first fight, if he fights on, he finally will come to the real American issue: representative government. He may start out like Mayor Fagan for good government, or like Folk to prosecute boodlers, or like President Roosevelt to regulate railroad rates; before he gets through, he will have to ask the people to answer the question: "Who is to rule—the disinterested majority or the specially interested, corrupt few?" And to make their answer, the people have to beat the boss, who is the agent of the businesses that rule and are destroying representative democracy.

Mayor Fagan's letter to Governor Murphy raised the great question in New Jersey. It took at first the form that the gentle Mayor of Jersey City had given it, railroad taxation. The railroads tried to keep it down. Governor Murphy appointed a commission to inquire into the need of a change in railroad tax methods, but the Republicans nominated for Governor Edward C. Stokes, who resigned a directorship of a branch of the Pennsylvania Railroad to run, and the issue of the campaign was the Jersey City issue. And Stokes was elected, but he had had to promise, and public opinion and the outrageous facts forced from the commission a report for some change. And "some change" was made; enough to relieve Jersey City, but not enough to hurt the railroads.

The people of Jersey saw that the railroads drew that law, that the railroads dominated still their state government — the railroads and the Public Service Corporation. For, besides the railroad legislation, the Jersey City men continued their franchise tax fight. And, meanwhile, Tom McCarter had aroused the people of Essex County to resist his perpetual franchise "grabs" in the Oranges. Jersey City wanted to tax franchises; Essex reformers were for limiting them. Record saw that they both were fighting one enemy and he advised a union, and, because he was wiser than the Essex leaders, he and Fagan took up their neighbours' less essential issue. Everett Colby, a young Republican assemblyman from Essex, led the fight for limited franchises. He was beaten but the defeat showed what the state government represented.

So they went home to raise the real question. Fagan and Record to Jersey City, Colby and the Orange men to Essex. The Orange men had seen that Carl Lentz, the Republican boss of Essex County, who ruled them at home, was the agent, at Trenton, of the railroads and of the Public Service Corporation. They went after him. Lentz declared that Colby should not go back to the legislature; since he represented the people, not the corporations, he should not be renominated. But Assemblyman Colby said he not only would go back; he would go back as a senator, and he would take his nomination and his election from the people. Fortunately, George L. Record, far-sighted, practical reformer that he is, had engineered through the legislature a primary election law. The people had a chance to control their parties, and the Republicans of Essex went to the primaries, and they turned the party over to Everett Colby. Then the whole people of Essex turned in, and they elected Colby senator and with him, a solid assembly delegation pledged to represent the public interests.

And Jersey City did likewise. After Dickinson and his mayor had given out the Murphy letter, the railroad-trolley rings went after the boss, and they got him. He began to insist in Jersey City upon some sort of compromise with the Public Service Corporation. The company wanted some new grants. The city couldn't get its old case into court; so what was the use of fighting? Why not settle it all out of court? Mayor Fagan hung back, but his cabinet persuaded him to talk it over with Tom McCarter. McCarter called, asking for perpetual franchises. The Mayor was willing to negotiate on the basis of a twenty-five-year franchise. McCarter said limited franchises were absurd in Jersey. There they stuck till Record suggested, as a compromise, a perpetual franchise with readjustments of the terms every twenty-five years. McCarter thought this opened a way to a settlement; so did the Mayor; and Dickinson, feeling that he had "delivered his man" (the Mayor), sailed for Europe. But it wasn't settled. McCarter demanded fifty-year periods, and the Mayor, who had had misgivings all along, broke off the negotiations. The Public Service had its way. The Democrats controlled the Street and Water Board, and they passed McCarter's franchise for him.

But it was passed over the Mayor's veto, and

when Dickinson came home to hear that not his party but the Democrats had sold out to the Public Service, and that he was left, as before, in the ridiculous position of boss who couldn't deliver his Mayor, he was angry. And all through the next session he opposed the legislation asked for by his city. He joined the other bosses against the people, and, like Lentz, Dickinson went home to beat "his man" for renomination. Like Everett Colby, Mark Fagan accepted the challenge; he received the nomination for Mayor from the Republicans direct and he took the organization besides. Then he turned to the people with this appeal:

"I find myself, at the opening of the campaign, confronted by a threefold opposition. First, that of the Democratic machine and its absolute boss; second, the scarcely concealed and treacherous opposition of a Republican party leader, whose demands in behalf of his corporate clients I have refused to grant; third, the secret but powerful opposition of a combination of public service and railroad corporations, whose unjust corporate privileges are threatened by my reëlection. The opposition of the corporations and the reasons therefor, and the close business relations between them and the Democratic boss are well understood by the public. The relations between these corporations, or some of them, and the Republican boss, are not so well known.

"I explicitly charge that this Republican leader is doing everything in his power to defeat my reëlection; that his efforts to that end are jeopardizing the whole Republican ticket; and that this action is in the interest of the public service and railroad corporations. . . .

"These facts, and many others too numerous to mention, have convinced me that it is time to come out in the open and have a square stand-up fight against the Republican boss, the Democratic boss, and the trolley and railroad corporations which control them both. It is impossible for a public official to get along permanently with a boss, except upon terms of abject obedience and the sacrifice of self-respect. Personally I am tired of the experiment. I am sick of talk of party harmony, which means surrender of personal independence and of popular rights. It is time to fight the boss system itself, by which unscrupulous men get between the people and the public officials by control of the party machinery, betray the people, acquire riches for themselves, and attempt to drive out of public life all who will not take orders from the boss, and his real masters, the corporations.

"MARK M. FAGAN."

So the fight that fall, in Jersey City, as in Essex County and in New York, as in Toledo and Cincinnati, and Cleveland and Philadelphia, and in Ohio and in Pennsylvania, was a fight against the bosses. And as in those places, so in Jersey City, the people crossed all party lines to follow the leader, and they beat the bosses. Mark Fagan was reëlected Mayor of Jersey City, and he and Senator Colby and the reformers of Jersey combined against the interests which the bosses represented.

But never mind Jersey! What of Mark Fagan, the man who by following the facts, without a theory of reform, by tackling each obstacle as he approached it, came out upon the truth and gave his state its issues and aroused it finally to take part in the second war for independence that is waging all over this country? I have told simply the simple story of this simple man. The mystery remains. Why did Mark Fagan do it? That is what they ask in Jersey City, and that is what the commercial spirit of this Christian land asks of Folk and La Follette and Tom Johnson. What prompted them to do something for others? What are they after? What is there in it for them? And how and why do they win?

His bitterest foes — the grafters — concede Fagan's honesty. "Bob" Davis was the only one that offered any doubts on that point, and he offered them to me; he had none of his own. Pressed for facts, he admitted that Fagan was "personally on the square." The bigger grafters said Fagan was a demagogue. This is ridiculous. He addresses no prejudices, stirs no passions, makes no appeal to class; he seems to have no sense of class. His talks, like his speeches, are so plain that the wonder is that they count as they do count, winning for him, a Republican, a majority in a Democratic city. I asked the politicians to explain it. Mark has a relative, Jimmy Connolly, once a saloon-keeper, always a hard-headed politician. When Mr. Record confessed he could not account for it he referred me to Jimmy Connolly, and I asked Connolly:

"How does Mark Fagan do it?"

"You can search me," said he. "I've watched him, and I've listened to him, and I give it up. And you can ast anybody in this town; we've all ast ourselves and that is where you'll end up. You'll ast yourself. I don't know what he says, and I've listened to him, but he doesn't say nothing. Leastways, if you or the likes of me said to a fellar what Mark says, I can just hear the fellar say, 'Say, what ye givin' me, what?' 'Say,' he'd say, 'haven't ye got th' price of a drink in your clothes?' But when Mark says it, what he says, they fall down to it like dead soldiers. Nope, you got to find that out for yerself."

And an idea struck him. "Maybe you can," he said. "Now, maybe you can. I'll get a wagon and we'll go chase Mark out to the railroad yards, and you'll listen to him yerself, and maybe you can tell me."

Out to the yards we went, and we joined the Mayor. He was going up to a group of men, who stopped work, wiped their hands on their clothes, and formed a shy group.

"I'm Mark Fagan," said the Mayor as shyly. "I have tried to serve you honestly and faithfully. I don't know how well, but you know my record. That's the way to judge a man — by his record. And if you don't understand anything in it, I'd like to have you ask me about it. If you think I have done right in most things, I'd like to have your support."

That was all. They shook hands, saying nothing, and he moved on.

"Understand that?" said Connelly at my elbow. "Every one of 'em 'll vote for him. Why? What's there to it?"

Mark climbed up into the switch tower and began: "I am Mark Fagan ——"

"You needn't waste your time here," said the tower man, looking around steadily. "I know you're Mark Fagan, and I know what you're doing. And I'll vote for you till hell freezes over." He flung over the switch, and Mark retreated, abashed.

"He knows me," he said wonderingly to me when he came down. Of course they all know the Mayor, but the Mayor can't call them by name; he hasn't a good memory for either names or faces, and I saw him talk to men he had talked to before. So there is no flattery, and no familiarity, and that was one point which missed Connolly, who couldn't understand why those men didn't laugh or josh the Mayor. "Why don't they give him a song and dance?" he said.

One man in a group I joined before the Mayor reached it did say he was going to "have some fun with Mark," and the others in a mood for horse play, dared the bold one to ask Fagan for "the price of a drink." I thought the man would, but when Mark came up, saying, "I am Mark Fagan; I have been Mayor for two terms, and I have tried to serve you," etc., etc., the bold man was silent; they were all respectful, and the psychology was plain enough.

The Mayor speaks, what Connolly calls "his little piece," with dignity, with the grave dignity of self-respect, and you feel, and those men feel, the perfect sincerity of Mark Fagan.

But that didn't satisfy Jim Connolly, and it wouldn't satisfy anybody in Jersey City. It didn't satisfy me, and since nobody else could help me, I went to Mark himself. I went to his home with him, and I asked him questions. He squirmed, and it wasn't pleasant for me; but I had a theory I wanted to test. Maybe it wasn't right to probe thus into the soul of a man, and maybe it isn't fine to show what you see. It hurt Mark Fagan, that interview, and the report of it will hurt more. But I am thinking of those of us who need to see what I saw when I looked in upon the soul of Mark Fagan.

Why had he done the things that had been done for Jersey City? That was the main question. He said he hadn't done those things, not alone. His cabinet had done them. He gave full credit to his associates, and he gave it honestly, as if he wished to be believed. But, as Record says, whatever of knowledge and resources he and the rest contributed to the Mayor, it was the Mayor who furnished the courage, the steady will — the transparent character.

"What is your purpose, Mr. Mayor?"

He elaborated his idea of making Jersey City pleasant. He talked about clean streets, good water and light service, and schools. "Now the schools — I think the schools shouldn't be shut

up when school is out. Don't you think it would
be nice if the mothers could go there, and the
girls, and learn to sew and other things? I'd
like to have a gymnasium in the schools; and a
swimming tank. The schools ought to be the
place where the people of the neighbourhood go
to read and hear lectures, and hold meetings,
and for the children to play. Do you think that
is foolish?"

He hadn't read of the efforts elsewhere for
these ends. He was glad to know his scheme had
struck others as feasible.

"I don't see why things shouldn't be useful,
like that, and pretty. Do you think it would be
foolish — I haven't talked about this to the others,
but do you think it would be so foolish to have
flowers in the schools?"

"Why do you care about other people?" I
asked. "You seem to like men. Do you really?"

His look answered that, but he went on to talk
about his boyhood and his experiences as an
undertaker. These would make anybody like the
people, he thought.

"What do you mean by the people?" I asked.
"The poor people? The working people? When
you address a crowd, do you appeal to labour as
labour, to the unions, for example?"

"Oh, no. I never do that. I mean everybody.

The poor need the most, and most people over here work, but by people I mean men and women and children, everybody."

"Railroad presidents? Do you hate the railroads?"

"No," he said, reflecting. "They do a good deal that is wrong. They corrupt young men, and they don't care anything about Jersey City. They should stop corrupting politics, but you can't expect them to look out for us. We must do that." He paused. "I have hated men, almost, some of these corporation men, but I don't any more. I used to hate men that said things about me that weren't true, that weren't just. But I've got over that now."

"How did you get over it?"

"I have a way," he said, evidently meaning not to tell it.

"You must have been tempted often in the four years you have been in office. Have you ever been offered a bribe?"

"Only once, but that was by a man sent by somebody else. He didn't know what he was doing, and I didn't blame him so much as I did those who sent him."

"But the subtler temptations, how did you resist them?"

"I have a way," he said, again.

This time I pressed him for it; he evaded the point, and I urged that if he knew a way, and a good way, to resist political temptations, others should know of it.

He was most uncomfortable. "It's a good way," he said, looking down. Then, looking up, he almost whispered: "I pray. When I take an oath of office, I speak it slowly. I say each word, thinking how it is an oath, and afterward I pray for strength to keep it."

"A silent prayer?"

"Yes."

"And that helps? Against the daily temptations too?"

"Yes, but I — every morning when I go up the steps of City Hall, I ask that I may be given to recognize temptations when they come to me, and — to resist them. And at night, I go over every act and I give thanks if I have done no injury to any man."

"When you were considering whether you would give out that letter to Governor Murphy, why did you say, 'Let the consequences go'?"

"Well, when anything is to be done that I think is right, and the rest say it might hurt my political career, I ask myself if such thoughts are tempting me, and if I think they are, I do that thing quick. That was the way of the Murphy letter."

"They say you want to be Governor of New Jersey?"

"I know that I don't," he said quietly. "I have asked myself that, and I know that I don't. I don't think that I would be able to be the Governor; I mean, able to do much for people in that high office."

"What do you want to do, then?"

"Why, what I am doing now."

"Always? Do you mean that you'd like to be Mayor of Jersey City all your life?"

He looked up as if I had caught him at something foolish or extravagant, but he answered:

"If I could be — if I could go on doing things for the people all my life, as Mayor, I should be very happy. But I can't, I suppose, so I shall be satisfied to have done so well that whoever comes after me can't do badly without the people noticing it."

"Well, what do you get out of serving others, Mr. Mayor? Try to tell me that truly."

He did try. "I am getting to be a better man. You know I'm a Catholic ——"

"Yes, and some people say the Catholics are against the public schools. Why have you done so much for them?"

He was surprised. "I am Mayor of all the people, and the schools are good for the people."

"Well, you were saying that you are a Catholic ——"

"Yes, and I go to confession ever so often. I try to have less to confess each time, and I find that I have. Gradually, I am getting to be a better man. What I told you about hating men that were unfair to me shows. Some of them were very unfair; from hating them I've got so that I don't feel anything but sorry for them, that they can't understand how I'm trying to be right and just to everybody. Maybe some day I will be able to like them."

"Like them also! What is it, Mr. Mayor, altruism or selfishness? Is it love for your neighbour or the fear of God that moves you?"

He thought long and hard, and then he was "afraid it was the fear of God."

"What is your favourite book, Mr. Mayor?"

"'The Imitation of Christ.' Did you ever read it? I read a little in it, anywhere, every day."

I wouldn't tell Jimmy Connolly, nor "Bob" Davis, nor Sam Dickinson, nor, to their faces, could I say it to many men in Jersey City; I'd rather write than speak it anywhere in this hard, selfish world of ours, but I do believe I understand Mark Fagan, how he makes men believe in him, why he wants to: The man is a Christian, a literal Christian; no mere member of a church, but a

follower of Christ; no patron of organized charities, but a giver of kindness, sympathy, love.
Like a disciple, he has carried "the greatest of
these" out into the streets, through the railroad
yards, up to the doors of the homes and factories,
where he has knocked, offering only service, honest and true, even in public office. And that is
why he is the marvel of a "Christian" community in the year of our Lord, 1909. And, believe
me, that is how and why Mark some day will
make his Jersey City "pretty." This gentle man
has found a way to solve his problems, and ours,
graft, railroad rates and the tariff. There may
be other ways, but, verily, if we loved our neighbour as ourselves we would not then betray and
rob and bribe him. Impracticable? It does sound
so—I wonder why?—to Christian ears. And maybe we are wrong; maybe Christ was right. Certainly Mark Fagan has proved that the Christianity of Christ — not as the scholars "interpret"
it, but as the Nazarene taught it, and as you and
I and the Mayor of Jersey City can understand
it — Christianity, pure and simple, is a force
among men and — a happiness. Anyhow, that
is all there is to the mystery of Mark Fagan; that
is what he means.

EVERETT COLBY, "THE GENTLEMAN FROM ESSEX"

AMONG the new political leaders whom a reviving democracy is raising up to beat the bosses (and perhaps the real rulers) of the Republic, is Everett Colby, the state senator from Essex County, New Jersey. Born in 1874, he was only thirty-two years old when he "busted" his boss; he shows what a young man can do. The son of Charles L. Colby, builder of the Wisconsin Central Railroad, he inherited wealth and the associations of big business; he shows what a rich young man may do if he rises above his class. And the gentleman from Essex was brought up in a class.

Imperial Kipling has raged at the "flanneled fools" of England. Did you know we had them? We have. There is a constantly growing class of rich men's sons who can throw as much strength, nerve and concentrated intelligence into sport as their fathers put into the game of life; but, having been brought up only to play, they can't work — "can't," not "won't." They don't know how; they don't know anything but games, and they cannot learn. Everett Colby was headed straight for this fate when a man got hold of him — J. A. Browning, a teacher who teaches. He took a small class of boys who had busy fathers and loving mothers: Harold and Stanley McCormick, Percy and John D. Rockefeller, Jr., and Everett Colby. Everett Colby was in the worst condition. The boy could only play. "He played hard," says Mr. Browning, "but it was sport, not work. He couldn't read till he was fifteen; he couldn't fix his attention. I got into his mind through his hands. He liked to play with tools. I let him. It was play till once I set him to making a bookcase for his mother. He finished that, and it was good, and it was work."

Young Colby was prepared for Brown, where he went to college with young John D. He still "played hard." He was a splendid young male when he entered; he went in for all the sports: tennis, golf, baseball; and, making the team, was captain in his senior year of the best football eleven Brown ever put into the field. But he worked, too, and he was graduated with his class, '97. In the next year, after the death of his father, he made a tour around the world; then he studied law and played polo; then he married and settled down in Llewellyn Park, Orange,

EVERETT COLBY

New Jersey. He didn't mean to stay there, but he got into politics. He became a Wall Street broker, but it was politics that saved Everett Colby.

Now, young Colby meant to go into politics. As a "little shaver" he used to go along with his father, who campaigned in Wisconsin as a railroad man. He dreamed that when he grew up he would be a politician, and, because the dream persisted, he went in for debating in college, and afterward for the law. But it was the scenic side of the game that appealed to him, the crowd and the excitement, the fighting, the speaking and the cheers. He says so himself. He was after glory, and maybe that is all he is after now. He doesn't pretend to know. But there lies the peculiar significance of the career of this rich young gentleman in politics. He simply wanted to go into politics — not to accomplish anything in particular; not to reform politics; not even with the thought of being practical in politics. He went in on the machine side, and he served "the party"; he put in his money; he took orders; and he obeyed the boss till he saw what politics meant. Even then he didn't revolt right away; he objected as a gentleman to doing things a gentleman couldn't do, but he "went along" till he discovered as an insider what we have discovered from the outside: that the evils of politics, so-called, were all parts of one system which is perverting our government from a representative democracy to a plutocratic tyranny. When this was beaten into his head, Everett Colby fought like a citizen and a man. Wherefore his experiences are not only the story of a new political leader, but an inside view of the System in action.

When young Colby spoke of going into politics, somebody advised him to see Carl Lentz. This German-American was the Republican boss of Essex County. Bosses were as natural to our young American as the north wind or the road to Newark, and he went to Newark and he saw Carl Lentz. He says the boss talked to him a long while. Colby doesn't recall what was said, but I can hear the boss drawing out and smacking his lips over an attractive young man of means; free with his money and, therefore, "useful"; the son of a railroad magnate and, therefore, "safe"; attractive and honest, therefore promising as a "good man" candidate, and cheap. All the boy wanted was to "make speeches"; he thought politics was oratory.

"He let me speak," Colby says. "Small meetings for a while, then I held the crowd at larger meetings. I spoke till the advertised speaker came, when, amid the shouts for him, I sat down unnoticed, but well satisfied with myself."

He was in politics, and having got in as many another fool young American has got in, he was taken up and taken in, as the rest are. Lentz flattered Colby; then he passed him on to Governor Voorhees, who flattered him. "Seeing the Governor" was honour enough for the year 1901, but when the Governor asked him if he wanted to get into politics and the young man said he did, and the Governor offered to appoint him to an office, the novice was overwhelmed with gratitude and modesty. He didn't know that to be a Commissioner on the State Board of Education was simply to be put to a harmless test — by the machine. Colby thought of his education and worried about his fitness, but he took the place, and he did very well, very well, indeed. Then Boss Lentz made him chairman of the executive committee of the Republican organization of West Orange.

"I thought Lentz was a great fellow," he says now, "a great man." Lentz loomed as large to Colby, probably, as Durham looked to a Philadelphian, Cox to a Cincinnati Republican, Ruef to a San Franciscan, or Murphy to a New Yorker. The bosses live on the images we create of them, out of our own silliness.

The chairmanship — "actual practical politics, with great responsibility" — came in 1902.

Of course, young Colby had to spend some of his own money, and he did. He was all right, Colby was. In the next year Lentz offered him the senatorship from Essex. That was too much. The young man, modest now, was sure then that he could not be a senator. In the first place he was under the constitutional age. That didn't matter. Lentz could "have that fixed in the Manual," where the statistics of legislators are kept. This sounded a little queer, like a rather unusual north wind or a bad road to Newark, noticeable, but still a perfectly natural phenomenon. Colby refused to go to the senate; but he consented to go to the assembly, so Lentz had him nominated, and elected, an assemblyman from Essex.

The education of this young legislator was begun promptly, and it resembled very closely the course of his education as a boy. He saw things with his eyes long before he saw them with his mind; he saw facts separately, but failed to combine them into the truth. He failed, as so many of us fail, for want of imagination, and his story is the story of thousands of young men who go into politics and go along till some day they wake up and find that they are part of a corrupted government.

One day, early in the session, Sam Dickinson asked Assemblyman Colby to introduce certain

excise bills.   Dickinson was Secretary of State
and Republican boss of Hudson County, a "great
fellow" like Lentz.   And, like Lentz, Dickinson
probably saw at once the uses of a fine, up-stand-
ing young gentleman to "stand for" a piece of
dubious excise legislation.   Colby looked over
the bills; they seemed to him to be merely a
weapon to help the Republican machine take away
from the Democrats the control of Democratic
Hudson County.   He hesitated.   He went to
see the Governor about it.   Governor Murphy
was a gentleman and the father of a friend of
Colby's.   The young assemblyman didn't know
that governors are usually mere figureheads for
the System; he felt only that he could trust the
Honourable Franklin Murphy.   And when the
Honourable Franklin Murphy pronounced the
bills "all right," Colby was reassured.   He introduced them in the House.

Colby's own pet measure — for every legislator thinks he must put some new law upon the
books — was a normal school bill.   Then Essex
County wanted to have passed a bill providing
for the purification of the Passaic River; of course,
an Essex assemblyman was for that.   But you
have to have votes to pass bills, and Colby's two
bills lacked a majority.   How could some more
votes be got for them?   Colby and some others

of his delegation went to the Democratic assemblymen from Hudson. Would they help? They would — if Colby and his crowd would withdraw his excise bills. Colby would see. He saw the Governor. The Governor saw Dickinson, and Dickinson consented to the dropping of the excise bills. A bargain was struck; Colby's and Essex County's bills were passed with the help of Democratic votes. And then Dickinson asked Colby to reintroduce his excise bills.

The young legislator was astonished. He had given his word, and he wouldn't break it. Dickinson had somebody else to do it, and when Colby threatened to fight, a caucus was called to bind him to it as a "party measure." Colby appealed to the Governor, and the Governor spoke to Dickinson, but in vain. The caucus was held. Colby protested that the party was bound by his bargain; not he alone, but the accredited Republican leaders had given their word to the Democrats.

"Your word to a Democrat doesn't mean anything," they told him in those very terms. His did, he answered. There was a scene, and amid cries of "Down with the traitor; up with the flag," Colby bolted the caucus. The party jammed through the excise bills, but Colby voted against them. He didn't see the iniquitous part the caucus plays in the perversion of representative government; he saw only his own honour, but that was enough for a gentleman. Wherefore the word of the gentleman from Essex is good with both parties in Jersey politics.

The boy disappointed his own boss, too, in that first year. George L. Record, the man behind Mayor Fagan, of Jersey City, was in Trenton with a primary election bill. This piece of legislation was to play a decisive part in a crisis of young Colby's career, but Colby didn't know that, of course. He was for it, as Edward C. Stokes was, because his instincts were right. Stokes, though the Pennsylvania Railroad man at Trenton, took charge of the bill and to him, next to Record, belongs the credit for its enactment. Some of the other ring men saw the danger to the System that lurked in the measure; Lentz especially was aroused; he couldn't make Stokes see it, but he ordered his own delegation to fight it. And to his young protégé he gave his orders personally.

"Colby," he said, "you're going to vote against that bill."

"No, Major," said Colby. "It's a good bill, and I shall vote for it."

The Major repeated his command, but the young assemblyman laid down the limitation of his subserviency.

"Major," he said, "you must not interfere with me on any but political bills."

As if a primary bill wasn't political! Bosses have their troubles; it takes time and patience to knock all the decency — or, as they would put it, all the poppycock out of a promising young man. Lentz had to stand by and see Colby vote for the primary bill, and· that bill became a law. But the honest young legislator, troublesome as he was, had his uses. For example, they won him easily to the support of a bill to require the consent of 20 per cent. of the stock of a Jersey corporation to bring a stockholder's suit. "It was an awful bill," he says now. "It was introduced in the interest of the United States Steel Company, and I knew that. But I was told what a great business this was, the steel trust, and how 'strike suits' were being brought against it. Strike suits were bad but that bill was worse. It was so bad, indeed, that even I saw my mistake before the session was over." It was so bad they couldn't raise a majority for it, and it was killed that year.

By the close of the session, young Mr. Colby had few friends among the leaders in his own party; they wouldn't speak to him, and one might have supposed that his political career was over. But this was all part of the game. Since the young man was rich, they couldn't buy him with money, so they were applying a little discipline "just to show him." If they could keep him under for a while, they would get him by and by through his ambition; he should have an office and honours. And as a foretaste of what was in store for him, in the next session the Honourable Everett Colby was made floor leader of the Republican majority in the House.

This was taking a big chance on the boy. This was making him responsible for all the dirty party work of the system, but they counted on "pride" and his "sporting blood" to see him through with it. And they handled him very carefully. They didn't tell him everything, and they didn't give him his orders harshly. They approached him through men he liked.

For instance, early in this session (1904) Percy Rockefeller came to Colby with the United States Steel's same old "20 per cent. consent" bill which had failed in disgrace the year before. We mustn't blame Percy Rockefeller; he seems not to have known what the bill meant. Indeed, the shocking thought is that he was innocent, and that some of his elders in Wall Street had got this boy to go to his boy friend, Everett, to ask him to introduce this bill which was so bad that even Francis Lynde Stetson, the great corporation's greatest counsel, told Colby afterward that he did right to keep clear of it. The System will sacrifice its own children to have its dirty work done! Everett Colby, fortunately, was "wise" enough to the purposes of the bill to explain them to Percy Rockefeller, and he sent his chum back to those who had sent him with the message that not only would he not father the thing, he would do his best to kill it if anybody else introduced it. And somebody else did introduce it, and when Colby, the leader, opposed it, the System sent its other messengers to him, not boys this time. No. Governor Murphy and ex-Senator (now Governor) Stokes, "the Penn's man." The Governor called Colby a "Puritan" for his scruples; he said the great corporations threatened to leave the state unless they were "treated fairly." And Stokes, backing up the Governor, said he, Stokes, would be willing to go on the stump and advocate a 50 per cent. law!

This opened a little the eyes of the young legislator. He didn't see the System yet, but he was learning to. These were the leading men of his state and of his party, and the young assemblyman had great respect for them.

"But," he says, "I saw then that they all were corporation men, and that they represented in politics the interests of corporations."

Seeing this, he opposed and he helped to beat

that particular bill, but he said nothing. "What could a fellow say?" He went on, and his education went on.

This was the session when the present issues of New Jersey politics were raised in their present form. Mark Fagan, the Mayor of Jersey City, raised them. The Christian Mayor went to Trenton with his corporation counsel, George L. Record, to ask in the name of his people for relief from the unendurable burden thrown upon them by the railroads. The railroads, with all the best (terminal, water-front) property in the city, paid practically no taxes to the city, only to the state, and then, on a valuation fixed by their own state board, at rates lower than the rates on other property. Record had drawn a bill to tax railroad property locally and at local rates. They were Republicans, Fagan and Record, and their party was in control of the state, absolutely; so they applied to the leaders of their party, among them, of course, to the Honourable Everett Colby. He liked Mayor Fagan, he says; he didn't like Record, but Mark Fagan, the "man of the people," intent only upon the needs of his city, walked straight into the heart of the rich young gentleman who, so far as he knew, was bent only upon a political career for personal glory. "I liked that man," he says, "and the condition of

Jersey City appealed to me. I wanted to help them, and I couldn't; at least, I didn't."

"Why ?" he said, repeating my question thoughtfully. Then he looked me straight in the eye. "I don't know that I can tell you, exactly. I will try to explain, if you will understand that I'm not apologizing for myself. There was no more excuse for what I did in this matter than there was for other things I did and — didn't do. The bill was bad; it was crudely drawn."

"Record admits that," I interjected. "Record says that at that time he had never heard of the main stem, and had no right understanding of the situation at all."

"Nor had I," said Colby. "But that doesn't let me out. It served me as an excuse at the time. The big leaders, seeing my bent toward the bill, told me it was badly drawn, and I grasped at this reason as at a straw. But why shouldn't I, the House Leader, have amended that bill? The need of the legislation was plain. Why didn't I fix the bill? I couldn't. You understand? I, a law maker, hadn't the ability to draw a good bill. Why, then, didn't I have some other, older legislator make the bad bill good? There wasn't a man in that House who could have drawn a sound tax bill to meet the most notorious need of the state. We were incompetent. Perhaps some of us might, once upon a time, have been legislators; but boss rule was so old there that we didn't, we couldn't think for ourselves. We had lost the art of independent thought and work. We were dummies. We took orders, we waited for orders, we depended upon orders. Dummy legislators, that's what we were.

"Oh, I was unhappy! I saw all this, but only dimly; I wouldn't let myself see it clearly. You know how a man jollies himself along with lies to save his face. The Democrats drew a better bill, still not good, and Fagan and Record accepted that; they had no pride in their pet measure; and they didn't care whether the Democrats or the Republicans got the credit of authorship. They wanted an income from railroad property in Jersey City. But the bill was buried in committee and I, the leader, should have got it out. I couldn't have got it out. And when the Mayor came to me and asked me why I didn't have it reported, I told him the truth. 'I can't,' I told him. I wasn't really a leader. I was the real leader's dummy.

"You understand that the crime was not that we wouldn't pass the bill, but that we wouldn't consider it. I was willing to vote against it, if there were good reasons. I wasn't against corporations. But why couldn't we have the bill out and debate it? That's what Mayor Fagan couldn't understand, and that's what I asked in the caucus. We had orders, that was all; no reasons, except the one I remember they gave me in caucus a year later on a similar bill. When I asked, 'Why not take it out and beat it in the open — if it's so bad?' they answered, in awed tones: 'Why, the Penn would raise hell.' There was the reason, the real reason."

There, too, was the truth about Jersey. When the Mayor who represented the people of the second city in the state asked that legislature to consider a bill in their interest, that Jersey legislature couldn't because it represented "the Penn," a foreign corporation. "The Penn" ruled that state, and the ruler would "raise hell."

Colby didn't see this. "I didn't want to see it," he says. But Mark Fagan saw it, and he made Everett Colby see it; made him grasp with his mind what his eyes reflected. Mark, the gentle Mayor, raised hell. Defeated, with eyes wide open and ears alert, he took in the truth. The thing for a "practical politician" to do was to "take his medicine," and go home and tell his people the lies he heard told to the public. But Mark Fagan had made promises, not only on the stump; he had gone about from house to house and had made his promises man to man, and for keeps. He couldn't go back home to his people with lies. He put the truth to Governor Murphy in an open letter, and this letter was read aloud to the House of Assembly. It was a silent House; the representatives had read in their newspapers what this meek Mayor, a Republican himself, had written to the Republican Governor about their party and themselves. But they listened again. Colby says that he sat low sunk in his seat, and each separate sentence, as the Democratic leader read it, fell like a whip upon him.

The letter said that the writer spoke "as Mayor of Jersey City, and also as a member of the Republican party. . . . The present session is drawing to a close," he said. "Its record is . . . disgraceful. Its control by corporation interests, in the assembly, at least, has been absolute." And those men knew this was true. "For that condition the Republican party is responsible." Everett Colby, leader, knew this was true. And as the letter took up the legislation, bill by bill, to show how everyone that was against a corporation failed, the party leader of the House could recall the orders he had got to make them fail. He heard Governor Murphy's comforting arguments and the bosses' tactful orders. He saw again Major Lentz watching in the lobby. What did it mean? Fagan asked that in his letter to Governor Murphy. "What is the meaning of all this?" And the letter gave the answer, and it is the answer we all must hear as those legislators heard it, writhing. "The answer is plain! A Republican legislature is controlled by the railroad, trolley, and water corporations." So this honest Republican Mayor wrote; but he didn't stop there. "And the interests of the people are being betrayed."

After the reading, silence hung on that assembly. "I sat where I was," says Colby, "stunned. It was my duty to reply. I was the leader. The others were waiting for me. And I? I couldn't say a word. It was all true, every bit of it. Nobody moved for a dreadful space of time. Then Tom Hillory got up, and he defended us, all of us. I felt mean. I was sore, sore at myself, you understand; not at the Governor, not at the Penn; not at anybody else. I was sore at myself. It was true. We were dummies; we betrayed the people who elected us."

"Do legislators commonly understand that?" I asked.

"They must. I don't know. They must and yet, how can they? It isn't easy to explain. A fellow is moved by a lot of mixed-up considerations. Take my case. I saw it as Mark Fagan described it. I had more facts than he had, knew it better than he, but I didn't go right out and fight. Neither did he. Why didn't we? We both supported the Republican party that fall, and the party was not changed. The truth, falling like that, didn't kill; it didn't even change things essentially."

The Governor appointed a commission to investigate taxes, and the platform promised some reform, if reform should prove necessary. But the Republican nominee for Governor was "the Penn's man," Edward C. Stokes. And Colby and Fagan supported the ticket; they were "loyal to the party" which one said and the other admitted "represented corporations" and "betrayed the people." Why did they do it? Why do men like John C. Spooner and Edward C. Stokes "go along"? They know, and their friends say, they grieve themselves sick. Why did Mayor Weaver "go along" so long in Philadelphia? Everett Colby says he had excuses for the world, and some for himself. "The commission was to investigate and report," and he, meanwhile, threw himself into a study of taxation. He broke away, finally; like Mayor Weaver and Mark Fagan, he made a stand in the end. And why did he do that? And why did Mayor Weaver and Mark Fagan do it?

The way Everett Colby will try, when you ask

him, to lay bare his motives is one of the convincing traits of the man.   He is instinctively honest, and his candour is obvious.

"You'll hear," he told me, "that I wanted to be Speaker, and that my defeat made me turn. There is something in that.   I think you understand that I don't want to think that that was all, and, as I recall it, I don't think it was decisive, nor just that alone.   That was only one of a score of things that made me see — and drove me to act. I simply don't know the exact weight of any one thing."

All he knows is, that from seeing things separately, with his eyes, he came to see them all together with his mind.   His friends put into his head the idea of the Speakership in the next session (1905).   "I didn't care much," he said. "I felt I hadn't done very well, and I was willing to wait."   But he wrote to his colleagues, and enough of "the boys" promised him their support to elect him.   When Major Lentz got wind of it, he told Colby he couldn't have the Speakership.   This was the System at work; the House leader hadn't "made good"; he was not yet "safe"; but that isn't what the boss said.   Lentz said Colby mustn't run because he couldn't be elected.   With those letters in his pocket, Colby knew it wasn't his colleagues that would make

it impossible to elect him. He didn't mention
to Lentz how many pledges he had; but neither
did he bow to the boss as bosses like to be
bowed to.

Now political bosses are not really bosses;
they are the agents of the real bosses, who are
business men, and when Colby got a telephone
message to come to the Newark office of U. S.
Senator Dryden, the young man, his eyes wide open
now, realized that he was to see one of the men
who represented one of the sovereign interests of
his state. Senator Dryden, the president of the
Prudential Life, was there, and with him was
Lentz. The United States Senator was the
financial head of the Public Service Corporation
in New Jersey; not the president; Thomas C.
McCarter is that. Dryden is the man back of
McCarter as he is the man back of Lentz; and that
is why he was a United States Senator; he represented one of the two great sources of the corruption of the state. He told Mr. Colby that he
couldn't be Speaker. Dryden is a pleasant-
spoken man, and he appealed to "his young
friend's" good feeling, explaining that since he
couldn't get the votes, it would weaken the pres-
tige of their (Essex) delegation to run and fail.
But Colby said he could get the votes. How did
he know he could? He knew it because he had

them in his pocket; and he tapped those letters.
This was unexpected, and the Senator exclaimed:
"But Tom McCarter says it won't do."

That settled it. Tom McCarter spoke for
the trolley business.

Colby consented not to run; he told them it
was all right. "But," he said, "I could be elected if
I could have the support of my county."

Major Lentz approved, as they went away,
the obedience of his young protégé. "That's
the way to talk," he said. Colby was "mad";
he hated the fraud of it all. "Why didn't they
give their real reasons? Why didn't they say
they feared that as Speaker I might not represent their trolleys?"

The next session was to be crucial. Colby
made up his mind to be a free lance. The Speakership denied him, he would decline the leadership
also. Without knowing what he meant to do,
he was going to be free to act as he might find it
right to act.

If Colby had begun his career at the bottom,
in local politics, he would have known of two or
three separate reform movements that had long
been going on in his county, and he could have
gone to these, combined and led them against the
machine. He does lead them now, but he didn't
go to them; they came to him. One of these

movements was in Newark, the metropolis of the
state. This city belonged absolutely to the business interests grouped about the Prudential Life,
the Fidelity Trust Company, and the Public Service Corporation, which, ruling through Major
Lentz, gave the city a government in which these
special interests came first, the common interest
of the city last. The Democratic machine stood
in with the Republican ring. Now and then,
when James Smith, Jr., the Democratic business
boss, had business differences with the Republican
business grafters, there was a political fight. But
all the opposition that counted at all came from
a few young men, with William P. Martin at their
head, who, mostly Republicans, got into councils
and opposed steadfastly the public utility grabs.
Their story is a story by itself, and a good one;
suffice it for the present to say these fellows were
battling against the enemies of their city, the
public service interest, all the while Colby was trying to get along with his party.

Several other movements were under way in
the suburbs of Newark — Bloomfield, the Oranges,
etc. These were "good-government," "good-
men-for-office" reforms till Tom McCarter
aroused these "communities" to opposition to the
real cause of all their troubles. Tom McCarter
is a fiery, red-headed politician, who, as president

of the Public Service, believes honestly that anything that helps business is right. He was extending his trolley system, and, desiring to go through parks and residence streets, needed franchises. Of course, he must have them, and of course he must have them for nothing, and forever. Frederick W. Kelsey, a park commissioner, opposed him till public sentiment was formed and then McCarter undertook, by the methods characteristic of privilege-seekers, to get what he wanted anyhow. There were scandal and mass-meetings. The New England Society took up Kelsey's old fight against business graft. Could the fight have gone on locally, with McCarter's franchises for issues, it might have developed good citizenship in the Oranges. But both sides appealed to the state.

Tom McCarter, finding that the local council, though corrupt enough and willing, lacked the nerve to vote for him what he wanted in the face of "mobs" of good citizens, decided to appeal to the legislature; and his plan was to create a Greater Newark, taking into the city which he could control the suburbs which were giving the trolley "so much trouble." And the men of Orange, finding that their representatives in the local council did not represent them (except when watched), determined not to reform themselves and their voters and their council, but to go also to the legislature. Their petition was a very modest one; they wanted "their" state to forbid "their" council to grant any franchise for a period longer than twenty-five years.

The average Jerseyman thinks his state is well governed. His local government is bad, but politicians run that and he sees the results with his own eyes. The state is a government by lawyers, whom he knows by reputation at least; these lawyers are counsel for business men, like Senators Dryden and Kean, ex-Governor Murphy, and Tom McCarter — the kind of men he knows as good business men, and they tell him the state is all right. When the good men of Orange, finding that Tom McCarter was back of the politicians who misrepresented Orange, set about getting their good state government to check Tom's chicaneries in Orange, the average Jerseyman learned why Senator Dryden and Governor Murphy and Tom McCarter called the state government "all right." The state government also represented "business," and it did not represent the average citizen of Jersey.

The men of Orange had to approach the state legislature through members of that body, and, naturally, they applied to their own Essex County legislators. What was their surprise to find that their own representatives wouldn't, nay couldn't, represent them! One by one they sounded them only to *see* that no representative of theirs dared touch their bill. Why?

Everett Colby was learning why. The men of Orange decided to ask him to take up their bill, and the Newark fighters were to support them. Would Colby do it? He didn't know. Before his fellow-citizens asked him, he heard of their intentions and he wasn't sure what he should do. He was aware of the feeling between the corporations and the people, not only in Orange but everywhere, and his disposition was not to take a side, but to listen to both, study the subject, and do the fair thing.

One evening ex-Governor Murphy gave a dinner. "Everybody" was there; all the business and political leaders and others, quite a crowd. When they rose from the table Colby went up to Tom McCarter to get the trolley side of the franchise question. He heard, he said, that the New England Society of Orange had a limited franchise bill to offer to the legislature, and wouldn't McCarter like to talk it over with him (Colby)?

"Now, you know," said Colby to me, "they could have fooled me easily. If they had had any tact, and had given me any reasonable argument, I think, in my ignorance, I would have been taken in. But, no; they ruled and they ruled, not by reason, but by command."

Tom McCarter did not want to talk it over with Colby. Irascible and dictatorial, the trolley boss bent his head forward at the young legislator, and, slapping his hands insultingly in his face, he said that anything but perpetual franchises in Jersey was "talk," "child's play"; and, raising his voice so that all in the room turned to hear, he cried: "We wouldn't touch anything else with a ten-foot pole!" With that he turned his back on Colby, and walked off.

"It wasn't a question," Mr. Colby explained to me, as he recalled this scene, "it wasn't a question of right and wrong as between two interests; it was, and it is, a question of who rules here."

Colby listened to his neighbours. He explained to them how difficult it would be for them to get any relief from their legislature, how little he could do; but they were agreeing on plans when McCarter drove home the lesson Colby was learning. This time it was at a luncheon at Trenton. The legislature had met, and again all the rulers of the state were present, the rulers and their dummies, the office-holders and legislators. This time Tom McCarter went to Colby; that is to say, the business boss beckoned the assemblyman to him.

"Colby," he said, "what's this I hear about you introducing a limited franchise bill?" He didn't wait for an answer. Raising his voice, as before, so that all could hear, he laid down the law of the land for legislators. "You introduce that bill," he bawled in his mad rage, "and you'll lose every friend you have in Essex County."

What did Tom McCarter mean? His brother made that clearer. The financial rings that rule Jersey often have to smooth over the troubles their quick-tempered trolley president causes with his "honest grafter" blunders. Uzel McCarter, Tom's big brother, and the head of the trust company through which (like the Big Three) the Prudential Life Insurance crowd finances its trolley and other schemes — Uzel, a diplomat, joined Colby that day on a train. He talked pleasantly, even flatteringly, to the young man. By and by the franchise subject happened to come up, and that led, naturally, to Colby's connection with the bill to limit trolley grants. Most unfortunate connection, that.

"We," said the banker, "we think you have a political future before you, and we don't want to see you throw it away."

There was more, but that was the point. Uzel McCarter was taking the young man who couldn't be bribed with money, or browbeaten by the bosses, up on the mountain to see the cities of the earth, and the young man understood it.

"It was a promise," says Colby, "and — a threat."

Undaunted, uncorrupted, the young man came down from the mountain to a study of the situation. He knew a limited franchise bill could not be passed, so he hit upon the idea of introducing a resolution to put the legislature on record. He drew one. He spoke of it to no one except Edward Duffield, the House leader, to whom Colby, as an ex-leader, owed that courtesy. Just before he rose he turned to Duffield and said:

"Now, Ed, don't be surprised, but watch. And look out that you don't make the mistake of your life."

And Colby offered a resolution to the effect that it was the sense of this House that perpetual grants of monopolies to corporations should not be made. Everybody looked to the leader. He sat still. The Speaker hesitated, then, with all eyes on the mute leader, he put the motion. Colby says, and I've heard men in other states who know legislatures well say, that if a body of elected Americans are not interfered with by business corruption they will do right nearly every time. That House that night, having no orders from the System and getting no sign from

"Ed," adopted that resolution with not one negative vote!

But before the Speaker declared the resolution carried, the lobby woke up. Governor Stokes's Pennsylvania man came rushing in out of breath; wanted to know what the —— thing meant anyhow. "Can't you give us time?" he begged. Colby knew that A. J. Cassatt would call down Stokes and that Stokes would call down his man, and that the Public Service lobbyist and legislators would catch it; and besides, he didn't want to join in a fluke, so he said: "Surely; we'll make it a special order for Thursday."

The next day a telephone message summoned him to one of the business-political leaders of the state, a man who usually had been able to "handle Colby."

"Everett," said this man, "our friends are awfully upset by this resolution of yours." Of course, he said, it had gone too far to be absolutely withdrawn — by Colby, but "our friends will fix up an amendment," and "if you will accept this amendment, they'll let it pass." "*They*'ll let it pass!"

"You don't mean to tell me," Colby exclaimed, "that they are to determine what bills shall pass!"

"Now, Everett," said this gentleman, "you ought to know by this time how all these things are."

The amendments were absurd, ridiculous, impossible. Colby refused to accept them, and he meanwhile had been busy seeing his colleagues. The Speaker and four-fifths of the members were for the resolution. Yet, when it came up again on Thursday, only ten men voted "yes"!

This was only a preliminary skirmish in the long fight of that session of 1905. It was a defeat, but it was better than a victory since it aroused public interest and attracted to Trenton citizens and committees of citizens to take object lessons in a "good business government" in action. The Orange men — on hand in force — insisted upon having their limited franchises bill introduced, and Colby presented it. It went to committee for burial, but there were hearings on it, and Colby says the sight of citizens delivering carefully prepared arguments to a committee of legislators whom he knew to be dummies with no will of their own, no minds of their own, no ears for anything but the orders which they already had received to "hang onto that bill" — this spectacle, common as it was, and typical of all our legislatures from the youngest state to Congress itself, the humiliation of it struck deep into the growing intelligence of the young legislator. And evidently it made an impression on Jerseymen; the papers described the scene mercilessly, and the rumble of popular indignation finally scared the rings. Major Lentz is said to have told Governor Stokes that if some bill wasn't reported, "that fellow Colby would make a lot of trouble" for him (Lentz) in Essex. So the Pennsylvania Railroad threw over the Public Service Corporation. Stokes gave orders. A substitute bill was drawn, for a commission to investigate; that was all, but just before final adjournment this old device to gain time was reported and rushed through. And, even then, Tom McCarter told the Governor he had no right to let such a thing happen when "our great interests were against it." And Governor Stokes did not sign it for weeks; and then he appointed a commission typified by ex-Governor Murphy, the chairman.

A railroad tax bill, promised in the Republican platform, was introduced with the permission (as I happen to know) of Mr. Cassatt of Philadelphia, but it was in the form prescribed by "the road." It taxed second-class property (buildings and ordinary real estate) at local rates, but not the "main stem" (the roadbed). This would relieve Jersey City somewhat, but it would not satisfy Mayor Fagan or any other citizen who believed in "equal taxation."

And after it was passed, another bill was run out and jammed through, prescribing that the first bill should not materially increase the total tax of the railroads. This was made "the Governor's bill," but Colby opposed it and introduced another to tax the main stem like any other real estate. Of course, Colby's bill was beaten, but its defeat left equal taxation an issue in Jersey politics.

Another fight that showed things as they are, was over a bill to promote Tom McCarter's scheme to bring into a Greater Newark all the suburbs which did not respond to trolley corruption. Bloomfield was one of these. The people there had held the trolleys at bay; annexation had been proposed to them, and they had voted it down. In this session of 1905 some "leading citizens" of Bloomfield applied to the legislature for another referendum on annexation, and the trolley pretended to have nothing to do with it. But it had. Those leading citizens were stockholders and friends of stockholders in McCarter's company; Major Lentz "steered" them; and for more direct evidence, there was the story of a friend of Colby. This man had been in the employ of the Public Service. He was against the bill, and "they sent for him." This was their bill, they told him. They wrote it, and they needed it as a step in their plan to absorb into Newark all the troublesome suburbs about the city; their employee

must get out of the way. Their employee told
them he was out of their employ and, being therefore free, would continue to fight them with this
added information to spur him on.

It was this bill that finally brought about the
declaration of war between Boss Lentz and
Assemblyman Colby. One day, when Lentz
was steering his "citizens' committee" about the
Capitol, he introduced Colby to them. And he
told Colby in their presence that he must work
for their bill. "They contribute to the campaign
fund"; that was the reason he gave, and it was
bad enough, but Colby knew that the real reason
was that Tom McCarter and Senator Dryden
wanted to control through Newark the destinies
of Bloomfield and the Oranges against the will
of the inhabitants of those places.

David Baird came along as they were talking.
Baird is the Republican boss of Camden, and the
agent there of "the Penn" and the Public Service Corporation.

"David," said Lentz, after introducing him,
"I want you to get your boys in line for that
bill."

"All right, Major," said David, "I will."

Colby wasn't so agreeable. He didn't say
much, but Lentz suspected him and his suspi-
cions were promptly confirmed. Colby happened

to meet about noon that day the chairman of the committee which had the Bloomfield bill in charge, and they went together to lunch. When they entered the restaurant there sat the Major with his citizens. The boss seemed gradually to work himself into a rage, for after staring angrily at Colby a few moments, he got up, stalked over, and "putting his head in between ours," Colby says, "and spluttering in my face, he demanded to know if I was opposing him in this." So far as Colby can recall, he and the chairman hadn't mentioned the bill, but he *was* opposing Lentz "in this," and he said so.

"That settles it," said the Major.

Not only "that," but everything settled it between Colby and his boss and the bosses of the boss. Tom McCarter had said Colby would lose every friend he had in Essex; Uzel had warned him to take heed for his political future. "It was fight," says Colby now. "I went home from that session burning hot with indignation. But I didn't think about *my* political future. That had sunk into a small detail of a situation which was bigger than the political ambition of any man. I saw that the legislature, yes, and the government in nearly all of its branches, was ruled absolutely by our Jersey corporations. And despotically, unscrupulously, too; in the interest of their business, they were corrupting all of us. Hadn't they nearly corrupted me?"

The question was what to do. Colby didn't know what to do. He asked me what I would have done, and I pass it on to you who read this: What would you have done? And I ask the question to bring home to you the quandary of this young legislator and of his friends, and of the citizens of Orange and of Newark and of Jersey who wanted to fight. Lentz said Colby should not be renominated for the Assembly, and some of his friends proposed a fight in the party for the county committee. But Colby didn't want to run for boss of Essex; he wanted to make his appeal more to the people. This was an instinct, a democratic instinct which this rich railroad magnate's son has well developed in him. He proposed running an older man for senator, but the older man wouldn't run and the Newark, Bloomfield, and Orange men wanted Colby to lead their common fight. He was in doubt. He wanted to make the fight impersonal, and they adopted his principle to fight the boss, not Lentz; not the man, but the boss as an institution, as an agent of a corrupt oligarchy. But how?

"Then," said Colby, as he told me the story, "then came Record."

There's a good deal of feeling against George

L. Record in Jersey. He is the man who came to Mark Fagan when the kindly Mayor of Jersey City was at the first crisis of his administration, and Record helped Mark Fagan. From suspecting him, Mayor Mark came to lean upon him for his economic policy, and they and their Jersey City cabinet have influenced Jersey politics and the Jersey legislature more and more healthfully than any other one force in the state. Yet, while none denies the perfect honesty of Mark Fagan, many men distrust George L. Record. And you may recall that Colby, two years before, when he took to Fagan, "disliked" Record. But when "Record came," he told Colby just what to do and how to do it. Colby is very handsome in his acknowledgment of the service Record rendered them in Essex, and his friends confess, though more grudgingly, that Record is a man of resources. But nobody can see what Record gets out of it for Record. They think he wants to go to the United States Senate. I hope he does; this long, lean, thinking Yankee from Jersey City might accomplish something even in the United States Senate. But Record is another story, and it doesn't matter now "what Record is after."

When he came to Colby, he came suggesting that since Colby had made one good fight at Trenton, he should make another; and since he personified all the discontent that opposed the control of the state by the corrupt corporation of the state, he, Colby, was the man to run for Senator. How? There was the primary law. Record, the father of that law, suggested the use of it to beat the Republican boss in his own party. "But," he said, "don't stop there. Adopt a platform. Promise specific things and go to the people with these definite promises. And put up a full ticket: senator and assemblymen and county officers — everything."

Mark Fagan has in Jersey City a "group plan" of government. A picked lot of fellows get together, discuss, and agree upon policies and plans. Colby took that idea, and he accepted also the suggestion to join issue with fighters in other counties. So two groups, one from Essex and the other from Hudson, came together and out of their deliberations grew a platform and what is known as "The New Idea Movement."

They adopted Colby's Orange issue: limited franchises; Record's: franchise taxation; Fagan's: equal taxation; and Colby, Record and others added one new one: an expression at legislative elections of a popular choice for United States Senators.

It isn't necessary to follow the campaigns, for there were two — the first a fight at the primaries for the nomination for state senator, the second the general election at the polls. Both were anti-boss fights. Colby opened with an announcement of his candidacy, backed by a statement of his programme. The boss and the ringsters laughed. They laughed till the first mass-meeting was held. That was expected to fall flat, but the opera house was filled to overflowing and Fagan, Record, Colby and Martin aroused the crowd to tremendous enthusiasm. But the best thing Colby did was to adopt Fagan's method of meeting the voters face to face. Fagan told him how to do it. Colby asked him. The young club man thought there was some mystery about talking to workingmen, so he invited Mayor Mark to luncheon to get his secret. The Mayor was puzzled.

"Why, Mr. Colby," he said, "I can't tell you how to do that. I can tell you when you will find working-men at liberty to listen, and I can tell you how they feel about some of these great questions. But I can't tell you what to say to them. You must say just what you think, and, Mr. Colby, if you don't feel from the bottom of your heart a real interest in people you might as well stay at home."

"And that," says Colby, "is about the best advice I ever got. The instant he said it I knew it was right.   After that I went out to my noon-day meetings and I didn't try to find out what they thought.   I told them what I thought about things."

Colby's class suffers from class consciousness, as much, if not more, than labour does.   If he had gone forth as a rich man to the poor, or as a capitalist to labour, or as a business man offer-ing a good business administration to a people incompetent for self-government, he would have had to buy votes or be beaten.   But going as he did, as a man to men, and promising things that were directed at the reform, not of politicians and the police, and dirty streets, etc., etc., but of the grosser vices of his own class, even though he did not mention class, those people sized up "this rich young club fellow" as they sized up the ex-gilder and undertaker, Mark Fagan, and they put their faith in him as the Missourians did in Folk, as the people of Wisconsin did in La Follette, and as the people of San Francisco did in Heney.   The American people seem not to know the difference between clean streets and dirty streets, but they do know the difference be-tween hypocrisy and sincerity, between pluto-cracy and democracy.   They'll help you beat the boss if you'll show that you see as plainly as they do who is back of the boss.

The machine blundered.   The bosses always

blunder when, as they put it, "they go up against a new game," and the New Idea was a new game. Colby made use of Record's primary law to print his name, as candidate for the senate, after the names of his delegates. Lentz wouldn't do that. He wanted to elect his delegates, then dictate as of old, all the candidates to be nominated by the convention. Governor Stokes warned Lentz. Colby thought he saw signs of the Governor's interference against him, and he went to Mr. Stokes to ask that "he keep his hands off."

"Why," said the Governor, "all I have done was to tell Lentz that if he didn't name a man against you, you'd beat him."

Colby's crowd worked early and late. As time went on and the excitement grew, men who never had taken part in politics joined in what they agreed was the "greatest game they ever sat in at," the great game of politics. Everybody was welcome, and everybody was happy. It was a popular election, every man's election, and they won. Won? The completeness of their victory at the primaries astonished them. They carried everything. The next morning Major Lentz told Colby the convention was his, Colby's, and Colby might "run it" to suit himself. Very gracious, indeed, was this defeated boss, but he hoped (and he hopes) to be boss again.

"I've been thinking," he said to the victor, "that maybe I ought to resign. What do you think, Colby?"

"I think you might as well, Major," said Colby, who thought Lentz meant what he said. But Lentz didn't mean anything of the kind.

"Well, I won't," he answered in a huff. "I didn't mean resign the chairmanship of the county committee; I meant as manager of the campaign."

Colby said he and his crowd nearly went to pieces on this very point. They held their convention, and they nominated the whole legislative and county ticket. That had all been planned in advance. But what next? What about managing the campaign? Lentz had the county committee, and the county committee usually ran county campaigns. Colby and his group meant to have their fight made by a joint committee, but their plans were indefinite.

"We hadn't thought it out," Colby says, "and we made a bad blunder."

The county committee was to have a meeting, and it was the custom for candidates to go and be presented. Colby left town intending not to recognize the committee, but he was telephoned for by some of his best friends. As a victor he must not show ill-will, etc., etc. So Colby went to the meeting. In the course of the formalities,

Lentz said something about the campaign being run as usual, and, Colby says, "I should have jumped up then and there to declare that it would not be run as usual. I didn't. Don't know why I didn't, but I didn't. I just hadn't my wits about me, and I let it pass."

The next day the papers were full of the "Love Feast." "Colby and the boss were together." Colby thinks this was a very "bad break," and so do some of his friends, but mistakes don't count in these criminal days, and he corrected his promptly. He came out with a letter demanding that his own, not the county committee, should run the campaign. This was a repudiation of the organization. Lentz refused to give up, so he ran one campaign, and Colby's committee, with William P. Martin for chairman, ran the other. The machine men cut Colby at the polls, but he won in spite of them. The normal Republican majority in Essex County ranges from ten to twelve thousand. Colby's was 19,986, and some of the other men on his ticket ran a few hundred ahead of him.

The election of Everett Colby and his ticket ranked in significance with the victories that fall of Jerome in New York, of Weaver's ticket in Philadelphia, of Judge Dempsy's for Mayor of Cincinnati, of Tom Johnson in Cleveland, of

Brand Whitlock in Toledo, of Pattison in Ohio,
etc. They all were anti-boss fights. Some of
them, like Pattison's and Dempsy's, were minority party fights against the majority party boss;
some, like Jerome's and Whitlock's, were against
"both the bosses" and "all parties"; Colby's,
like La Follette's and Folk's, was within the
majority party. No matter how made, these
fights were all against the boss, and the boss fell.
What next?

The political boss is nothing but an agent of
the business bosses back of him. Some of these
anti-boss leaders know this; some do not. Those
that do may get somewhere; the others won't.
Colby is one of those that can see beyond the boss;
that is one reason why he would not make his
campaign a personal fight against Carl Lentz.
He saw, and he sees, and some of the men with
him see, the powers behind Lentz, and he is proceeding now, deliberately and intelligently against
them, the real enemies of the state, its active rulers,
the class which corrupts it, and its officials, and its
people for the sake of the privileges obtained or
to be obtained from the state.

Look at their programme of bills again. In
themselves they might not interest you and me
very much, but look behind those bills. To
"limit franchises" and "to tax them" — these

will bring these New Jersey leaders in direct, open
conflict with the Prudential-Fidelity-Trust-Public-
Service interests. To "tax the roadbed of
railroads" like any other real estate is to challenge a most profitable privilege of the Pennsylvania and other railroads. To let voters pledge
their legislators to candidates for the United
States Senate — that is to make the United States
Senate represent the people. All the resources
of the railroads, trolleys, and other public utilities,
and of all the "protected" businesses of Jersey
and of the United States will be called into play
to defeat this kind of reform; for this is real reform.
It is not a little tap at superficial evils; it is a stab
at the source of all evil in all our politics. It aims
at democracy, at the restoration of truly representative government. It is "radical"; it is "dangerous." If the corporations do to Colby in
Jersey what they have done to La Follette in Wisconsin, they will stir up envy and hatred against
him; they will befool his followers with false
arguments or buy them with money or office or
"business"; and they will embitter his life, public and private, too, with misrepresentation and
slander. If the fight is fought to a finish, every
trick known to expert manipulators of legislatures
and public opinion will be tried, but the rings
didn't believe it would be fought to a finish. Can

you guess why? One of them told me what their faith was founded upon.

"We'll get Colby," he said. "We'll get him before the session is over. He wants something. Every man wants something. It's all a matter of finding out what he wants. He may not know what it is himself, but we'll find out; and he'll get it and we'll get him — or his crowd, or both."

There is no conceit about Colby, no bluster, and when I told him this, he did not clench his fist and set his jaw. He pondered a moment, then he said:

"I wonder if they will."

Colby knows the tremendous power and the infinite ingenuity of the interests that will oppose him, so he wondered, as you or I may, what is going to happen to him. He is as open-minded to the truth about himself as he is to the truth about corruption, and because he is open-minded, and because he can confess his mistakes when he sees them; because he takes fences as he comes to them, and because he says he "will go any length to put a stop to the corruption of men and government," it is likely that the Gentleman from Essex will fight to a finish. What the end will be in Jersey, Jerseymen must decide; they will have to watch the struggle and choose between those representatives who represent them and those who do not. But the rest of us should watch, too. Everett Colby is a national leader; the Jersey fight is a national fight. The arena is local, but others are making the same fight elsewhere; the fight we all must make, sooner or later — the fight to restore the government of the people to the people.

BEN LINDSEY, THE JUST JUDGE

I. "THE KIDS' COURT"

IN the County Court of Denver, one night, a boy was arraigned for larceny. The hour was late; the calendar was long, and the Judge was sitting overtime. Weary of the weary work, everybody was forcing the machinery of the law to grind through at top speed the dull routine of justice. All sorts of causes went to this court, grand and petty, civil and criminal, complicated and simple. The petty larceny case was plain; it could be disposed of in no time. A theft had been committed; no doubt of that. Had the prisoner at the bar done it? The sleepy policeman had his witness on hand, and they swore out a case. There was no doubt about it; hardly any denial. The Law prescribed precisely what was to be done to such "cases," and the bored Judge ordered that that thing be done. That was all. In the same breath with which he pronounced sentence, the Court called for the "next case" and the shift was under way, when something happened, something out of the ordinary.

A cry, an old woman's shriek, rang out from the rear of the room. There was nothing so very extraordinary about that. Our courts are held in public; and every now and then somebody makes a disturbance such as this old woman made when she rose now with that cry on her lips, and, tearing her hair and rending her garments, began to beat her head against the wall. It was the duty of the bailiff to put the person out, and that officer in this court moved to do his duty.

But the man on the bench was Ben B. Lindsey, the celebrated Judge of the Juvenile Court of Denver. He wasn't celebrated then; he had no Juvenile Court. He was only a young lawyer and politician who, for political services (some aver, falsely, for delivering a vote for a United States Senatorship) had been appointed to fill out an unexpired term as County Judge. Lindsey didn't want to be a judge; he had asked for the district-attorneyship. His experiences on the inside of politics had shown him that many things were wrong, and he had a private theory that the way to set the evils right was to enforce the law, as the law. But another man, Harry A. Lindsley, had a prior claim on the district-attorneyship, and Ben Lindsey had to take the judgeship or nothing. So he had taken it (January 8, 1901), and he had been administering justice — as

Justice — for several weeks when that woman cried out against his "Justice," and his "bailee" moved to uphold the decorum of his court, the dignity of the Law. And — the Judge upheld the woman.

"I had noticed her before," he says now. "As my eye wandered during the evening it had fallen several times on her, crouched there among the back benches, and I remember I thought how like a cave-dweller she looked. I didn't connect her with the case, any case. I didn't think of her in any human relationship whatsoever. For that matter, I hadn't considered the larceny case in any human way. And there's the point: I was a judge, judging 'cases' according to the 'Law,' till the cave-dweller's mother-cry startled me into humanity. It was an awful cry, a terrible sight, and I was stunned. I looked at the prisoner again, but with new eyes now, and I saw the boy, an Italian boy. A thief? No. A bad boy? Perhaps, but not a lost criminal. I called him back, and I had the old woman brought before me. Comforting and quieting her, I talked with the two together, as mother and son this time, and I found that they had a home. It made me shudder. I had been about to send that boy to a prison among criminals when he had a home and a mother to go to. And that was the Law!

BEN B. LINDSEY

The fact that that boy had a good home; the circumstances which led him to — not steal, but 'swipe' something; the likelihood of his not doing it again — these were 'evidence' pertinent, nay vital, to his case. Yet the Law did not require the production of such evidence. The Law? Justice? I stopped the machinery of justice to pull that boy out of its grinders. But he was guilty; what was to be done with him? I didn't know. I said I would take care of him myself, but I didn't know what I meant to do — except to visit him and his mother at their home. And I did visit them, often, and — well, we — his mother and I, with the boy helping — we saved that boy, and to-day he is a fine young fellow, industrious, self-respecting, and a friend of the Court."

This was the beginning, the Judge will tell you, of his practice of putting juvenile offenders, not in prison to be punished, but on probation to be saved. It wasn't. The Judge is looking backward, and he sees things in retrospect as he has thought them out since, logically, with his mind. If you should take his word for it, you would get the impression that this first "probation case" was the beginning of his famous Juvenile Court, the most remarkable institution of the kind in all the world. And if you got that impression in just that way, you might do as the reformers of some twenty-five states and a few hundred cities have done — you might lose the significance of Judge Lindsey. You might learn his methods and miss the man. You might imitate his "kids' court," and make a mistake with both the "kids" and their "Jedge," as they call him. And you certainly would do, as Denver desires to do, and Colorado — limit the meaning of Judge Lindsey's life-work to the problem of the children.

Ben Lindsey's "methods" are as applicable to grown-ups as to kids. Man has a way of inventing devices to help him to be a man; a spear, an army, the Church, political parties, business. By and by the aid to his weakness comes to be a fetish with him, a burden, an end in itself, an institution. He decorates his spear, keeping a commoner weapon to hunt with. His army returns from fighting his enemies to conquer him. Priests declare the Church holy and, instead of ministering to men, make men minister to the Church. Political parties, founded to establish principles for the strengthening of the State and its citizenship, betray principles and manhood and the State for the "good of the party." Business, the mere machinery of living, has become in America the purpose of life, the end to which all other goods — honour, religion, politics, men, women and children, the very Nation itself —

are sacrificed. And so with the laws and the courts. Jurists and legislators note and deplore the passing of respect for the Law and of faith in the courts, and they wonder why. It is largely because we laymen think we observe that legislation purporting to be for the common good is bought for the special evils; that laws enacted to help us are manipulated to our hurt; and that our courts, set up to render justice, either make a worship of the letter of the Law or violate the spirit thereof to work deliberate injustice. As for the penal code, nourished by the centuries to prevent crime, it is operated as escapes for the strong criminal or as instruments of society's revenge upon the weak.

Ben Lindsey's great, new, ancient discovery is that men are what we are after, men and women; and that everything else, business and laws, politics, the Church, the schools — these are not institutions, but means to those higher ends, character and right living. He began with the laws; the Law he was prepared to revere. He saw that the Law was capable of stupid injustices and gross wrongs; and setting humanity up on the bench beside his authority, he has reduced the Law to its proper, humble function — the service of men and of the State. He has drawn the sting of punishment out of the penal code, stamped

out the spirit of vengeance; he has tried to make
his Court a place where the prisoners at the bar
are helped to become good men and useful citizens. His greatest service has been to boys and
girls, but that is only because he found in children
the most helpless victims of our machine system
of "businesslike justice." He has created in his
Juvenile Court a new human institution, the
beauty and use of which is spreading imitative
"movements" all over the land. But, wonderful
as his creation is, this man should not be known
as the founder of another institution. That might
become, like certain societies for the prevention
of cruelty to animals or to children, only another
"end in itself."

Judge Lindsey is a man, a brave, gentle man,
who is re-introducing into life, all life, and into
all the institutions which he can influence, the
spirit of humanity. As he puts it in his "Problem
of the Children," "these great movements for the
betterment of our children are simply typical of
the noblest spirit of this age, the Christ-spirit of
unselfish love, of hope and joy. It has reached
its acme in what were formerly the criminal
courts. The old process is changed. Instead of
coming to destroy, we come to rescue. Instead
of coming to punish, we come to uplift. Instead of
coming to hate, we come to love."

That the man has this more general significance is shown by the gradual, apparently accidental way in which he developed his "methods" and his Court. He didn't think them out with his mind. That isn't the way big, human things are done in this big, human world of ours; they are felt out with the heart. The man Lindsey had heart, and the cave-dweller's cry reached it, and when the Judge felt her agony, he found himself. That was all. His judgment in this case was but the beginning of Judge Lindsey's practice of putting heart into his business. He didn't know what probation was when he said he'd take care himself of the cave-dweller's boy. We have seen that he hadn't thought of being a judge, and the idea of a Juvenile Court hadn't dawned upon him. It took other cases to "set him thinking." The other cases came.

One day a "burglary" appeared on his calendar. The Judge says he looked around curiously for the burglars. He saw none till the case was called. Then three boys were haled whimpering before him, three ordinary, healthy American boys, from twelve to sixteen. What had they burglarized? A pigeon-loft. A pigeon-loft! Yes, your Honour, they broke into a pigeon-loft and were caught red-handed stealing pigeons. That was burglary; there was no doubt about the crime.

What was to be done with the burglars? They
were to be sent to the reformatory, of course;
the Law prescribed the penalty. The Judge
shook his head, "No."

He didn't say so in court then, but he tells now
how he was recalling the time when he, as a boy,
went robbing a pigeon-loft. He didn't actually
commit "burglary," but he would have if he
hadn't lost his nerve. He was "scared"; the other
kids had told him so, and it was true. And they
left him, in contempt and ashamed, while they
robbed the coop. So he wasn't an ex-convict,
not because he was a good boy, no; nor because
he was "smaller than them," though that was a
plea set up in the gang in his behalf. He wasn't
a burglar, like these boys before him now, simply
because he didn't have as much "sand" as
they had. Was he going to punish them as
burglars, "send them up" for crime, to live among
criminals? No.

But the complainant had a view to present.
A worried, old, persecuted man, he told how boys
were forever stealing his pigeons; how he had
"laid for them" again and again; how they generally escaped; and how, finally, after many failures, he had caught these three. He wanted them
punished; he begged to have them "sent to jail."

There was something familiar in the appear-

ance of the poor old pigeon fancier, and the Judge
questioned him: where he lived; where his barn
was; just where the pigeon-loft was; what his
name was; whether he had a nickname. The old
man answered, peevishly, but fully enough for the
Judge to learn what he wanted to know. This
was the very man, his were the pigeons, his loft
was the same old loft which he, the Judge, and
his gang had burglarized years ago. And now
the Law expected him, a Judge, to send to prison
these boys who were no worse than he was; nay,
who were better, for they had the "sand" he
lacked! If he, the Judge, had been sent up for
burglary he might not have become County Judge,
and if he didn't send up these boys as burglars,
they might become county judges, or — since they
had more "sand" — something better.

But there was the Law; what about that?
The boys had committed a crime; what was the
Judge to do with them? He didn't know; he
would have to "think it over." And he thought
it over. He went back to first principles. What
did the complainant really want? Only to have
his property protected. And what was the law
against burglary for? To protect property by
preventing burglary. Wasn't there any other way
to achieve these common ends except by punishing these boys as burglars? And if he put them

in prison might not other boys go on robbing the pigeon-loft? The Judge says it is "out of the mouths of babes" that he has learned wisdom. He took the prisoners into his chamber, and he talked with them.

Now, the Judge's talks with boys and girls are regarded with superstition by some people; he gets such wonderful results — the truth, for example. Children who lie to their parents, their teachers, and the police, tell him everything. The police started a story that Judge Lindsey is a "hypnotist," and others speak wisely of his "method." His "method" is very simple; he employed it, before he knew it was a "method," with his Italian "thief" and his first trio of "burglars." Friendship is the key. Judge Lindsey talks to boys as one boy talks to another.

His personal appearance helps him. The "Jedge" is a short, slight, boyish-looking young man, open-faced, direct, sincere, and he lays off the ermine, figuratively speaking, very readily; indeed, he hardly ever puts it on now, even on the bench. In chambers he comes right down to earth, using boy-talk, including slang. For this he has been criticized by good people who think of English as an institution, to be kept pure. The Judge answers that he has something else in mind than the purity of the language. He has

found "after four years' experience that the
judicious use of a few of these slang terms not only
does not hurt the boy, but actually helps him, and
wins his confidence," and, since the boys are what
he is after, he declares he will "continue to talk
to the boys to a certain extent much the same as
they talk with one another."

As a matter of fact, it is an instinct with the
Judge, a part of his simple naturalness and his
native desire to understand others, which prompts
him to say "fellers"; "ah, say, kids, let's cut it out."
When he called in his burglars, it was no judge
that asked them if they belonged to a gang. It
was no fatherly elder, wisely pretending to a
superior sort of interest in the habits and cus-
toms of their "crowd," and the limits of their
range or habitat. It was "one feller askin' th'
other fellers, on the level now, all about swipin'
pigeons." The reason he, the Judge, and his
gang robbed the coop was to get a certain variety
of fan-tail pigeons which the old man wouldn't
sell, and he understood it when the boys explained
that what they were after, really, was to get back
some of their pigeons which had joined the old
man's bigger flock. Also, however, the boys understood the Judge when he reflected that it wasn't
right to go and "rob back" your pigeons; that it
annoyed the old man, wronged him, and hurt the

boys. Maybe the old man was grouchy, but, gee, the coop was his, and "swiping" wasn't "square." It was sneaky, it was weak to steal. So he proposed to stop this "weakness" of this gang; not only of the three that had been caught, but of the whole gang.

Now, the Judge teaches respect for grown-up law by himself invariably showing great respect for "kid law." It is against the law of Boyville to "snitch" (tattle). So he wouldn't let them tell him who the other "burglars" were. "But, say, fellers," he said, "you bring in the other kids, and we'll talk it over, and we'll see if we can't agree to cut out stealing altogether, and especially to stop swipin' pigeons off the old man."

That was fair, and it was human. They went away, and they got the gang. And the gang entered into a deal with the "Jedge"; "sure they did." Who wouldn't? And do you think they would go back on a Judge like that? Sure they wouldn't, and they wouldn't let any other feller go back on him either; not much; not if they could prevent it; and they thought they could. And they did, as they reported from time to time.

It was this case, which, coming home so personally to him, set the Judge thinking. "It seemed to me," he says, "that we were not proceeding just right in such cases. I didn't know anything about it, but it looked wrong to charge these boys with burglary. It was unnecessary under the Law, too; the school law of 1899 permitted children to be brought to the County Court as 'juvenile disorderly persons.' And here they were being arraigned as thieves and burglars. We were dealing with the thing the child did, not with the child; and the child was what should concern us. I don't blame anybody in particular. I had been at fault myself. A good many children were brought into my Court, and I had been following the thoughtless routine. The fact is, I was pretty free in sending boys to the Industrial School at Golden till these special cases awoke my special interest. Then I began to consider the situation generally. I found that there was no system about juvenile cases. Some were sent to the District Court, others to the Justice Courts, others to mine. We all were 'trying' the boys for the 'crimes' they had committed, finding many of them guilty and sending them away. It was absurd; it was criminal, really. The thing a child had stolen was treated as of more importance than the child. This was carrying the idea of property to an extreme. It was time to get back to the idea of men and women, the men and women of to-morrow, and obviously some system of character-building was needed in the Court. Fortunately, there were laws in existence under which juvenile offenders could be brought into court as 'dependent,' 'neglected,' or 'delinquent' children, and these laws were enough as they stood for the starting of a Juvenile Court. We hoped to get other laws later; but those that we had would enable us to treat the children, rather than the children's crimes."

Judge Lindsey went to District-attorney Lindsley with the request that all children's cases be brought to his Court; and that they be accused there of delinquency instead of the particular crimes for which they were arrested. The District-attorney was willing. Lindsey's request was regarded as "queer," but nobody wanted the bother of these "kids'" cases, so the Judge was permitted to found his "kids' court." And he founded it, and it is the "kids' court," their very own. It is run in the interest of the "bad" boys and girls, and therefore of the state, and the children needed the Court, and so did the state.

While the Judge was "thinking," the question arose in his mind: "What sort of a place is the Industrial School where I have been sending boys so freely?" He went to Golden to see. Nobody up there remembered ever having been visited before by a judge on the bench, and this Judge saw boys with the ball and chain on them. He began a quiet reform of the reformatory. Then he asked himself what kind of places the jails were. One Sunday evening he visited the City Jail.

"It was a dirty, filthy place," he says. "The plaster was off the walls, which were crawling with vermin."

He went over to the County Jail. The conditions were much the same, but what stirred up the Judge's "thoughts" to the bottom of his heart was the sight of boys in the same cells with men and women "of the vilest type." A little further inquiry showed him that these children were allowed to associate freely with grown criminals. Locked up with them in the County Jail, they visited the men in the bull-pen down in the City Jail. The boys liked to listen to the "great criminals," and the great criminals liked to brag to the boys. It was a school of crime. The men told the boys how they "beat the police" and, filling them with criminal ideals, taught them how to commit "great" crimes.

"I found that in the five years before I went on the bench, 2,136 Denver boys had been in these jails for periods varying from a few hours to thirty days, and," the Judge adds in his mild way, "I was satisfied the influence was not good. But that was typical. This was being done all over

the country, and it is now in many places. Every
boy who makes a mistake or, if you will, every
child that shows any tendency to crime is sent
to a school where crime is taught. Is it any wonder that juvenile crime is on the increase?"

And the Judge found that juvenile crime was
on the increase generally in the United States.
He engaged the services of a clipping bureau, and
he quotes, in his "Problem of the Children," some
of the results: "Five Thousand Boys Arrested
Last Year" (in one city); "4,000 out of 16,000
Arrests Last Year Were Boys Under Twenty" (in
a city of less than 150,000); "Bandits Caught Mere
Boys" (a frequent head line); "Over Half the
Murderers Last Year Were Boys"; "Boy Burglars
Getting Common"; "Thieving Increasing Among
Children"; "Desperate Boy Bandits Captured"
(aged twelve, thirteen, and fifteen). And he cites
the Van Wormer boys of New York; the Bid-
dles of Pennsylvania; the car-barn murderers
of Illinois; the Collinses of Missouri; the boy
murderers of Nebraska; the Youngblood murderers of Denver; the boy train-wreckers of the
West, and the reform-school boy murderers of
California. The phrase "mere boys" indicated
that the news editors regarded juvenile crime
as exceptional and remarkable; it isn't. Three-
quarters of the crimes committed in the United

States, the Judge says, are done by boys under twenty-three!

"And why not?" he asks. "The children of parents who die or fail in their duty are taken by the State and sent for their schooling into the streets or jails where they pick up false ideals and criminal arts. With few exceptions, all these boy criminals named above, whom society has sent to the slaughter-house to be killed, had been sent to jail in their teens by society for other crimes. And most of them were first imprisoned as little children."

In other words, our criminal court system does not prevent, it fosters crime. Our "businesslike" procedure of heartless, thoughtless "justice" makes criminals. What should the State do? The Judge says that when the State gets hold of a "bad" child, it takes the place of the parent, and like a good parent, it should try to mould that child into a good citizen. He gives an illustration in his "Problem of the Children."

"We recall the case (and it is one of hundreds)," the Judge says there, "of a young man who had been in the criminal courts at the age of thirteen. At twenty he shot down a policeman who was heroically doing his duty. Suppose that at the age of thirteen that boy had been studied, helped, looked after, and carefully handled; would that policeman be maimed for life, or dead, a young wife and child a charge on the community, and a strong, robust young man a charge on the State for life? Perhaps not, and even so we could have felt better about it, and in the sight of God less accountable. Was the State responsible? Yes, even more than the boy, for he was in jail in the plastic stage. The State had him in time, and it did nothing — not even try. The State treated him as a man, this boy. . . Strange that if his money or property were involved he could control none of it; he would need a guardian in that case. A boy's property is important. But his morals — the boy, the man in embryo, the citizen to be — needed no guardian. This boy needed no help. He needed punishment. He needed retribution, and so as a boy he got what men got, that which is often barbarous even for men. I have seen them, eleven to fifteen years of age, in the same bull-pen with men and women, with chains about their waists and limbs. And I have seen them crowded together in idleness, in filthy rooms where suggestiveness fills the mind with all things vile and lewd. Such has been too often the first step taken by the great State in the correction of the child."

Judge Lindsey founded his Juvenile Court to correct and save to the State the children who were caught up in the meshes of the criminal law, and his first step was the correction of himself and of the Court. Having to start with only the idea, which was really little more than a sentiment, that the welfare of the child prisoner was the chief consideration, he had to institute proceedings to meet the needs of the child. What were those needs? The Judge didn't know, and he had no theory; he had to find out for himself. How did he go about finding out? Very simply, very naturally. He asked the child.

One of the first, most obvious observations he made was that children came into Court with either tears or defiance in their eyes. They hated the policeman, and they feared the Judge, and since the "cop" and the Court were the personification of justice and the State, these young citizens were being reared in the spirit of dread and hatred of law and authority. This was all wrong, and yet it was perfectly natural.

"The criminal court for child-offenders," writes the Judge, "is based on the doctrine of fear, degradation, and punishment. It was, and is, absurd. The Juvenile Court was founded on the principle of love. We assumed that the child had committed, not a crime, but a mistake, and that he deserved correction, not punishment. Of course, there is firmness and justice, for without these there would be danger in leniency. But there is no justice without love."

The Judge drove out fear from his Court, and hate and brutality; for awe, he substituted confidence and affection. How did he do this? By coming down off the bench to the boy. Since the boy was the centre of interest, the Judge subordinated his own "dignity" and the whole machinery of the Court and even the "stolen property," to win back the prisoner at the bar. The good of the boy, obviously paramount in the mind of the Court, was made paramount in the mind of the boy, who was led to feel that everybody cared about him, that everything done was done for him in his interest. "Of course," he says, "the Law is important, but the vital thing is the relationship established with the child. The case from the boy's standpoint must be understood." Each case, the Judge means. He seeks to get for himself a personal, sympathetic understanding of each separate case. There are no hard and fast rules. No fixed routine will do the work. The Judge didn't turn away hate, quiet fear, and dry tears by any "methods." When a child is brought weeping or scowling before him, Ben Lindsey is dragged off that bench by his heartstrings, and when he sits on a stool beside the boy in trouble, or goes for a walk with him, or takes him home to dinner or "out to the show," this is no art thought out by a wise man. This is nothing but a good man putting into his work what he wants to get out of it — "faith, hope, and love."

To understand the case of Ben Lindsey, it is necessary to study it as he advises us to study the cases of boys — from the boys' standpoint. He tells in one of his articles how a young fellow of twenty, who was under sentence for murder, regarded the old criminal court. This boy had been arrested at the age of twelve for stealing a razor to whittle a stick. "It was this way," he explained to Lindsey. "The guy on the high bench, with the whiskers, says, 'What's the boy done, officer?' And the cop says, says he, 'He's a bad kid, your Honour, and broke into a store and stole a razor.' And the guy on the high bench says, 'Ten dollars or ten days.' Time, three minutes; one round of a prize-fight."

In Judge Lindsey's court, in the beginning, when boys still came there with sorrow and gnashing of teeth, they saw no "guy with whiskers, on a high bench" asking the "cop" questions. They saw a clean-cut young man come into court, go up to the first boy to be "tried" and ask: "What's the matter, my boy? You been making a mistake? Well, lots of fellers make mistakes. That's nothing. I've made mistakes myself, worse'n yours, I guess." Then turning to the policeman, he asks: "What is it, officer?" The policeman tells about the crime, say theft. "Stealing isn't right," says the Judge, and he appeals to the boys in the court room, "Is it, fellers?" Putting his hand on the boy's shoulder, he gives him a shove back and a pull forward. "It's weak to swipe things." That hurts. Boys learn in the street that it's smart and brave to steal, and the only evil thing about it is getting caught. Lots of men take this view, too, but Judge Lindsey sets up another standard. "I know how it is," he says. "It's a temptation. It's a chance to get something easy, something you want; or something you can sell to get something you want. Wanted to go to the show, maybe. Well, it takes a pretty strong feller to down the desire to take the chance and see the show. But it's wrong to swipe things. 'Tain't fair; 'tain't brave; it's just mean, and it hurts the feller that steals. Makes him steal again, and by and by he is caught and sent up — a thief. Now you ain't a thief, and you don't want to be. Do you? But you were too weak to resist the temptation, so you were caught. Ought to cut it out. Not because you were caught. That isn't the reason a feller oughtn't to steal. It's because it's mean and sneaky, and no feller wants to be mean and sneaky. He wants to be on the square.

"But what are you crying for? You've been crying ever since I began to talk to you. Afraid of being punished? Pshaw, a feller ought to stand up and take his medicine; but we don't punish boys. We just try to help 'em get strong and be square. Even when we send fellers to Golden, it isn't for punishment; it's only to help a kid that's weak to get strong enough to control himself. So we aren't going to punish you. I believe you can control yourself without going to Golden. We'll see. But first off, a kid ought to be strong enough and sufficiently on the square to tell the truth about himself. Ought to tell not only about this time, when you're caught, but all the other times, too. You wait, and after court we'll go back in chambers and we'll have it all out, just us two."

This is rather reassuring, isn't it? It proved so to the children who sat waiting their turn at the first sessions of the Juvenile Court. There was no terrorism in it, no trace of hardness, there were no awful forms. The children felt the difference. "The Judge, he gives a feller a show," said one boy to me. And as they saw the proceedings in court, so the children heard about the scenes in chambers. These were the best of all, best for the kids and best for the Judge. There is where Lindsey saw into the hearts of children, and where they saw into his.

"Never let a child get away with a lie on his soul," the Judge says. "A clean breast is half the battle." Children are wonderful liars, but the Judge thinks he can tell when they are lying and they admit that he has an instinct for the truth. One foundation for their respect for him is that with all his kindness he isn't sentimental; and he isn't "easy." "You can't fool the Jedge," the boys say, and the police tell, as an illustration, the story of a "tough kid" on whom all the Judge's appeals seemed to fail. He "lied straight," and since the Judge will not help (try) a boy who will not tell the truth, he told the officer to take the boy away. On the way back to jail, the boy changed his mind. He asked to be taken again before the Judge. "You're right, Judge," he said, "and you're game, too. I lied to you; I lied like a horse thief; and I couldn't fool you a little bit. You've beat me, Judge, and I'll tell you th' truth." And he did.

The Judge in chambers reasons with the boy that while it is wrong to "snitch" on other fellows, it is all right to "snitch" on yourself. The boys understand this. It is made clear to them that there is no punishment, only "help for a feller if he needs it," and among the most interesting experiences that the Judge has to tell, are the discussions he has with boys as to whether they "need to go to Golden."

There's a little, old, young, big man, called "Major," whom I saw in command of the battalion at Golden. He is somewhere between twelve and sixteen, but with an old, old face; very tiny of stature, but very tall in dignity. He never smiles, so sober and sensible is he. But he had what the kids and their Judge know as the "movin'-about fever." The Major had come honestly by it. He had no home, and he wanted none, for he could range all over the West, from Chicago up into Idaho and down into New Mexico, and always, everywhere, he was known, for his pompous dignity, to hoboes, cow-boys, miners — to all men as "the Major." The Judge gave him trial after trial, and it was no use; the time always came when the Major had to "move on." If they must move, the Judge lets boys go, but he expects them to call on him to say good-bye and be pledged to write to him regularly and not to steal. Well, once when the fever was coming upon the Major, he called on the Judge. The Judge urged the Major to down the temptation. The Major tried, but he couldn't; he confessed that he was too "weak" to resist. Then the Judge suggested Golden; they would help him there, all right, to stay. The Major received the suggestion thoughtfully. He raised objections which the Judge answered, but they separated without a decision, and the Judge says that for a week or two he and the Major weighed ponderously the mighty question, till in the end the Major agreed that perhaps he'd better go up to Golden and be helped to cure that moving-about attack and thus learn to "stay put." That's how the Major came to go to Golden, and that's how he won the rank and title which the "movin'-about" world had given him as a "little shaver."

And that's the spirit in which the Judge in chambers persuades boys to "snitch up" on themselves and look upon the reformatory as a help. As they begin to tell him things bit by bit, he expresses no horror, only understanding; he sympathizes with a feller. If a kid describes how he saw an easy chance to steal and not get caught, the Judge exclaims: "Gee, that was a chance. That's certain. But 'tain't square, Hank." "Mistake" after "mistake" is confessed, "weakness" after "weakness"; no crimes, you understand, for the kid and the Judge, they see things through the kid's eyes, with all the mitigating circumstances. And so they come to discuss the question whether the kid can "cut it out." The Judge is sure the boy can, surer than the boy, but then, it's up to the boy, because the boy has to do the hard work of resisting. The Judge can "only help; th' feller has to do the business himself." "Interest is everything in a boy's life," the Judge says sagely. "If you want his loyalty, excite his interest." Well, the game of correction is interesting, especially when you are the centre of the game. It's one of the most interesting games "a feller" ever played, and the Judge has a fascinating way of playing it. Having done something wrong, you try to do something that's right, positively right. This is the Judge's great doctrine. He calls it "overcoming evil with good." There's nothing "sissy-boy" about it. You have done an evil thing; you are not, therefore, bad, only so much weakened. So you go and do a good thing. This not only balances the evil; it "strengthens a feller."

Now then, a good thing a feller can usually do right away is to go out and bring in some other kids that are "swipin' things." You mustn't tell the Judge who the other fellers are. That would be snitching. But it's all right to get the other fellers to come in and "snitch up" on themselves just as you have "snitched up" on yourself. That gets them into the game; helps them and, since the more fellers there are in on it, the easier it is for you — it helps you.

One of the early cases in the Juvenile Court was that of seven boys brought before him by a policeman who had caught them wiring up signal-boxes, hopping cars, stoning motormen and conductors, and otherwise interfering with the traffic of the street railway. The boys were either tearful or sullen, and they denied the testimony of the officer and his witnesses. The Judge took them into his chambers. There he cleared away all ideas of punishment, and got down to the truth. The Judge could see that it was fun, but also he could see that what was fun for the boys was trouble for the conductors and motormen; it made life hard for them, delayed them, and got them home late. The boys hadn't thought before of these railroad men as human beings, only as "fair game," as "fellers what'd give you a chase if you held 'em up." So the Judge gave the boys a good view of the men's side of the fun, then he said:

"'Tain't fair, is it, fellers?"

"No, sir."

"Well, what do you say to cuttin' it out?"

They agreed. But there was more for these boys to do than simply to quit themselves. There was an evil deed done to be overcome with good. There was the gang.

"Will you fellers bring in the rest of the gang to-morrow?"

"Sure they would." But they didn't. The seven turned up the next day without their "crowd."

"The other fellers was askeared to come," they reported.

"Well, what are you going to do?" the Judge asked the seven.

They believed that if the Judge would write a letter to the gang, they would come.

"A warrant," said the Judge, seizing the chance to take the terror out of another instrument of the Law. "I'll write you out a warrant, and you shall serve it on the gang. But what'll I write?"

One little fellow spoke up. "You begin it," he said; "begin by saying, 'No kid has snitched, but if you'll come, the Judge'll give you a square deal.'"

This showed what the matter was, and it brought home to the Judge the force of his own feeling against snitching.

The Judge began the "warrant" as the little fellow suggested, and thus he ended it, too. The boys took it, and evidently they served it, for the next day the gang came pouring into the court, fifty-two kids. There was a talk, straight talk, like that which he gave the seven. Only the Judge put more faith into it. He was going to see if they couldn't get along out where that gang lived without any policemen. The peace of the neighbourhood was to be left to the gang, but the gang had to play fair, and give him a square deal.

"For," said the Judge, making a personal appeal to their honour, "I have told the company that I would be responsible for their having no more trouble. The company don't trust you kids; and they say I'll be fooled. They said you'd go back on me. But I said you wouldn't, and I say now that you won't. So I'm depending on you fellers; and I don't believe you'll throw me down. What do you say?"

"We'll stay wit' you, Jedge," they shouted. And they didn't throw the Judge down. They organized, then and there, a Kid Citizens' League, and the League played square with the Judge.

It will be noticed that Lindsey made effective use in this case of the "gang" which the police and all prematurely old reformers seek only to "break up." The "kids' Jedge" never thought of breaking up such organizations. His sense is for essentials, instinctively, and there's nothing wrong about gangs as such. They are as natural as organizations of men. The only trouble with gangs is that they absorb all the loyalty of the members, turning them from and often against the home, the Law, and the State. But that happens in grown-ups' gangs, too. Railroad and other corporations are gangs which, in the interest of their "business," corrupt the State. Churches are "gangs" whose members submit to evils because, if they fought them, the church might be hurt. So with universities, and newspapers, and all kinds of business organizations. Tammany Hall is only a gang which, absorbing the loyalty of its members, turns it, for the good of the gang, against the welfare of the city. Judge Lindsey simply taught the members of his kid gang what many gangs of grown-ups have to learn, that they are citizens also, and he turned the loyalty of the Kid Citizens' League back to the city, using the honour of the gang as his lever.

Another similar case came up when two boys were brought in by a policeman from the Union Station. The policeman said they belonged to a gang the members of which stoned him wherever they saw him. Why? Well, he was trying to keep them out of the station and off the grass around the station. What were the boys doing at the station and on the station lawn? They

explained, and they explained with many mani-
festations of hate for the cop. They were there
to sell papers. It was their place of business,
and everybody had acknowledged it — not only
all the other newsboys, but everybody else — till,
one day, some other bigger boys with red caps
appeared there selling papers and things. Then
"this cop chased us off." Why? Why had the
cop suddenly interfered with their business? It
was his turn to explain, and he explained that the
railroad company, having come to realize that the
trade in newspapers at the station was profitable,
had decided to take a share in it. The concession was let to a man who employed the boys
with red caps. The man wanted a monopoly.
So the policeman had received orders to drive off
the other boys. He had obeyed. No explanation was given to the boys; no notice. They suddenly found themselves deprived of their means
of livelihood, and resenting it, blamed the cop
and — stoned him.

Thus it was all a misunderstanding, not a
"crime" at all, and the Judge undertook to clear
it up to the satisfaction of all concerned. Having explained it to the two boys under arrest, he
enlisted their services in behalf of the Court to
bring in the others who were "in it" but had not
been caught. The policeman, knowing how hard

it had been to catch two, was scornful of the Judge's confidence of getting the rest, but he was invited to be present at the hour appointed for the "round up," and he was not a little chagrined when his two prisoners returned with twenty-four other kids. The Judge lined up the gang on one side of the room, the policeman and his friends on the other. This was the Juvenile Court in session; let the Judge describe what happened:

"I proceeded to explain why it was that the owners of the station had a right to grant 'concessions' to the man who employed the boys with the red caps to sell papers and carry baggage to the exclusion of all others; why, if the company demanded it, they had a right to protection for their lawn; how all of this was justified by the Law, which secured the right of every man in the enjoyment of his property; how it was not the officer's doings, but the Law that required him to perform his duty; how, therefore, they had no real grievance against the policeman — rather their sympathies should be with him. After the sympathetic admission by both the officer and the Court that if it were our station and grounds all boys could play on the grass and sell papers there, there was gained for the policeman sympathy and loyalty. As 'little citizens,'

interested in a 'decent town of decent kids,' they
agreed not only to 'keep off' and 'keep out' themselves, but to keep other boys out; and everyone
agreed 'on the square' that he would give any
kid there leave to 'snitch' to me, if any boy broke
his word and was not square. Thus harmony
was established between their world and ours,
and we all pulled together one way."

As the Judge remarked to me, those boys did
what few men would do; they gave up their business "just because it was right." All that was
necessary was to make them understand the right
and their duties, and then to interest them in the
"game of correction."

The arena for the great game of correction is
the Court of Probation. Held every other Saturday forenoon, it is a picturesque and a very pleasant spectacle. All the "bad" boys in town who
have been caught committing mistakes or who
have "snitched up" on themselves, assemble
there to report. It isn't new. Like the Juvenile
Court itself, the "method" of putting children
on probation did not originate with Judge Lindsey. Yet he discovered it himself. As I quote
him as saying above, he didn't know about such
things. When he went first to the home of the
"cave-dweller" to investigate, he was performing
one function of a probation officer; and when he

went there again and again, he was holding a
court of probation. So with the three pigeon
burglars and their gang; he went to see them,
but there was no method as yet. It was only as
the cases grew that the Judge had to ask the
boys to come to see him, and then, finally, to
appoint a time and place where most of the boys
could meet all together with him; and that was
the origin of Judge Lindsey's Court of Probation,
the institution.

But there is more than that to the story of it.
The Judge feels that he suffered as "a little shaver"
from lack of approbation. He was born in Ten-
nessee and his family, well-to-do Southern people,
were brought to trouble and to Denver by
the War. His father died, and Ben had to work
hard as a boy. For a long time he had three
jobs: he carried newspapers in the early morning; worked all day in a lawyer's office; and,
after hours, served as janitor. Always slight of
build, he was often worn out; and nobody appre-
ciated it. He was only doing his duty, and it
nearly killed him — literally. He sank under
his load to the very verge of despair; and he learned
the value of a kind word of sympathy and good
cheer.

Many of the bad boys who came to his court
were lonely little fellows. They had no home and

no friends, and he found in their hearts a long-
ing which he knew all about. He gave them the
sympathetic hearing and the kind word he had
wanted, and "they drank," he says, "they drank
in my friendship as if they were famished."
Right there we have one secret of his "hypnotic"
influence over children. The Judge is proud now
of the fact that he has made himself a friend of
every boy in town, or, at least, of every "feller
that needs a friend," and he will tell you the
philosophy and the use of his method if you care
to listen. He will tell you how he learned from
the gangs that the members thereof did bad things
largely because some big fellow, who was bad,
or some leader of their own, suggested to them
evil and praised them for its accomplishment.
He will reason it all out for you, now, if you wish,
showing how by his method he has put himself
in the place of the big fellow; made himself the
fountain of praise, the source of approbation,
"the feller" for whose good words kids do good
things now. In short, Ben Lindsey is the actual
leader of most of the gangs of Denver. And the
loyalty which the boys give to him, he is giving
back to the State.

All this, however, is but the unforeseen result
of this kind man's native sweetness and strength.
The only definitely thought-out method is that

of having the boys bring reports from the schools. "If you want a boy's loyalty, excite his interest." It was easy enough for the Judge to excite the boy's interest; the problem was to keep it. In the early history of the court, before the new laws, he had no probation officers to follow up his cases, and since there was too much for him to do, he bethought him of the school teachers. The Judge has always been clear on the point that his Juvenile Court is merely supplementary, that the home and the school are the places where juvenile character should be moulded, and that he had to do only with those children who, for some reason, were not successfully treated in the regular way. Thus he was helping the teachers, and since he needed help, he went to the teachers for it, and he got it. The school teachers of Denver have been his mainstay. All that the Judge required of the teachers was a report as to how the boys in his Court of Probation were doing in deportment and studies.

"What I was after," the Judge explained, "was something for which I could praise the boy in open court. Believing in approbation as an incentive, I had to have their reports for the boy to show me, in order that I might have a basis for encouraging comment, or, if the reports were not up to the mark, for sympathy. It didn't

matter to me very much what the reports were
about. Some of the teachers couldn't see at first
why they should report on the scholarship of a
boy who was good at school and bad — a thief,
perhaps — out of school. But you can see that
these fortnightly reports were an excuse for keeping up my friendly relationship with the boy,
holding his loyalty, and maintaining our common interest in the game of correction he and
I were playing together. Since we had a truancy
law, the teachers were in touch and thus could
keep me in touch with every boy under school age
in the city, and their reports were my excuse for
praise or appeal."

Judge Lindsey's Court of Probation is thus a
Court of Approbation. It serves other purposes;
indeed, it is everything to the boys of Denver. It is the State, the Law, and Justice; it is
Home, School, Club, and Society; it is Friendship, Success, and the scene of Triumphs; it is
the place also where Failure goes for Help
and for Hope renewed. It is all that Judge
Lindsey is; all that he means to the minds of
the boys. For the Judge's personality makes it,
his and the boys', and they made it up out of
their own needs.

The boys assemble early, two or three hundred of them, of all ages and all sorts, "small

kids" and "big fellers"; well-dressed "lads" and ragged "little shavers"; burglars who have entered a store, and burglars who have "robbed back" pigeons; thieves who have stolen bicycles, and thieves who have "swiped" papers; "toughs" who have "sassed" a cop or stoned a conductor, and boys who have talked bad language to little girls, or who "hate their father," or who have been backward at school and played hookey because the teacher doesn't like them. It isn't generally known, and the Judge rarely tells just what a boy has done; the deed doesn't matter, you know, only the boy, and all boys look pretty much alike to the Judge and to the boys. So they all come together there, except that boys who work, and newsboys, when there's an extra out, are excused to come at another time. But nine o'clock Saturday morning finds most of the "fellers" in their seats, looking as clean as possible, and happy.

The Judge comes in and, passing the bench, which looms up empty and useless behind him, he takes his place, leaning against the clerk's table or sitting on a camp-chair.

"Boys," he begins, "last time I told you about Kid Dawson and some other boys who used to be with us here and who 'made good.' To-day I've got a letter from the Kid. He's in Oregon, and he's doing well. I'll read you what he says about himself and his new job."

And he reads the letter, which is full of details roughly set in a general feeling of encouragement and self-confidence.

"Fine, isn't it!" the Judge says. "Kid Dawson had a mighty hard time with himself for awhile, but you can see he's got his hand on his throttle now. Well, let's see. The last time, I talked about snitching, didn't I? To-day I'm going to talk about 'ditching.'" And he is off on the address, with which he opens court. His topics are always interesting to boys, for he handles his subjects boy-fashion. "Snitching," the favourite theme, deals with the difference between "snitching," which is telling on another boy to hurt him; and "snitching on the square," which is intended to help the other fellow. "Ditching" is another popular subject. "To ditch" a thing is to throw it away; and the Judge, starting off with stories of boys who have ditched their commitment papers, proceeds to tell about others who, "like Kid Dawson out there in Oregon," have "ditched" their bad habits and "got strong." I heard him on Arbor Day speak on trees; how they grew, some straight, some crooked. There's always a moral in these talks, but the Judge makes it plain and blunt; he doesn't "rub it in."

After the address, which is never long, the boys are called up by schools. Each boy is greeted by himself, but the Judge uses only his given or nickname. "The boys from the Arapahoe Street School," he calls, and, as the group comes forward, the Judge reaches out and seizing one by the shoulder, pulls him up to him, saying:

"Skinny, you've been doing fine lately; had a crackerjack report every time. I just want to see if you have kept it up. Bet you have. Let's see." He opens the report. "And you have. That's great. Shake, Skin. You're all right, you are." Skinny shines.

Pointing at another, he says: "And you, Mumps, you got only 'fair' last time. What you got this time? You promised me 'excellent,' and I know you've made good." He tears open the envelope. "Sure," he says. "You've done it. Bully for you." Turning to the room, he tells "the fellers" how Mumps began playing hookey, and was so weak he simply thought he couldn't stay in school. "He blamed the teacher; said she was down on him. She wasn't at all. He was just weak, Mumps was; had no backbone at all. But look at him now. He's bracing right up. You watch Mumps. He's the 'stuff,' Mumps is. Aren't you, Mumps? Teacher likes you now all right, doesn't she? Yes. And she tells me she does.

Go on now and keep it üp, Mumps. I believe in you."

"Why, Eddie," the Judge says, as another boy comes up crying. "What are you crying for? Haven't you made good?"

"No, sir," Eddie says, weeping the harder.

"Well, I told you I thought you'd better go to Golden. You don't want to go, eh? Get another job, you say? But you can't keep it, Eddie. You know you can't. Give you another chance? What's the use, Eddie? You'll lose it. The best thing for you, Eddie, is Golden. They'll help you up there, make you stick to things, just make you; and so you'll get strong."

Eddie swims in tears, and it seemed to me I'd have to give that boy "another chance," but the Judge, who is called "easy," was not moved at all. His mind was on the good of that boy; not on his own feelings, nor yet on the boy's. "You see," said he to me, "he is hysterical, abnormal. The discipline of Golden is just what he needs." And he turned to the room full of boys.

"Boys," he said, "I'm going to send Eddie up to Golden. He hasn't done wrong; not a thing. But he's weak. He and I have tried again and again to win out down here in the city, and he wants another trial. But I think a year or so at Golden will brace Eddie right up, and make him a strong, manly fellow. He's not going up there to be punished. That isn't what Eddie needs, and that isn't what Golden is for. Is it, fellers?"

"No, sir," the room shouted.

"It would be unjust to punish Eddie, but Eddie understands that. Don't you, Eddie?"

"Yes, sir, but" (blubbering), "Judge, I think if I only had one more show I could do all right."

"Eddie, you're wrong about that. I'm sure I'm right. I'm sure that after a year or two you'll be glad I sent you to the school. And I'll be up there in a few days to see you, Eddie, myself. What's more, I know some boys up there — friends of mine, that'll help you, Eddie; be friends to you. They won't want to like a kid that cries, but I'll tell 'em you need friends to strengthen you, and they'll stay with you."

All forenoon this goes on, the boys coming up in groups to be treated each one by himself. He is known to the Court, well known, and the Judge, his personal friend, and the officers of the Court and the spectators, his fellow-clubmen, all rejoice with him, if he is "making good," and if he is doing badly, they are sorry. And in that case, he may be invited to a private talk with the Judge, a talk, mind you, which has no terrors for the boy, only comfort. They often seek such interviews voluntarily. They sneak into the Judge's chambers or call at his house to "snitch up" that they are not doing well. And the boys who sit there and see this every two weeks, or hear all about it, they not only have forgotten all their old fear of the Law; they go to the Court now as to a friend, they and their friends. For Judge Lindsey had not been doing "kid justice to kids" very long before all Boyville knew it. The rumour spread like wildfire. The boys "snitched" on the Judge, "snitched on the square"; they told one another that the County Judge was all right.

The Judge tells many stories to illustrate the change that followed. Once as he approached a group of boys, one of them said: "There's th' Jedge, fellers," and two kids dived down an alley. The others gathered around the Judge.

"Who were those boys that ran away?" he asked.

"Who? Them? Oh," came the answer, "they're kids from K. C." (Kansas City); "they ain't on to the game here."

Another time the Judge was walking along the street arguing with me that stealing isn't a heinous crime in a boy, and that it shouldn't be treated with holy horror. Most boys swipe something at one time or another; and to prove his point, he halted before a "gang."

"Say, kids," he said, and, as they looked up, he asked: "how many of you fellers have swiped things?"

Every boy's hand shot up in the air. The Judge had proved his point, but he had proved also another thing. Those boys knew he was the Judge, yet they were not afraid to tell the truth. Or, to state the situation more completely: those boys knew he was the Judge and *therefore* they were not afraid to tell him the truth. Not all these boys had been in his Court; in fact, only one or two had; but that didn't matter. All the boys of Denver know of the Judge, and what they know of him is that *though* he represents the Law and the State, he is "all right."

One afternoon, a boy of about ten years stuck his head into the door of the Judge's private room.

"Is the Judge in?" he asked.

"Yes," said the Judge.

"Is this him?" the boy asked.

"Yes, my boy. I'm the Judge."

"Well, I'm Johnny Rosenbaum, and I came down here to see you."

"Yes? I'm glad you've come, John, but what did you come for?"

"Well," he said, "Joe Rosenthal, he used to come down here, and he 'swiped' things once.

And I 'swiped' something, and he said I better come down here and see you about it."

"All right, but what have you come to me about it for?"

The tears started. "Well," he said, "I came down here to tell you I'd cut it out and never do it again. And I thought I better get here before the cop did. Joe said the cop 'ud ditch a kid that swiped things, but that you'd help a feller to ditch the swipin'."

"Yes, I'll help you ditch swipin', but you're a mighty little boy; how did you find the way down here alone?"

"Oh," he said, "'most every kid I seed knew about it, and they passed me down th' line to here."

Johnny Rosenbaum was put on probation, and he began overcoming evil with good, as he proved one day in court. Sometimes the Judge will turn to the boys and ask whether any feller has done that week a thing good enough to make up for an evil thing done before. Once, when he asked this question, Johnny rose and said:

"Judge, some of the kids I run with was diggin' a cave, and we wanted a shovel, and they said: 'Let's go and swipe one.' So they wanted to put me into Mr. Putnam's barn where the shovel was, through a little hole that nobody but a little kid could crawl through. And I says, 'No, I gotter report down to th' Judge, and I told him that I'd cut out swipin' and when I got a chanct I'd do a good thing. Now is my chanct,' I says. 'I won't swipe th' shovel,' I says, 'and you mustn't,' I says to them. Now I ain't goin' to snitch on who the fellers was because they says 'All right, we won't swipe the shovel.' And I went 'round and I ast Mr. Putnam to borrow us the shovel, and he said he would. So we got the shovel on th' square. But, Judge, if I hadn't done that they would have swiped the shovel, wouldn't they?"

"Yes, John," said the Judge. "They would have swiped the shovel, and if you ever swiped anything in your life, you have more than made up for it by doing the right thing this time."

Another case of "making good" was that of Eli Carson. Eli told at a meeting how his news gang down in the *Post* alley were going to "swipe a box of cherries off'n Wolf Londoner's grocery store." "I says it wasn't square," said Eli, "and the other kids, they all allowed it wasn't either. Texas was th' kid that said first to swipe th' cherries; and he thought afterwards it was best not to do it. And I wanted to tell you, Judge, that I had done a good thing, but Texas he didn't want me to. But by and by Texas changed his mind, and says I could tell you. So I'm not snitchin', am I?"

"An experience like that," the Judge said by way of comment, "goes to show that my theory is correct, that all we need is an influence for good to counteract the influence for bad of the gang. For Texas is a well-known newsboy, and had Eli not been a member of our gang, coming to Court where he could tell his experiences in the presence of one hundred and fifty other boys, and be praised, why, then, Eli would have wanted to please Texas. As it is, he wants to please me and the Court gang; and Texas does, too."

Another instance of faith in the Court: The Judge had been trying a case all day. It was a grown-up case, difficult and slow, and when the adjournment came late, at six o'clock, the Judge was tired. As the court room cleared, however, he saw a child in a back seat. "He was so small," the Judge says, "that I thought someone must have gone off and forgotten him, and I told 'Uncle John' Murrey (the bailiff) to find out whose child it was. But when Uncle John spoke to him, the little fellow got up, and I saw he was almost ten years old. I called him up to the bench, and he came, and when he reached me he dropped his head on my shoulder and began to sob.

"Judge," he said, "I'm Clifford, and my

mamma don't live here, and I stay with my aunt down on —— Street, so I been swipin' things, I have, and I come here to 'cut it out.'" As the tears flowed more abundantly, he said he was sorry and would never do it again if the Judge would "give him a show," as he had another boy he named. The Judge took the little fellow back in his chambers; they had a long talk, and the boy, put on probation, reported regularly and well. "He turned out to be a splendid boy," the Judge says.

But the best example the Judge gives of the difference in results between the old criminal court system of vengeance and fear and the new method of friendship and service, is a story he tells of two brothers. "Both were wayward," he says. "The older was brought to the criminal court for some boyish offence in the days before the establishment of the Juvenile Court. He was flung into a filthy jail and herded with men and women, where he heard and saw vile and obscene things. He was dragged into court by an officer and put through the police court mill. He was only a little boy. He had been sinned against long before his birth. Both by heredity and environment he had been driven to lawlessness. But the State took no account of this. It had its chance to make a good man of him. He wanted bread; the State gave him a stone. It branded him a criminal, made him a criminal. It made the pressure of evil upon him inexorable. To-day he is a man and in the penitentiary.

"The younger brother was as wayward as the elder. Four years ago he was brought to the Juvenile Court, defiant and frightened, just as his brother had been taken to another tribunal. The policeman told me the boy was a very Ananias, and I replied that, given the same conditions, he (the cop) would probably have been the same, and the officer went away convinced that there was no use bringing the boys to the Juvenile Court, where the Judge 'did nothing to them.' The policeman would count as nothing the many hours during many weeks that I laboured for that boy. He told me the truth; he convicted himself, but no stigma of conviction was put upon him, and he was not punished. He was put on probation, and encouraged to do his best. He was made to feel that the State was on his side; that the forces of the Law were working for him rather than against him; that the Court was his friend, his appeal when he was in trouble. And that Morris, as I will call him, did feel perfect faith in the Court the Law, and the State, he proved once in an amusing way.

"One day I was trying an important will case.

Millions of dollars were involved. The door opened cautiously, and Morris poked his freckled face in, piping up that he wanted to see the Judge. The bailiff started to shoo him away, but I called in the boy. I ordered a recess. No doubt the distinguished counsel were shocked; certainly they looked shocked. But a live boy looms larger than a dead man's millions to me, and when this boy came into my Court, unafraid, smiling, and sure of justice, I remembered the flash of fear and hatred that I once had seen on this same freckled face. So I beckoned Morris up to me, and I heard his case then and there. He was in business. He sold newspapers, and his place of business was a certain busy corner where he dealt not only with pedestrians, but with passengers on passing cars. The 'old cop,' it seemed, had let him 'hop the cars,' and all had gone well till a new cop had come there. The 'new guy,' as Morris called him, had ordered the boy off the corner. 'Thinks 'cause he's a cop he owns the whole town,' said Morris, who was losing about fifty cents a day. The case stated, I asked Morris what he would have me do.

"Evidently Morris had been reading, as well as selling, his newspapers, for he was ready with his answer.

"'Judge,' he said, 'can't you gimme one o'

them there things they call 'junctions against de fly cop?'

"I gave him one. Why not? I called for an injunction blank, and on it I wrote a note to the policeman. I told him about Morris; not much, but enough to make him understand that the boy was one of my probationers who was trying to 'make good'; that he was bringing me good reports from his teachers; and that I hoped the officer would give the boy all the leeway possible. To the boy I explained that the officer represented the Law, as I did, and must be respected accordingly. Morris went away gleefully with his writ."

And the writ "worked." The Judge says that the next time he saw Morris, he asked the boy about it. Morris said he had "served it all right."

"An' say, Judge," he said, " it worked fine. De cop liked to 'a' dropped dead when he read it. He tinks I got a pull wit' de Court, so he wants to be my friend. And I don't know but I'll let him in." The Judge spoke for the cop. He told Morris he must be a friend of the policeman, and the boy reported later that he had "let the cop in." And he had. The Judge learned that they became good friends.

In his comment on this incident, the Judge

attributes the difference between Morris and his brother to one thing: "opportunity." "The State," he says, "surrounded the boy who is in the penitentiary with everything to make him do evil; hence the State must support him now in the penitentiary. The State surrounded Morris with every influence to make him do right; hence he is growing up a good citizen who will support the State." There is a great difference there. But I want to point out another "difference," a "method" of the Judge to which he does not refer in anything he ever says about the celebrated injunction case of Morris, the "bad" boy, *vs.* the new cop on his corner. Recall what the Judge wrote into that injunction. How did he make the policeman obey the writ which the boy served on him? The Judge simply told the policeman about the boy. Having told the boy about the cop, he related enough of the history of the newsboy to get the cop interested in the boy and in the game of correction which he and the boy were playing together. In other words, Ben Lindsey, the man of heart, reached for the heart of the policeman, and since the heart is a vital spot, it is no wonder "de cop liked to 'a' dropped dead."

This, then, is Judge Lindsey's "method." It is an old method. He didn't discover it. A great religion was founded on "faith, hope, and love" once. That was long ago. The only new and interesting thing about Lindsey's experiment is that he finds that this ancient, neglected method "works" — works, too, as I said at the outset, with grown-ups as well as with children, with cops as well as with kids. It has won his fight for him. Yes, he fights. The kids' Judge has had to fight, and, as we shall see, he has fought. The fight isn't finished yet. The "bad" men of Colorado haven't been taught by their State and their courts to see things as the bad boys of Colorado are learning to see them. They also go to the courts for injunctions, and *some of them* get their writs. Ben B. Lindsey is a man with a man's fight for men on his hands, and he is the kind of man that finishes his fights. He will win with good men or — he'll wait and win it with bad boys. For his bad boys will grow up some day, and they know what the State can be to a feller and that "there can be no justice without the love of man for man."

II.   WHAT MAKES "BAD" CHILDREN BAD

If you care to take the measure of Christian civilization in the United States to-day, reflect for a moment frankly upon the meaning of this fact: There is opposition to Judge Lindsey. That men like Heney and La Follette, Everett Colby, and (even) Mark Fagan, should have to fight for the right to do right, is significant enough of the power of evil among us; but Ben Lindsey! This man is so just and so gentle; his purposes are so pure, his work is so beautiful, so successful, and — you would think — so harmless, that no one would expect to see any man's hand raised against the Judge of the Juvenile Court of Denver. Callous souls might show indifference, but why opposition? And such opposition?

The two bosses of the two political parties conspired together once to keep Judge Lindsey off the bench. At another time, some men tempted him to disgrace with a woman! Legislation is proposed (and has been passed) to divide his Court and thus limit his power as a judge to serve the children of his county. Physically delicate, the only rest this overworked man takes is when he travels, as he does, thousands of miles to tell people what wonders "justice with love" has done for the "bad kids" of Denver. This time-off he justifies on the ground that his lectures further the cause of the children elsewhere, and bring in money to carry on his plans for his own "Court gang" at home; and he spends thus all

he makes from these lectures, and out of the
$4,600 which the county pays him, he retains
some other judge to fill his place while he is away.
I ask the thousands of men and women who have
heard Judge Lindsey tell his stories of boys and
girls, to consider what it means, that powerful
men in Colorado have drawn a bill that shall
"put a stop to this little whipper-snapper's running around all over the country lecturing." This
is hate. And the other attacks upon him and
his work show a deeper-seated opposition. Why?

There's a reason. There are two reasons.
One is that Judge Lindsey does not confine himself to saving the children that are "lost in crime";
he began early to inquire into the causes of juvenile crime. He asked what made bad children
bad. That led him to a study of the conditions
of child-life; that led him to the conclusion that
the typical environment of an average Christian
community was such that even little children could
not be good; and that led this man to attack those
conditions. In other words, Judge Lindsey has
sought not merely to cure but to prevent the evils
of child-life.

"Don't tear down all the time," men shout
at reformers. "What we want is reconstructive
work." It was Lindsey's "reconstructive work"
that threatened to "hurt business."

There we have one all-sufficient reason why he has to fight; but there's a second: Ben Lindsey does not limit his labours to the cause of the children. He is celebrated for his juvenile system, and in Denver you hear that he is "a philanthropist, and if he would stick to his philanthropic work, he might go on forever." That's a lie. But, as I said, this man should not be known only as the founder of the Juvenile Court; he is doing a man's work for men. The "kids' Judge" of Denver was elected as the County Judge of Denver, and as such he dealt out justice to bad men as well as to bad boys, and when by accident one day he discovered evidence of graft in his Court, Judge Lindsey forced the grafters to trial and to conviction.

Ben Lindsey does his duty, his whole duty as a man, as a citizen, and as a public official, and that's what makes him a menace to Things As They Are in Colorado and in the United States. Like Heney, and La Follette, and Colby, and (even) Mark Fagan, Ben Lindsey is up against the System, and, therefore, like them and like every honest man you hear of in this land, the just Judge has to fight.

A large part of the opposition to Judge Lindsey, especially at first, was honest. It was ignorant, but sincere and natural. For, you understand,

Lindsey's methods are applied Christianity. Without thinking much about it he was putting into
practice in actual life, and, of all places, in the
criminal courts, the doctrine of faith, hope, and
charity. In a Christian community this was
revolutionary and, "as it was in the beginning,"
caused a great rumpus. The Bar was shocked.
When the Judge, searching the juvenile mind for
causes of juvenile crime, saw fear of the Law
and hate of the Court in the eyes of the little prisoners and, looking about him, realized that there
was reason for this dread, we have seen how he
threw off authority, came down off the bench,
subordinated the machinery of justice to the good
of the boy, and for routine and vengeance substituted sympathy and help. He took the boys' view
of boys' "mistakes," and when he sent a "feller"
to the reform school at Golden, it was only upon
his own confession and for his own good. The
boys understood, but the lawyers wagged their
heads: the lawyers, I mean, who regard the Law
as a sacred Institution. When they saw a judge
who was "a lawyer, and a good lawyer," sweeping
aside technicalities and ignoring "good practice" to get at the real, human interest of the
prisoner at the bar, they were deeply pained.
But the Judge, who understands men as well
as he does boys, understood this feeling, and

he was patient to explain, and, since this was an honest opposition, he overcame it. He tells the story:

"I sent a boy to the Industrial School on the charge of 'needing correction for his own good.' The boy had made a clean breast of it to me, and we had such a perfect understanding, that boy and I, that he had taken his commitment papers and gone off by himself to Golden. Then appeared Counsel employed by his parents, declaring that he had been dealt with without due process of law, no jury trial, etc., etc. He (the lawyer) said he would apply for a writ of *habeas corpus*. I assured him I could make no objection, but that the boy had been guilty of two or three offences constituting technical burglary, so that while he might be released for the purpose of obtaining due process of law, this process would not only make the boy a burglar and a thief, but would return him, so branded by the records, to the place whence he might be brought upon the *habeas corpus* writ.

"The case," says the Judge, "was never brought." Lawyers still lift their brows at Judge Lindsey's "loose practice," but though he has dealt with more than five thousand children's cases, the question of due process has been raised but once since — at home. A Boston judge demurred not long

ago. Lindsey lectured there, teaching his doctrine that the boy is more important than the
Law, and that where justice, blindfolded, made
criminals of "bad" boys, justice with love saved
them to the State. "God forgive the people who
brought that man here!" exclaimed the Boston
judge. And the next time a young criminal was
brought before him he "showed how to deal with
such cases." The boy had thrown a snowball
at a man, and the Boston judge sent the prisoner
to jail for thirty days "on the evidence." But
Lindsey's doctrine had taken hold of the public
mind; the newspapers investigated the case very
much as Lindsey would have done, and —
on the facts — Boston public opinion reversed
the Boston judge. He had made a mistake.
He was right, in a way, this law-worshipping
judge; it wouldn't do to let men like him exercise
their human feelings. But Boston was right, too;
such men shouldn't be allowed to deal with the
children of men. Even blind justice isn't revenge.

The penal instinct is strong in man, and Denver felt, for a long while, as this pagan judge felt.
Grave fears were expressed everywhere of Lindsey's "leniency," as men called his Christianity,
for, of course, no one recognized it for what it was.

"What the little devils want is a good licking,"
said the grown-ups, "or the jail."

"No," the Judge replied, "all they lack is a fair show and — understanding." And he gave the boys and girls a "show and understanding," and they showed that they understood. He had to fight the doubts of their elders, but he believes in fighting. "The world needs fighting men," he teaches. "Every good, great man was a fighter." So he enlisted the children in his fight for a "decent town of decent kids," by telling them how he was called foolish for putting faith in "bad kids." But also he teaches that "a good example and loving service — these are the weapons of peace." And this, likewise, the kids understood. The difficulty was to make their elders understand, but he was patient, and the children helped him.

A city official of high degree, exasperated by the outrageous depredations of a "gang up his way," called on the Judge once to send to prison three of the boys that were under arrest.

"Born criminals, that's what they are," said the official, and some of their acts were "burglaries."

The Judge talked with the boys. He got them to bring in the others, and among them was the son of the official of high degree!

"Your son isn't a born criminal," said the Judge, "and neither are the others."

He sent none of the boys to prison. The Judge

taught them some elementary lessons about crime and, putting them on their honour, let them go "on probation." Their "crimes" ceased.

The Judge says his service in the Juvenile Court has taught him many things about children, but the information he has gained there about parents he characterizes as "amazing." He ranks fool fathers and incompetent mothers among the first causes of the troubles of children, and if you add vicious and negligent parents you have nine-tenths of all his children's "cases" accounted for.

"Children don't rebel at authority," he says, "only at ignorant authority," and there is where many parents fail. "Every father and mother ought to know more about their own children than anyone else. Perhaps, in most cases, they do, but it is amazing how often they don't. And the reason they don't is that they haven't enough love for children to understand them, and not enough character to hold their respect. Their children lie to them, and it is the parents' fault. I recall hardly a single case in the thousands I have dealt with when we did not get the truth from the child; yet in hundreds of these cases the children had lied to the parents. Why? They were afraid of their parents; they were not understood at home."

The reference here is not to the parents of the poor "bad kids"; they also have their faults, and the Judge has had his troubles with them. But the poor have in poverty an excuse for neglect, and where one parent is vicious, the other is pathetically glad, usually, of help such as Judge Lindsey gave. The poor are "down on" the Society for the Prevention of Cruelty to Children, of New York; but for Judge Lindsey, of Denver, they will fight — even at the polls. He won over the poor easily enough.

His hardest honest battles were with the well-to-do father who "had no time to fuss with his boy," except now and then to "lick him,"and the vain and frivolous mother who "just knew that her nice little boy" or her "nicer" little girl "wouldn't do such things." Now, the Judge finds that all children are pretty much alike at bottom; they all are "nice," but the Old Harry who is in their parents is in the kids, too; and the Judge doesn't mind. The Judge has a sneaking, human prejudice against "little prigs"; he rather favours husky lads and mischievous little girls who, if they can do wrong, can do right with equal energy. But the "nice" parents are forever making prigs and snobs of their children or proving to them their elderly assininity.

"I remember a gentleman," the Judge relates,

"who was most violent in his complaints to me about boys in a certain (fashionable) district who swiped ice-cream and other good things to eat from back porches, and he declared he had forbidden his boy to go with the suspects. He was the surprised dad of one, the worst of the gang. I had to find it out for him. He should have known it himself. He was too busy downtown all day, and at night too busy denouncing his neighbours' children. He is busier now studying his own son.

"The mother of a very well-to-do family once swept into my chambers, highly indignant that I had sent to the school for her boy who had been, with others, complained against for a serious offence. I had preferred not to send an officer to arrest him. 'I would have you to understand,' she excitedly declared, 'that my boy is no thief; he never did anything wrong in his life.' She knew it because she heard her boy say his prayers every night at her knee. And she knew how he came to be so falsely accused. For she said: 'I know Mrs. A. across the street has been lying about Frank. She is a mean, contemptible old thing. She told Mrs. B. that he did so and so, and I know it is a lie, because Frankie told me so.' I had never heard of Mrs. A. before," the Judge says; "I had got at the truth from the boys them-

selves, and Frank had told me all about his part
in it. Indeed, we had just finished our talk, and
Frank was in the next room waiting for the type-
writer to copy a note I had dictated to ask his
father not to lick the boy. Frank feared his
father, and I knew that the licking would be, not
to correct the boy, but to sate the anger of the
parent and salve his wounded pride. Children
know, and I know, and you know how many a
licking is as selfish as that. Well, as the mother
ended her tirade, the boy came back with the
letter to be signed. His face fell when he saw
his mother. 'Now, Frank,' I said, 'tell your
mother what you have told me.' He did. She
sank into a chair with a frightened little sigh: 'Well
who would have believed it?' Another mother,
in an exactly similar situation, after nearly faint-
ing away, suddenly arose and, with the image of
Mrs. A. plainly in her mind, persuaded her little
Frankie to repudiate his confession and stick to
the lie. Her little Frankie didn't turn out as well,
but the one I saved from a 'lickin'' has been a
princely little fellow ever since this, his first real
lesson.''

Experiences like these would make an ordinary
man feel like "licking" Frankie's busy father
and humiliating his silly mother, and Judge Lindsey has some very healthy, human feelings about

such things, as he shows by the way he writes of them. The man has humour and heat, but also he has charity and infinite patience. He was as gentle with those parents as he was with their children. Having discovered early that many parents thought less of their children than of what their neighbours might say, the Judge provided privacy. We have seen him calling up boys in his Probation Court by schools, and addressing them by their first or "nick" names. This he does to spare not only the pride of the boy, but the vanity of his father and mother. And so he abolished criminal records in the Juvenile Court, not only to save a boy from growing up with a rogue's name to burden him, but to shield his family from "disgrace."

But the best example of his practice of privacy and consideration for both parents and children is his method of dealing with girls. He himself seldom speaks of this part of his work, and the reason is that he finds it is a sex-problem. Some women, who themselves are students of delinquent children and who admire Lindsey's service with boys, say that he errs with girls.

"Little girls steal, lie, and do all the other things that boys do," they say. "The police don't arrest them as often, but the problem of the girls is as various and as complex as that of the boys."

However that may be, Lindsey finds the sex-problem big enough to alarm him; and he says his observations are borne out by men who know in other cities.

In brief, it is another case of parental ignorance and Anglo-Saxon prudery. Parents do not like to tell their children the essential, natural facts of sex; they think *their* children too innocent. The result is that their children learn them at school or at play from other people's children, "bad" boys and "forward" girls, who impart all this knowledge in the very vilest form. And the Judge, probing into the doings of boys and girls brought before him for other things, discovered that these lessons had taken a practical turn; that in certain schools, where the thing got started, it had spread to include, in one case fifteen, in another nearly all the little girls in the school. What did he do about it?

First, he got the truth. Girls lie more readily and more obstinately than boys, but he persuaded them to tell all about it. And this he accomplished by affecting no horror of the subject. He treated it naturally. He didn't take the course the world would have taken, and especially the women's world — he didn't make the poor little girl feel that she was lost forever and ever. As with boys, he called it "all a mistake," and a mistake that could be retrieved. Having the truth, he called in the mother. It is a fact for mothers to ponder that no children wanted mamma and papa to know; they would get no such candour and no such sympathetic understanding at home as they got from their Judge. But the Judge insisted, and after an hour with the child, he often had to spend hours with the mother to prepare her to be motherly. She was horror-stricken; she thought of the disgrace; of what Mrs. A. would say. But the Judge had foreseen all that. He had other women calling on him the same day, other mothers and unmarried women. The shocked mother's good name was shielded, and she and her daughter were brought together. For once, no lies, no vanities, no hypocrisies, and no false modesty stood between them, and therefore there was no lack of a perfect understanding. In one case the Judge was so stirred by the extent to which the schools had been cursed by this evil that he called a "meeting of mothers." No one knew what it was for; mothers not involved were invited with those that were in trouble; school teachers and other women; some of the "best" women in town. There, all together, the women of Denver were informed, warned, and instructed in private. It was beautifully done. No names were mentioned, of course, not even the name of the school, and no breath of the purpose of that meeting ever leaked out.

The head of one of the public utility companies once marked Lindsey for defeat, and one of his executive staff remonstrated.

"Oh, no," he said, "not Lindsey."

"What!" exclaimed the magnate. "You, too? Everywhere I turn it is, 'Oh, no, not Lindsey.' My wife is for Lindsey, my mother is for Lindsey, my sisters are for Lindsey. And now you are for Lindsey. What is it that makes everybody and everything fight for this judge?"

Everybody doesn't fight for Judge Lindsey; only those are for him who know how he has conspired with them in secret to help their little boy or their little girl. But these are legion. Poor and rich, "everybody" has knowledge of private calls made by this man; of hours, days, weeks spent on the case of somebody's bad little boy whom they have seen afterward being "good" to "show 'em that th' Jedge is dead right in bankin' on th' honour of a kid." Opposition? That of the parents of Denver melted like one of Denver's summer snows.

All the opposition to faith in mischievous boys soon disappeared, but there remained the **fear** of this treatment for "really bad" boys.

The police represented the old policy of vengeance and prison. When the Judge received official permission to deal with all juvenile cases, and they saw what his treatment was — faith and hope and love — they snorted. The town snorted with them, and when the police held back its "criminals born," public opinion backed the police. But the Judge is a politician, too; he knows the game, and he went after the police. How? He might have exercised his authority, and he has done that since, in his fights with the dishonest opposition of the police. But this was honest opposition, this that came first. It was nothing but the natural conservatism of human nature, and he was patient with it. He reasoned with the police. He "showed them." He got the bad boys to help him "show 'em," just as the "nice" boys had helped him show the "good" people up on the hill. Judge Lindsey came down off the bench to go into the jails and bring into his Court the "criminals born"; and he brought them there, and there he gave to them also trust, encouragement, and service, and, like the good boys, the bad ones gave him back faith for faith, hope for hope, and for his love, their loyalty, and — his greatest triumph.

That is what most of the admirers of Judge

Lindsey call his practice of trusting young "criminals" to go alone to Golden. Other triumphs of his seem to me to be greater, but certainly the sight of "a convict," and a boy convict at that, receiving his commitment papers from the Judge and passing through the streets, taking train and changing cars to get to Golden, and there delivering himself up — this is indeed a spectacle to see. And it is a common spectacle in Denver. Judge Lindsey hardly ever sends an officer with a boy now, and out of the hundreds he has trusted, only three have failed him. One of these I saw. He was "Eddie," the boy I told about in the first part of this story, who was hysterical, and the Judge had doubts about him; indeed, he put him privately in charge of a "tough kid" who was going also to the school, and it was the tough kid who reported by telephone from the station where they changed cars, that "Eddie can't seem to make it, Judge. He don't say he won't, but he cries, and I guess he ain't strong enough."

Another of the three failures was a boy who was started twice, and when the Judge reproached him for his weakness, suggested a way to beat himself. "Try me by another road, Judge," he said. "This road goes right by my old stamping ground, and when I see th' gang playin' 'round, I can't help it. I just have to drop off th' car." The Judge gave him tickets over another route, and that night received word that the boy had "made it."

Well, this practice of the Judge was begun on an impulse in this first, honest conflict with the police. They had caught two "dangerous young criminals," boys with records for serious crimes and jail breaking, and the Judge, having found them in the cells, talked with them. One night the Judge telephoned to the warden to send over two of the boys. An officer brought one. "I think," the Judge says, "that the warden's idea was that it was dangerous to send two at one time without handcuffs on them, and the police knew it offended me to have them come into my Court or my chambers with young fellows handcuffed."

When the officer came in with the boy, he spoke in an undertone to the Judge, warning him that the prisoner was the "worst in the bunch," and that every time he had brought him to. that room, the boy had eyed the window with the fire-escape.

"Better let me stay here," said the officer. The Judge said he would take his chances. "All right," said the officer, and he smiled, "but we shall have to hold you responsible. You know

what it has cost the county to catch this prisoner."
The Judge knew, and he promised to give a
written order of court, if necessary, and the
officer left.

It was ten o'clock at night, dark and cold.
The boy, sixteen years old, was strong, and his
face was not very prepossessing. The Judge
is built like a flower, but he had worked hard
on this boy, and he believed in his "method."
So when the door closed behind the officer, he
went straight up to the boy.

"Henry," he said, "the officer who brought
you here says you had your eye on the fire-escape,
and that you are looking for a chance to 'skip.'
He said he wouldn't be responsible for your
return to jail if I made him leave you alone in
this room with me. He said that you'd be down
that fire-escape quicker'n a wink. Now, I don't
believe it. I believe in you, Henry, and I hope
you believe in me."

With that, the Judge went to the window
and, throwing it up as high as it would go,
he said:

"There, Henry, there's the fire-escape and the
night and two hours the best of it, for I'll promise,
if you decide to 'duck,' not to report to the Warden
till twelve o'clock. Now, then, if you think you
are not worth saving, not worth helping — if

all the hours I have spent with you in jail are to go for nothing, you 'scoot.' I'll not interfere. I leave it to you. I can't save a fellow, you know, not by myself; I can only help a fellow to save himself, if he wants to. If he doesn't want to, and I can't convince him that he ought to want to, then I do not see much hope. So, go or stay, as you wish, Henry."

"Do you mean that, Judge?" the boy asked, and the Judge thinks his impulse was to go.

"You know what I mean," he answered, and for a moment the two looked at each other.

"Then," says the Judge, "I thought I saw a peculiar shadow cross his face, and I believed he understood. I went back to my table and sat down. I must confess it was an anxious moment for me. I wasn't sure that I had made on that boy the impression I hoped to make. He looked so hard. And he wavered there. I hardly dared to look at him. I thought of the ridicule of the police, of the failure and what it would mean: the defeat of the policy I was coming to believe in. And there that boy hung, swinging, actually swinging. Well, he had a certain peculiar swinging gait, and when he made a lurch for that window, my heart rose in my throat. His hand went up in the air, and I thought he was gone. But no — the hand that went up seized the window and brought it down with a slam and a bang. Then the boy came and sat down at my table.

"'Judge,' he said in a very simple, almost boyish way, 'I'll stay with you. I never had nobody talk to me like you. I'll do anything you say for me to do.'"

So they talked. The Judge told the boy he might have to go to Buena Vista (the penitentiary), and they discussed that. And they discussed crime and the police, till it was time for Henry to go back to the jail. And then — the Judge sent him back alone, and he went back alone, and he took voluntarily his place behind the bars!

It "worked," this "method" did, so the Judge adopted it as a method. It would strengthen the boys. He told the police that he proposed thereafter to trust all prisoners to go alone to Golden. The police laughed. It is said that they passed the word to put up a job on the Judge. At any rate, the next boy for Golden was Billy B., a chronic little runaway, and with the two policemen who brought him in came two reporters. The officers excused their double patrol by pointing to a brand-new shine-box which Billy carried as evidence that he meant to "skip." That kid had given them a two weeks' chase, they said, and *they* weren't taking any chances on him. The Judge might, they implied, but there were the two reporters to bear witness that, if Billy skipped, it was no fault of the police. As a matter of fact, one of the reporters told the Judge that the papers had been "tipped off to send them out and get a good story on the Judge."

When the case was called, everybody was laughing in his sleeve, everybody but the Judge and Billy B. The Judge was anxious, and the boy was sobbing in a corner with his shine-box hugged to his breast. Billy was only twelve years old. He had no father, and his mother was a washerwoman. He had learned early to tramp. The Judge had worked with him, but when the "movin'-about fever" got hold of Billy, Billy had to move. And he had the fever now. He admitted it to the Judge, and when the Judge said he must go to Golden, the little fellow burst into tears. He had visions of stone walls and iron bars, with a policeman standing over him with a club all the rest of his days. That is what prison means to boys, and Golden was prison to Billy. So he dropped on his knees and begged the Judge not to send him away, promising pitifully "never to do it again." Billy was simply afraid.

"Billy," said the Judge, "you are crying because you are scared. What are you scared of?
Me? Why should you be afraid of me?
Haven't I given you a square deal? Haven't I
given you every chance I could, helped you every
way to be a good boy at home?"

"Yes," Billy sobbed, "but ——"

"You can't be a good boy at home. You
don't get a fair chance at home. You want to
move on all the time, and by and by you'll just
be a 'vag.' Now, you don't want to grow up
to be a bum; do you? No, you want a chance
to learn a trade and be a man."

The Judge explained at length that Golden
wasn't a reformatory or a prison. It was only
a school, a good industrial school, where a poor
kid that hadn't a chance at home could learn a
trade. "Why," said the Judge, "I've been there.
I like to go there. And I tell you everybody up
there just loves a kid that tries to do his best,
and they help him. Nobody hates a kid at
Golden. No, siree."

By and by, the tears ceased to flow. The
Judge described the school, its shops, its mili-
tary organization, its baseball nines, and then,
as the Judge relates, "when fear vanished,
and interest began, I appealed to the boy's
nobility, to his honour, pride, his loyalty to me."

Judge Lindsey seized for this purpose the very preparations the police had made for their "joke on the Judge." He introduced Billy to the reporters.

"What do you think the cops have told these reporters, Billy?" he said. "They have told them that that fool Judge was going to trust little Billy B. to go to the industrial school all by himself, and that they were going to have the laugh on the Judge because they knew Billy better than the Judge did. They say they know you'll never go, and they are saying what a fine joke it will be to have the reporters write a story to-morrow telling how the Judge trusted Billy, and Billy threw the Judge down, ditched his papers, and ran away. And, gee whiz, it would be tough if I did get thrown down. But I'm not scared. I believe in you, and I'm going to trust you. I am going to give you these, your commitment papers, and your railroad ticket, and we'll see whether you stay with me or stay with the police. I want these reporters to tell just what happens, so it'll be up to you, Billy, to go to Golden or skip."

As the Judge proceeded, Billy's head began to go up in the air. By and by he pushed the cold tears out of his eyes, and when the Judge ceased to speak, those eyes were blazing.

"Judge," he said, "you know John Handing, don't you?"

The Judge hesitated.

"You know, Judge; the kid th' fellers call Fatty Felix."

"Yes, yes," said the Judge.

"Well," said Billy, "he's my chum, Fatty is. Now, here's my shine-box. You give that to Fatty, and you gimme them papers. I'll show 'em. You trust me, and I'll stay wit' ye, Judge, and we'll fool 'em, all right."

And off went Billy B., twelve years old, out of the court-room, down through the streets — the streets he loved — to the car; then over three railroads to the little town of Golden where, asking his way, he climbed the long, lonely hill road to the industrial school — just to show a doubting world that "it" works.

Was the world convinced? No. The grown-ups marvelled, and even the boys sneered. The Judge "fixed" the boys. He heard that they called Billy B. a "chump" up at Golden, so he went up there, and he told the story in a speech which made Billy B.'s face shine like his old shine-box. That speech, repeated again and again, at Golden and in Denver and all over the State, has made it an honour to go alone to Golden: a test of pluck, loyalty, and self-control. And, on the other hand, to "ditch your papers and run," is a disgrace in Boyville now. A boy called on the Judge one day with an offer from the gang to "lick" any kid that ditched his papers or in any other way went back on the Judge, and the Judge had some difficulty in explaining why that wasn't "square."

Wonderful? Yes, it's wonderful, if you don't see what "it" is, and Denver didn't — at least, official Denver didn't. The Judge saw that he had to "win out" with what the world calls "young criminals born," so he watched for a chance; and the chance came.

"One morning," he says, "the newspapers reported the capture of Lee Martin and Jack Heimel, two notorious boy burglars known as 'The Eel,' and 'Tatters.' They were the leaders of the River-Front gang of sneak thieves, pickpockets, burglars, etc., and they had done time in the reform school and jails in Colorado and elsewhere. The newspapers, having told all about them and their crimes, went on to say that these criminals had amply qualified for a long term, and they should therefore be tried in the criminal court, not before the new-fangled, grandmotherly juvenile department. Here was my chance and a challenge.

"I visited the jail. The boys were in separate

cells, handcuffed to their benches. They had just come out of the sweat-box where the police had been bullying and threatening them for hours in an effort to make them tell on the other members of the gang, and they were bruised and battered. Tatters looked more like a pirate than the fifteen-year-old grammar school boy he was. A picture of uncleanliness, he scowled at me out of sullen black eyes, and the sinister effect was increased by the livid bruises on his swarthy face. I talked with him, but could get nothing out of him. His lips were padlocked, for he was plainly suspicious of me.

"Lee Martin presented a very different appearance. He was slight, fair, and scrupulously neat, despite the unutterable prison filth. About him was an air of childish innocence hard to reconcile with his established reputation as the most expert and reckless boy criminal within a thousand miles. There was something peculiarly winning about him. I have never met so interesting a boy, or one so full of vital, human experiences learned in the hard school of life. He had gentle, blue eyes, just now glaring with hate. It was an expression I was to see in them often during the next few months, for hatred and revenge were then the dominant emotions of his life.

"As I stepped across the cell, he drew himself up with an odd touch of dignified pride peculiar to him. He was only a little boy, hunted and run to earth like a wolf, cuffed and kicked and flung into a dark cell prior to being railroaded through the court to the reformatory, but he was staunch and 'game' still to his comrades.

"'I ain't no snitch,' he flung out before I had said a dozen words.

"'Good for you,' I told him. 'There's always good in a fellow that won't snitch on his chums.'

"He looked at me, greatly surprised but still suspicious. He asked me who I was. I told him. 'Are they going to try me in your Court?' he asked. I answered that he would probably be tried in the criminal court. 'They'll send me up, all right,' he said with conviction. 'Would you?' he demanded. 'I'd give you a square deal,' I told him. He sneered in my face."

Not a very promising beginning, was it? The Judge did not give up. He called again on the boys, and again and again. He told them the truth. He told them he was labouring to have them tried in his Court, and why. He talked about his Court, and what it meant; how it was opposed, and why. He had no secrets; he kept nothing back. He discussed crime, his view of it, the police view of it, the world's. He didn't know who was right. "Gradually their suspicion of me disappeared," the Judge says. "They came to regard me and my Court as engaged in a fight for them against the hated police." The Judge let them think that. It was true. He explained how it was true, how "the police were not to blame," not the policemen. They were reared in a school that taught them that it was their duty to fight crime with crime, craft with craft, violence with force, and maybe that was the only way. Certainly, "fellers" like Tatters and the Eel made it hard for the police. Hadn't the boys added to the work of the "cops," and to their worries?

They had indeed. The Judge laid down the kid law, which was the criminal law, about "snitching"; how snitching on the other fellow was wrong, but snitching on yourself was all right, if you believed what you told was to be used to help you. This they understood, and as their confidence grew, they began to snitch on themselves.

They told the Judge their stories, and they were amazing stories of crime and of hate. "The Eel especially hated anything in the nature of legal machinery with a bitterness that amazed me," the Judge says, "till I had heard his story." And then the Judge tells the Eel's story. His father was foreman in a machine-shop, honest enough, but brutal to the boy, who loved his mother, who loved, but was too weak to help, her son. He "bummed" the streets day and night, dodging his father, who cuffed and cursed him whenever their paths crossed. Lee ran away, and to keep himself became a sneak thief. Before he was ten, he had "bummed" his way from Chicago to Denver and become a "pretty slick thief." Arrested now and then, and railroaded by the law, he was patted on the back in the jails by hardened criminals who taught him to pick pockets. Caught at this, he learned burglary from burglars in the jail and, at the age of twelve, nearly killed himself trying to blow a safe. The "Bull-pen" had shown him how, but he put the powder in the wrong place. He was full of courage. An experienced "hobo," he travelled twenty-five thousand miles in one year on brake-beams till, tiring of that, he learned to sneak into Pullmans and hide and sleep in a vacant upper berth. Once he was awakened by an exclamation from the porter: "Good Lawd, they's a kid in heah!" The Eel tells the rest: "I flew th' coop when the coon guy went to tell th' conductor. That ditched me in a town they call Reno, Nevada. 'Course, I was broke. I touched a guy for a half and bought me a cane and some

chewing-gum. I walked into a bank and up to
th' guy in th' monkey cage. I says I wanted
work, and when he went to see de head guy, I
rammed th' gum in de end of my cane, shoved
it through the cage, and swiped a twenty that
stuck to th' gum. Then I hiked out on th'
express that night."

Where did the boy learn that trick? In jail.
That's where the State taught him his trade,
and, when he had learned a new crime, he could
break out and try it. Twice he had broken jail,
cleverly, boldly. Once when an officer, Roberts,
tried to recapture him, Lee smashed a lantern
in the man's face and then led him a chase through
a back yard where clothes-lines hung in the dark.
Caught under the chin by a line, the officer
turned a "flip-flop," and the boy got away;
not unscathed, however; the officer fired several
shots at him, and one hit the boy in the hand.

To kill that policeman was one of the vows
the boy had made to himself. "He tried to kill
me. I was only a kid, and he tried to kill me.
I'm going to kill him one of these nights."

The Judge listened to these stories, noted
what they meant, and he sympathized with the
boys. But that isn't all he did. He sympathized
with the Law and with the policeman, too. He
showed the boys just where he thought things

were wrong in the Law and in the courts, and the boys came to understand. It wasn't easy to correct the teachings of the jails and the police and the home and the streets, but this man did it with those boys. He showed them, for example, how the officer, Roberts, was acting in good faith, doing his duty, and how he must have been exasperated with the Eel. And the Eel saw it. And when the Judge saw that he saw it, he brought the boy and the officer together, and — they are good friends now.

So with the Law; the Judge explained what the machinery of justice was for. It had been perverted from its true function, justice, to vengeance, but it could help a fellow, and he proved it, the Judge did. He got the cases. And he got them with the consent of the police. One captain who was loudest in his protestations, said:

"You can't baby Lee Martin, Judge. He's been in jail thirteen times, and it hasn't done him any good."

"No," said the Judge, "and if I fail, I'll still have twelve times the best of you. You've failed with him your way. It's my turn now. It has cost the city in officers' fees alone, $1,036 to make a criminal of him. Let's see what it'll cost to turn him into an honest boy."

The captain ran over a list of his crimes. The

Judge brought out a longer, more correct, type-written list.

"How in the world did you get that?" the officer asked, astonished.

"They've confessed to me everything."

"How did you do it? We couldn't sweat it out of them."

"I made them see that I was their friend," the Judge said, "and that I wanted to use the information for and not against them."

It was a strange, new point of view to the police, but they saw that there was something in it, so they tried the boys before the kids' Judge.

The evidence was plain. Burglary was the specific charge, and the police proved it; the Judge was convinced formally of what he knew (for the boys had told him all about it). What did the Judge do to the boys?

He put them on probation. Yes, to the horror of the police and the town, he did by these bad boys just as he did by good boys; he gave them a "show." What was the result?

A day or two later the boys called on the Judge. With them were two others, "Red" Mike and Tommy Green. The Judge understood; these were members of the River-Front gang, for whom the police were on the lookout. But nothing was said about that. "We had a general talk about crime," the Judge says, "and the principles of the Juvenile Court." The Judge was expectant, so were Lee and Tatters, but it was left to the newcomers to do their own snitching, and they did it. After a while, "Red" turned to Tommy. "Don't you think it's about time we were snitchin' up?" he asked. Tommy allowed that it was, and then followed what the Judge calls "a snitching bee." "And," the Judge adds, "I had two new probationers for my Court." A week or so more, and these four called with a fifth "kid," and he, a "soft, mushy one," as the Judge describes him, he also "snitched up." Another period, and the five brought in two more. That finished the "criminal" list of the River-Front gang. "Not one of these boys had snitched on another," the Judge says. "Each one had told only on himself."

All those "young criminals" were put on probation, "and," says the Judge, "six out of the seven have stuck. The seventh made the pluckiest fight I ever saw before he slipped back, and I still have hopes of his ultimate success."

What does the Judge mean by a plucky fight? "A plucky fight" means what the Judge means by probation — the game of correction, the game of overcoming evil with good. These young criminals had not only to be good; they couldn't

be good. That's too negative for husky kids,
and the River-Front gang were a husky lot.
The Judge says boys are bad because, while
they have lots of opportunity to do wrong, they
have none to do good. So, as in the case of mischievous boys, he gave these criminals opportunities to do good. There were other "fellers"
starting on careers of crime. If they were
allowed to go on, they would be caught, jailed,
and made criminals by the police, who, though
they didn't mean to be, were really criminal-
manufacturers. The game was to beat the police
and beat public opinion by showing the opposition
that the Judge was right about kids, that "there
ain't no bad kids." So the game was for the
River-Front gang to bring in kids that were
going wrong, get them into the Court gang, and
thus prove by the good they all could do together that "it" worked. And "it" did work.

The loyalty of the River-Front gang to the
Judge as leader of their new gang was superb.
It was mistaken sometimes. Once when Jack
Heimel's mother was away, he slept in a cheap
boarding-house. A drunken man cried out that
he had been robbed, and he accused Jack and a
friend of Jack's. The lodging-house keeper
knew Jack and, of course, believed the charge,
so, sending for the police, he placed himself in

the door to bar the way out. Jack made a dash, hit the man behind the ear and, dropping him, leaped out and away with his chum. The police searched for them all night, but couldn't find them. The Judge found them. When he went down to Court the next morning the boys were "layin' for him." Jack explained:

"We didn't take th' money, Judge, but I had to hit de guy, because, you see, if de cops had 'a' jugged me, me name would 'a' been in the papers, and then, wouldn't they say that this was de feller what de Judge ought to 'a' sent up and didn't? And, say, wouldn't dat 'a' got you into trouble, and maybe lost you yer job?"

It developed afterward that the drunken man hadn't lost the money at all, so Jack Heimel was cleared, and that was his last "scrape." He got a job as a mechanic in the railroad shops and, loyal always, his last report to the Judge was that he had sent East for a book on mechanical engineering. He was rising, and he feels to this day that his success means much, not only to him, but to the Judge and the Court gang, and the methods thereof.

The Eel had a hard time. "This boy, whom the police called a depraved criminal, has done more to discourage crime," the Judge says, "than any ten policemen in the city." He brought in boy after boy to "snitch up," and he helped keep his own gang straight. "Red" Mike slipped back once. Arrested for robbery, he escaped, and the police were after him. The Eel was troubled. He called on the Judge. He knew where "Red" was hiding, and he knew the Judge knew he knew, but the Judge asked no questions. He and Lee simply talked the matter over till they agreed that it would be better for "Red" to come in and surrender than to be driven deeper into crime. And a day or two later "Red" appeared at the Judge's house, "ready," as he said, "to take his papers and go to the reformatory."

Lee became an unofficial officer of the Court, and the Judge used him freely. Once a boy stole a pocketbook from a woman in the store where he worked. The Judge sent for Lee. "Something ought to be done," the Judge said, "to get that boy back in the right path." Lee went after him. He found him in a cheap theatre, "treating a gang," brought him voluntarily in, and — to-day the boy is a trusted employee in that same store.

Another time, Teddy Mack, a fourteen-year-old "criminal," who was arrested for stealing a watch, sawed his way out of jail and got out of

Denver. All summer the police searched, and the Judge and Lee Martin often talked over the case. One day Lee said:

"I'd like to get that kid for you, Judge. I'll bet he's down to the fair at El Paso. You send me down there, and — I won't be a 'snitch cop,' but I believe I kin get him to come in."

The Judge gave Lee five dollars, and the boy went across the line to the bull-fight. There was Teddy. The two boys took in the fair together, but Lee talked "crime, and the principles of the Juvenile Court" to Teddy, and back these two came together to the "Jedge." Teddy "snitched up." The Judge gave him twenty dollars to redeem the watch he had pawned for three dollars, and when Teddy returned with the watch and the exact change, he was sent to deliver the watch to the owner and to admit that he was the thief. That settled the case, and that settled Teddy. "We had no more trouble with Teddy Mack," the Judge says, "though he had been one of the worst boy thieves in the city."

The boy with whom Lee Martin had the most trouble was Lee Martin. He could not settle down. The habit of "bumming," developed in him from early childhood, was too strong, and every once in a while that "movin'-about fever" would get him. "It was like a thirst for drink," the Judge says, "and I told him that when he felt it he must come to me. Once or twice when I saw that the call of the road was too strong to be resisted, I let him take a ride as far as Colorado Springs and back." But that didn't always satisfy him, and he would throw up his job and "skip." It hurt him to do this; it was regarded as disloyalty to the Judge, and that was awful.

"One Sunday evening," the Judge relates, "word reached me that Lee was going to 'fly out.' This worried me so much that I started for his home. I found his mother in tears. The Eel was gone.

"'He just couldn't stand it any longer, Jedge,' she apologized. 'He lay on the floor there and sobbed just like he was in a high fever. "What'll the Judge think? What'll the Judge think?" he kept saying, an',' the woman added, 'he told me to tell you he'd write.'

"I went home much troubled, but the promised letters reached me, one from Albuquerque, then another from El Paso, a rapid succession of them. They were like wails from a lost soul. He implored me not to think he had 'thrown me down.' That was the burden of them all. He was coming back, he said; he just had to get on the move for a while, but he hadn't thrown me down. I wrote him not to steal, and he didn't. When he came back a month later, he showed me a letter from a man he had worked for to prove it."

There is more of the story, more triumphs, and more disappointments, and there are more stories just like it, of other gangs. For all the time the Judge was devoting himself to the "River-Fronts," he was giving himself with the same devotion to his other "cases." And there were failures as well as successes, and the police and the cynics clung to the failures. As the Judge says, however, the failures were really weak boys. "The husky kids, the kind the cops call 'dangerous,' they stuck with me; they showed the police that there 'ain't no really bad kids.' Bad? I believe," the Judge said, smiling, and he quoted Riley:

> "'I believe all childern's good
> Ef they're only understood —
> Even bad ones, 'pears to me,
> 'S jes as good as they kin be!'"

He smiles as he quotes, then the smile disappears, and he adds, "And that's so of men, too."

"Yes, but," you say, "there *are* criminals born?"

"Yes," he replies, "there are criminals born, and there are criminals bred, minors and majors, too. But who bears them, and — what breeds them? What makes bad boys bad? What makes bad girls bad? And what makes men and women bad?"

That's his answer, another question: one question; the fortunate, fatal question which got Ben Lindsey into his fights with the dishonest opposition of Denver, the fights which — because he won them, he and the children, and because they led him straight to the cause of crime, juvenile, and grown-up, too — have made the "kids' Jedge" of Denver one of the leaders of the great war that is going on in Colorado. The outside world couldn't understand why the people of his state wanted the Judge of the Juvenile Court to run for Governor; nor why he was willing to take the nomination. The reason, as we shall see, was that Ben Lindsey is no mere philanthropist, but (in the true sense of the word) a politician; no mere saver of little victims of wrong, but a man leading men to destroy the opportunities for evil-doing, and to give all the children of men a "show" to "do good."

III. BATTLES WITH "BAD" MEN

Early in the history of Denver's Juvenile Court, a boy was arraigned for stealing lumber and sand from a contractor. The contractor was indignant; he "wanted to know whether Judge Lindsey was going to coddle that kid or protect the property of the citizens of Denver from thieves." The Judge said he would take the case under advisement. He did. He took the case "for a walk and a talk."

Once out of that stiff old, stuffy old court room, the tears dried up, and the two got acquainted.

"What did you want the lumber for, kid?" the Judge asked.

"We were building a shack in my back yard, and we needed more boards than we had."

The Judge used to build shacks, and he and the kid discussed the different kinds you could build. The Judge bragged about some he'd put up. But he never used sand in a shack.

"What did you swipe the sand for?" he asked.

"Well," said the kid, "girls can't build shacks. They can keep house in 'em after they're built, but my sister and the other fellers' sisters, they wanted something to do till the shack was done. So while we was gettin' the boards, we seen the sand, and we swiped a little pile for the girls to play in."

And coming into the back yard, the kid showed the Judge the shack and the sand-pile — abandoned now. All work was suspended, pending a decision in their case. The kid wanted to know what the Court was going to do to him. The Judge said he'd take the case under advisement, and he did. He took a walk down to the contractor, and he told said complainant all about the shack and the sand, and the contractor furnished all the lumber and sand necessary to finish the job in that back yard. As for the children, they "cut out" all "swipin'."

The Judge kept the case under advisement, however. He kept on walking around in back yards, and talking with young "thieves" and "builders." He saw many signs of energy and enterprise, and nothing to do; nothing good. Everywhere was private; nowhere to play. Everything was property to steal. The grown-ups had "hogged" everything, and children had nowhere to play and nothing to play with.

The Judge set about organizing a juvenile association of grown-ups to furnish materials for young builders to build with; playgrounds to build on; water to swim in; jobs in the beet fields for vacation kids that had to work, and mountain trips for the rest. In brief, the Judge's Juvenile Association for the Protection and Betterment of Children, which he is trying to make a national organization, originated out of his discovery that society had forgotten to provide children with opportunities for good.

But society provided opportunities for evil. Denver offered plenty of these, and the children knew them all. "I was amazed to hear what children knew," the Judge says. "I talked to them, and I walked with and among them; I visited back alleys at night, hung around cheap theatres, visited the tenderloin and the slums. Standing in the shadow just outside of saloons, I saw children come with pitchers in their hands, sent there for beer by their parents, and while they waited, I heard men tell obscene stories. The children listened, boys and little girls. I talked with the boys, and I found that they understood everything that was vile. You see, I was trying to get at the causes of criminality in children, in children whom I found responsive to the noblest sentiments of honour and fair dealing. Well, I thought I saw what the causes were: the problem is one of environment; manifold opportunity for evil and none for good; and then, back of this, certain social and economic conditions. What could I do to relieve these conditions? I asked myself that again and again. My Court could correct the evil done, some of it, but how could I prevent the evil from being done?"

Perfectly simple and logical, all this. The Judge had no answer ready, but he attacked the worst condition, one that stirred him to his depths.

He found that the Denver saloons had wine-rooms, and that not only boys, but girls, were allowed in them and ruined. The law forbade these places to women, but the law wasn't enforced. Why? Everybody knows, in a general way, why. Denver is a typical American city government, and Lindsey, a former member of the Democratic State Executive Committee, knew, in a general way, the reason for a "liberal" excise policy. It helped business. When cowboys and miners and other visitors came to town, they wanted to have a good time, and it was good for all business to help them spend their money. But the Judge saw that however good for business it might be to neglect to enforce the wine-room law, it was bad for the children; and he put that view of it before the Police Board. He knew well the president, Frank Adams, and the members of the Board. Frank is a Democrat, like Ben, so Ben urged Frank to enforce the law in the interest of the children. The Judge also addressed the Chief of Police. The Chief couldn't do anything but refer the letters to the Board, which wouldn't or, at any rate, didn't, do anything. The Judge then proceeded in his own way to compel the Board to enforce this law.

Colorado is a great place for injunctions. The "interests" there use the courts very much as

in other states they use legislatures and governors.
The brewers own the saloons, and brewing is an
interest. It "contributes" to both parties. The
brewers and the dive interests got out a writ en-
joining the Police Board from enforcing the law.

Judge Lindsey says the Police Board got out
the writ against itself, and there was some ground
for this suspicion. In the first place, the attorney
for the brewers was the Democratic State Chairman. In the second place, Frank Adams, who
is a member of the Adams family, famous in
Colorado politics, was the "iceman" in Denver.
There were other icemen, but the saloons generally
bought of him. So he may have been doing his
customers a favour, on the side. But certainly
the brewers were interested, for they warned
Lindsey that if he went on making trouble for
them, they would defeat him for reëlection.
No matter about that, however. Judge Peter
L. Palmer — of whom it has been said that he
would "enjoin the birds of the air from flying
and the fishes of the sea from swimming" —
Peter L. Palmer held that since, under the constitution of Colorado, women had the same rights
as men, the law forbidding them the wine-rooms
was unconstitutional. Wherefore he enjoined the
Police Board, and the Police Board obeyed his
order. Judge Lindsey didn't. He fined a dive-

keeper in the face of it, and the Supreme Court of the United States upheld his ruling.

It takes time to go through the courts, however, and while the case was pending on appeal, girls were being haled into the Juvenile Court as "incorrigible"; and they did look "bad." But the evidence showed that they had been made bad in wine-rooms.

"And I found that these wine-rooms were 'protected' by the police," the Judge says. "I tried time and again, with Frank Adams and with the other commissioners and with the Chief of Police to get the wine-room keepers arrested, and in vain. Children they would bring in, the boys and girls, but no adults. I investigated further. I called on the Humane Society, and the Secretary, Mr. E. K. Whitehead, told me of the most horrible details. He also had complained in vain to the police. Then I went out and I saw some of these things. I saw sixteen boys gambling in one place, and when I reported it to the policeman on the corner, he insulted me. I wrote about this and about the wine-room to the Chief and to the Commissioner. No answer.

"One Sunday I went to visit one of my probationers, and I found him cursing his mother vilely, with an amazing command of oaths. Looking about, I saw that it was partly a house of assignation, partly a home for the very poor, and all the children were masters of men's language. Looking further, I saw, ten feet from the door of this house, the rear entrance to a wine-room — wide open, though it was a Sunday morning. I went to the mistress of the house of assignation, and she, hardened though she was, told me that this wine-room had supplied more than one bad place with inmates. Only a week before, she said, she saw two girls halt at that wine-room door. One was afraid to go in. The other was urging her, and while they were talking three men came out, seized the reluctant girl, and dragged her in. The next day the woman heard groans and sobs across the way, and she went to see what was the matter. She found the girls in the cellar, naked and drunk!

"My God!" the Judge exclaimed, "where was the policeman all this time?"

"Oh!" she said, "he knew all about it. He was in there, too, drinking with them!"

"It would be hard for me to repeat," the Judge says, "all the things I saw and heard that harrowed my very soul. But they were the causes, this crime and vice and this police partnership, of many of the woes and troubles that come into my Court."

What could he do? The Judge knew that

besides the "ice" and the brewers' contributions, there were other powers back of all these conditions. The railroads ruled the state, the railroads and the mine-owners and the American Smelting Company. Under them, in Denver, and for them, were all the public utility companies which, having grants of privileges, rewarded the people of the city and state by corrupting their government. "It's necessary," they say. Now the corrupt business interests that ruled Denver and Colorado ruled partly by ballot-box stuffing, and it was the dive-keepers, thieves, loafers — all the hangers-on of vice and crime — who did the stuffing. Lindsey, who long had known this, realized now that he had nowhere to turn to appeal for some little consideration of the children of his town, except to the people of his town.

He invited the Police Board to visit the Children's Court on Saturday morning, May 24, 1902. He also invited reporters. Frank Adams didn't come, but the other commissioners did, and the bailiff gave them seats in the jury-box. There the children could see them, and they could see the children, and there were some two hundred children on hand that morning: two hundred "bad" boys who knew all about everything, including that Police Board. When they were all ready, Judge Lindsey entered and took his place on the bench. He looked over his gang of kids, and then he spoke to those officials, typical American officials.

"I have asked you gentlemen to come here and look at these boys," he said. "There are also girls in this city who report on Fridays," he added. The commissioners looked at the boys, and the Judge went on to say that while these children were brought there as delinquents, it was not alone the children who were delinquent. "Parents, in many cases, and adults who violate the law, and particularly police officials who refuse to enforce the law, they are more responsible than the children," he said.

He illustrated: "It became the duty of this Court recently to send a young girl to the Industrial School. She was not depraved or vicious; she was capable of being a good, pure woman with any kind of favourable environment. But she was subject to temptations. What were these temptations? The wine-rooms; not one, but many. She was induced to enter such places. You knowingly permitted them to run in violation of the law. Yet the child is punished and disgraced. You and the dive-keeper, the real culprits, you go scot-free."

The Judge — from the bench, mind you — said this to those commissioners. Then he spoke of a young man who had lost his life in the same place where this girl was ruined. He told the rooming-house woman's story, and he described also her terror lest the police should learn that she had informed on the dive-keepers! Then he described what he knew of gambling by boys.

"I have seen a pitiful, gray-haired old lady, bent with years, her face dimmed with tears, pleading in this Court to recover the all she had on earth, lost by a son in a gambling hell tolerated by you. And here in broad daylight those who conduct the place come, and they tell of the open game of this young man and the loss of that money, and this they do with the prosecuting officer passing in and out. . . . It is nonsense to talk about these things not being known to your Board. It only subjects you to contempt and ridicule."

Frank Adams had been appealing to the Judge in the name of "business" and "the party," not to "rip up" the liquor question. The Judge answered that appeal now with another:

"Flesh and blood, body and soul, the future of little children is so sacred," he said, "that it is a monstrous sacrilege to permit any other consideration to interfere. . . . I know it is unusual to speak thus publicly, but all things usual have been done, and something unusual is justifiable. I therefore beg of you in this public manner, in the presence of these children, for their benefit, that you earnestly and diligently war upon these places. . . . I assure you that you will have then the good will and respect which are denied you now. That is worth more than all the vaunted boastings of all the devil's agents in this town. It is to these that you are catering now, and until you break the spell they have over you, you will be storing up misery, hell, and damnation for the present and future generations."

It was a terrible arraignment, there before those children, whose eyes bored into those officials. There was silence for a moment; then one commissioner, Charles F. Wilson, rose to answer. He said the Board had closed the place where the Judge had seen the boys gambling. The two hundred boys looked at the Judge; he hesitated. Didn't he know about that? Some of the boys did, and one of them sprang to his rescue. Leo Batson, twelve years old, rose, and pointing his finger at Commissioner Wilson, he said:

"Yes, you closed it up, but you opened it up again, like you generally do. It was open inside of a week. And it's open now, 'cause I seen boys in there myself."

There was silence when Leo sat down. The boys looked at the commissioner. He was still a moment, then he went on without answering the boy. He referred to Peter L. Palmer's injunction. It was the Judge's turn.

"The issuance of that injunction was without sense or precedent," said Judge Lindsey. "And it didn't tie your hands. You could have brought your cases to my Court. In this tribunal you will find the whole power of the Court on the side of the law."

The newspapers all turned "yellow" with this story, and that settled the matter for the time being. The tip was passed that the police couldn't "stand for wine-rooms where young girls went—for a while."

The Judge went on walking and talking with the children, and he listened, too, and the things they suffered kept his feelings aroused, while their wisdom "put him wise." It was appalling, what these children knew.

"Huh, business men! They steal, too!" said a cynical little thief one day when the Judge held out to him the prospect of growing up to be a "respected business man," if only he would stop stealing. "Don't the street railway swipe franchises? And the gas company and them, don't they steal 'em? Guess I can read. And my boss,

that's kicking to have me sent to jail, don't he
sell cheap jewelry for eighteen carat fine?"

In this and similar cases the Judge had to reach
down below the teachings of the world of business
to the nobility born in the "born thief," to save
him. "It's mean to cheat and steal," he said,
and it was the success of this appeal that convinced Ben Lindsey that human nature was good
enough to go to war for.

Of course, he didn't realize at first what he
was warring against. Brought up in a perfectly
conventional way, his notions of life and economics
were perfectly commonplace; but when men
came to him and in the name of "business,"
"the party," and "property" besought him not
to fight so hard for the children, he began to see
that the enemy of men, as of children, was not
men, but things. Once he and a police captain
had a dispute in chambers over the custody of
some boys arrested for stealing bicycles. The
police wanted to hold the boys. Why? The
Judge couldn't make out till the officers said
something about the owners of the wheels wanting
to "get back their property."

"Oh," said the Judge, "I see the difference
between you and me: you want to recover the
property, while I want to recover the boys."

The Judge recovered both.

A cotton mill was set up in Colorado. That was a new industry, and the men who established it were applauded for their "enterprise, which could not but benefit the whole State." To compete with the South, however, this mill had to employ child labour. The kids' Judge heard that they were importing large families and setting the little children to work. Colorado had a child-labour law, and the Judge went to the mill to see if the law was being violated. It was, and the conditions were pitiful.

"These imported people were practically slaves," he says. "They had come out under contracts, and the children, unschooled, toiled at the machines first to liberate their parents, then to support them."

The Judge warned the milling company, but that did no good, so he had criminal proceedings instituted, and not only against the superintendent, but against the higher officers also.

This is not the custom in the United States, and the president of the mill, who was also one of the big men in the Colorado Fuel & Iron Company, called on the Judge to explain that he was a respectable citizen. The Judge suggested that it wasn't proper to try to influence a judge in a pending case, but the president "didn't want to do anything improper"; all he wanted was to remind the Judge that a conviction in the case would make him (the president) a criminal. "And I am no criminal," he said. The Judge replied that he was if he broke the law. But the president didn't break the law. If the law was broken, it was by his superintendent, and it was all right to fine his superintendent. But the president was a gentleman and a "big man."

"I'd rather fine you than your superintendent," said the Judge. "He is only your agent, and, as you intimate, you wouldn't mind if he were punished. So I'll punish you as I warned you; I told you that if he persisted in violating the law for you, I'd hold you responsible."

"But, Judge," he said, "if you are going to keep up this fight, we will close the mill!" And he proceeded to tell what a great industry it was; how many people it gave employment; how much good it was doing to the city (he meant the business) of Denver; and how much money had been invested in it by himself and other capitalists.

"His point of view," the Judge says, "was perfectly plain. Money was sacred, men were of no account. If business went well, children could go to — well, let us say, to work. And he blamed me, not the Law, not the State; he had no fear of these. I, personally, with my queer regard for men and women and children — I was a menace to business."

"I warn you right now," he said to the Judge, "that if this thing keeps up, we will shut down the mill, and you will have to share the consequences."

And Judge Lindsey replied: "We are here to protect the children and to enforce the Law, and all I regret is that the penalty isn't imprisonment instead of a fine, so that I could be sure of preventing you from employing young children."

And the Judge persisted, and the mill was closed down. Other causes contributed, but Lindsey never shirked his "share of the responsibility."

What is more, Judge Lindsey had the child-labour law made stricter. He can put "money" in prison now if it hurts children. He had to fight business and politics and the police to do it, but he did it; he and the kids and the men and women of Denver.

We have seen that the Judge set out to correct the evils of child life under the laws as they stood. He had been making notes, however, of legislation he wanted, all the while he was walking and talking and trying cases. For example, the Juvenile Court existed by the courtesy of the District-attorney, who was a machine man; Lindsev gave himself the legal right to demand all children's cases. He had exercised discretion; he gave himself explicit authority to exercise discretion. He had found adults at fault for the criminality of children; he drew a paragraph making parents, employers, business men, and all other grown-ups amenable to the criminal law for neglect, abuse, or temptation of children. This is his now famous "contributory delinquency law against adults." Needing probation officers, he authorized the appointment of them, and since the police and the Sheriff and the District-attorney were all tied up with the liquor and other business interests, he gave his probation officers certain police powers. The child-labour law was only one item in the legislation Judge Lindsey went after.

The Judge's bills were most important legislation, and to put them through he had to proceed most carefully. He began in the convention, by taking a hand in the nomination of legislators. His enemies fought him there, and they beat his man, but he came up on good terms with the others. They introduced his bills and started them through the mill, very quietly. Hardly any notice was taken of them. Apparently the lobbyists didn't do their work well, for the interests were amazed after it was all over to see in the new laws "what Lindsey had been up to." An officer in one of the telegraph companies said the "interests" would never have let either the child labour or the adult delinquency bill pass if they had known of them. The Judge had learned that the messenger service was a degrading influence for boys; they were sent to all sorts of vile places, saw all sorts of vile things, and caught respectable citizens in predicaments the knowledge of which made the boys cynical and vicious. So he advised, and he still advises, both boys and parents against the messenger service. But he wished also to have a club to hold over the companies; wherefore he had drawn into one of his bills a clause including officers of telegraph companies under the "adult delinquency law." The companies, suspecting the Judge, twice sent a lawyer to the capital to see "Lindsey's bill," and he saw one bill, an inoffensive one, never the other. He didn't know there was another. It was the other that "hurt our business," he said. Thus beaten, the companies never dared to move for a repeal; they surrendered, and, calling on the Judge, came to an understanding with him about what they might and might not do with boys.

There was a fight on these bills, however.

It is known among the good citizens and bad kids of Denver as "the fight against the jail." After moving along regularly through the Senate, the Judge noticed that his bills suddenly stuck in the House. "What was the matter?" the Judge inquired. The clerk couldn't explain. One evening a reporter called at the Judge's house.

"Judge," he said, "Frank Adams is fighting your bills. His brother Billy, you know, is a power in the Legislature. They don't dare come out in the open and fight you, but they are telling it around that you are crazy on the children subject, and that the boys fill you up with lies!"

"What had I better do?" the Judge asked.

"Stir 'em up," said the reporter. "Give me an interview and tell all about the jail."

"That's grand-stand playing," the Judge said, smiling.

"It's appealing to public opinion," said the reporter, "and that's against the rule of graft, but what do you care? You aren't a grafter."

The Judge made out a statement, but it was too mild. The reporter rejected it, and with the facts the Judge told him and what he and all police reporters knew, Harry Wilber (for that was the reporter's name) did what newspaper men love to do when they get the chance — he wrote the truth, and he wrote it to kill. United

States Senator Patterson's paper, the *Rocky Mountain News*, printed the interview in red, and it was sensational. The Judge says it gave him a sensation himself. But it was true, so he "stood for it." Frank Adams answered it with a denial. The boys were liars, he said, and as for Judge Lindsey, he was crazy.

"I knew then," says the Judge, "that I was up against it. I must make good. So I wrote to the Police Board offering to hold an inquiry. They were willing, they answered, but not then. I wanted it then, and I ordered it for two o'clock the next day in my court room. And lest the Board, recalling the last time they met the boys, might not come, I invited also the Governor, the Mayor, the District-attorney, other officials, fifteen ministers and rabbis, and others. I didn't expect many to come, but they all accepted, even Governor Peabody — all but Frank Adams and the police commissioners. The Board sent a dummy to represent it."

It was Saturday morning when the Judge got his acceptances, and he had to hurry. Calling in a friendly deputy sheriff, he asked him to get ten witnesses named on a list he had made of boys who had been in the jails. "I must have them by two o'clock," the Judge said. The officer declared it impossible. He should have had two days' notice. The Judge was in despair, but he ran over his list till he came to the name "Mickey."

Mickey was a street boy. He had been in jail often, and the last time was only a month or so before. After he got out, he and the boys in with him had called on the Judge to complain. They stated their case. They were running through the street when one of them knocked over a sign to which some shoes were attached. The man in the store rushed out and sent the policeman after the boys. They had stolen his shoes, he said, and the policeman arrested them. The boys hadn't taken a shoe, and absolutely the only evidence against them was the fact that one of the boys needed shoes! His feet had come through his old ones. They were thrown into cells among criminals, bums, and drunks, then put all together in one cell next to drunken women of the street. During the evening one of them broke a window, and when the jailer came and cursed and kicked them about, they wouldn't tell who had done it. In a rage, the man knocked down one of them and, when the rest scattered and ran, pursued, and bowled them over with his great keys. They were detained a week and then released without a hearing.

The Judge had the boys examined by a physi-

cian, who found evidences enough that they had
been beaten. But the Judge went down to the
jail, and he learned the truth there from his
regular sources of information. Satisfied of the
justice of their complaint, the Judge went with
the boys to lodge a protest with the Police Board.
The commissioner refused to believe the boys'
stories. It was this case, and many, many cases
like it that had convinced Judge Lindsey that
the jails were not only schools where older criminals, male and female, taught boys crime and
vice, but places where the police practised brutal
injustices which made the boys hate the police,
dread the law, and despise everything that we
mean by "civilized society." It was the experiences of boys like Mickey and his gang which
had prompted the Judge to write the bill which
had been held up, the bill providing a detention
school and forbidding juvenile offenders to be
held in jail at all.

"This was Mickey's fight that I was making,"
the Judge says, as he tells the story, "and I knew
I could count on the little chap. I asked the
officer if he could get me Mickey. He said he
could, and I begged him to go and tell the boy
I needed help."

In a few moments Mickey burst breathlessly
into the Judge's chamber.

"What's the matter, Judge?" he asked.

"Mickey," the Judge said, "I'm in trouble, and you've got to help me. I helped you. I went down and I made a fight for you fellows. Didn't I?"

"That's what you did," said Mickey. "Betcher life you did."

"Well, now you've got to stay with me." And he told Mickey what he wanted — all the kids he could find that had been in jail. "The officer can't get them; says there isn't time enough. Can you?"

"Can I? Well, you watch me! Don't you worry about the kids, Judge! Gimme a wheel, and I'll get kids, kids to burn!"

The Judge went out, and he and Mickey borrowed a wheel. It didn't fit, but Mickey hopped on and went spinning down the street.

"It was a relief to me to see him go," the Judge says, "but my worry wasn't over. The invited officials began to arrive before Mickey returned. At ten minutes before two, when the Governor appeared, there was not a kid in sight. The entire company had assembled in my chambers before I saw sign of any witnesses, and I was troubled. It was painful. I knew I could count on Mickey, and the kids generally, but suppose he couldn't find them!"

But Mickey found them. Just at two there was a murmur outside. It grew into a hubbub which, as it came down the hall, developed into an alarm. The Judge's guests were startled, and even the Judge wasn't sure. It sounded like a mob, and up the stairs it rattled, then down the upper hall toward his chamber. As it approached, the Judge knew. He flung open the doors, and there were thirty or forty boys, with Mickey radiant at their head.

"Here's the kids, Judge. Got more'n I thought I would."

"Bully for you, Mickey!" said the Judge. "You've saved the day."

"I told ye I'd stay wit' ye, Judge."

The Judge took the "mob" into a side room. There he told them what was up. They were to tell the truth about the jails. "The police say you have lied to me," he said. "If you have, I ask you now to tell the truth. But tell it. Tell it as you tell one another. Tell it in your own words. They may be bad words, but these gentlemen want to know the truth. So tell them all. Tell them what you see — the dirty things; tell them what the older prisoners say, and what they do to you."

He put Mickey in charge. "Pick out your best witnesses, Mickey," he instructed him,

"and send them in one by one." And Mickey
began to sort his witnesses. As the Judge left
the room, he heard Mickey say, with a shove,
"You get back there, Skinny, you've only been
in five or six times. Fatty Felix has been in
twenty-three times and ——"

Mickey led in his witnesses, one by one, Fatty
Felix, Teddy Healy, Teddy Mack, and the
rest, till the Governor and the ministers cried
"enough!"

Those boys told what was what. They told
of lessons in crime by older criminals; stories
they had heard there of injustices by judges
and of cruelties by the police. They showed up
the world as the criminals see it and as those
criminals showed it to the boys. And they also
related scenes of vice and foulness too revolting
to repeat. And those boys made that company
of grown-ups believe them, too. Once or twice
the police representative interrupted, but, as the
Judge says, "Teddy Healy's answer, direct,
awful, and yet innocently delivered, made the
matter ten times worse." The officials dropped
all thought of cross-examination. Once a minister asked Mickey about the visits of the clergy
to the jail.

"Never saw one," said Mickey. Then he
remembered. "Oh, yes, seen the Salvation Army

there onct, but they sang 'Praise God from Whom All Blessings Flow,' and we'd heard that before, and besides, there didn't seem to be no blessings flowing our way."

It was the officials' turn to smile, and the ministers, they also ceased to cross-examine. The boys were left to talk, watched by Mickey and frankly guided by the Judge. It went on for an hour or two, then a preacher rose.

"My God," he said, "this has gone far enough! It is too, too horrible!" And, as he left, Governor Peabody got up.

"Gentlemen," he said, "I never in my life heard or knew of so much rot, corruption, and vileness as I have learned this day from these babes — almost — and I want to say that nothing in my administration will be so important to me as signing Judge Lindsey's bills. I don't care to read those bills. If he says they are designed to correct these conditions, I am satisfied. And," turning to the representative of Frank Adams, he added, "if Judge Lindsey is crazy, I want my name written right under his as one of the crazy people. And as to those boys lying, anyone who says they have been lying to-day must be himself a liar."

With that the meeting broke up. The Judge went back to the boys, and he thanked them and Mickey. He was careful to explain again what it was all about. "'Skill in handling marble is as nothing to skill in handling men,'" he quotes, and he wished to be sure that no false impressions were left in these boys' minds. "I am fighting for a decent place to keep kids that are too weak to be on the level," he said. "The jails are not decent; and Mickey, you boys have beaten the jail to-day, you and all the good kids in Denver. Go out and tell them so, for it is their victory."

That was true. It was a victory. The pulpits rang with the story the next day. The men and women of Denver heard, and so did the grafters, and the grafters felt the effect in public opinion. Lindsey's bills came up from the bottom and were passed and signed and made part of the laws of Colorado within a week. And now other states are copying them.

Reformers, whose notion of reform consists in "getting a law passed," are often amazed to find that their good law does no good. The reason is that neither public opinion nor public officials enforce the new laws. Lindsey had waited for his legislation till he had the support of public opinion, and then he enforced his new laws; he, and the boys and girls, and public opinion.

They were effective laws. They gave the

Judge control of the whole children's case. He proceeded gently to the enforcement of his power. He had written into the laws full authority to exercise his discretion, with adults as with children, and he did this because he meant to be human and charitable to men as he had been to children. It had worked with the children; he would try it on their elders. So he was firm but not unkind.

When the police brought in a boy for getting drunk, the Judge asked for the man who sold the boy the liquor, and the police had to fetch the man. Sometimes the Judge fined him; sometimes he imprisoned him; sometimes he suspended sentence. For he talked to the men as he did to the boys, and if he found that they hadn't thought of the evil they did by carelessly serving boys and girls with tobacco and liquor, the Judge explained it to these saloon-keepers. And if he thought they were impressed, he put them also "on probation." That gave him a hold on them, which prevented crime and vice. For the Judge knew what was going on. He had thousands of eyes. The boys and girls watched for him. When the Judge had got his legislation, he told the children that the new laws were their laws — enacted for them and by them; for Mickey and his "gang of jailbirds," who carried the day, represented the children of

Denver. The children, therefore, must obey these laws and help enforce them. He broadened the doctrine of "snitching on the square." It was mean to spy; it was wrong under the law to "get a man to break the law and then peach on him." No child was to be "smart" and hunt for evil. But when a man sold cigarettes and liquor to children, that man was "making kids bad," and for a pitifully small profit, too. Wherefore, the thing for a kid to do was, first, to warn the man, then, if he didn't "cut it out," to tell the Judge.

This was a very delicate part of the Judge's policy, and many a man will shake his head over it. We all despise spying. But boys despise it more than men, and I know no better way to prove that the Judge made it clear and right than by stating that the boys of Denver, the "big fellers," approved the doctrine and practised it. Take the "Battle-Axe gang" of Globeville, for example. Globeville is a suburb of Denver, and the Battle-Axes were the toughest "fellers" over there. Their leaders were three brothers, known as the Cahoots — "Big Cahoot," "Middle Cahoot," and "Little Cahoot." The whole gang frequented dives, drank, smoked, chewed (they were named after their favourite brand of plug tobacco); they did everything that men did, and other things besides. The Judge got hold of this gang, in the usual way; one or two were arrested, won over, and persuaded to bring in the rest. They all came, and were interested in the game of correction. The good they could do, the Judge told them, was to help enforce the laws of the kids' Court. They did it, too. They had trouble at first. One day Big Cahoot went to a saloon where some of the little fellers in his gang had bought tobacco. He told the man about the law and asked him not to sell to any Battle-Axes. The saloon-keeper, taken aback, became angry, and started for the boy. Big Cahoot wasn't afraid. He stood his ground; there was a fight, and the young tough was kicked out into the street. But he told the Judge, and the Judge sent the man to jail for fifteen days. After that it was easier for the boys, who are still reporting to the Judge that the law is respected "over in Globeville" and that "the Battle-Axes are doin' all right."

One curious development of this policy was that many of the liquor dealers, having been made to understand what all this meant to the children, came to like the Judge and to help him to carry out his policy. The Baker case will illustrate.

One day a girl was brought in. She told her story; it was a wine-room story, and the Judge had the wine-room keeper, Baker, arrested. He tried him in the Juvenile Court, and sent him up for sixty days.

"The girl I kept on probation," he says, "and I was talking to her one day — the day before Christmas — when I was told that a boy, Paul Baker, wanted to see me. Putting the girl in a side room, I had the boy in. He was a handsome, wholesome little fellow, and he came up to my table, halting, but with a frank look on his face.

"'Judge,' he said, 'you put my papa in jail, but everybody says that you like boys and do all you can to help a boy. So I came to ask you to let my father come home for Christmas.'"

He began to cry, and the Judge spoke.

"Yes, I like boys," he said, "and I like men, too. Do you think I dislike your father? Not a bit! I was sorry to put him in jail. And did it never occur to you that it wasn't I that put him in jail? It was the Law. And the Law is right. Do you know what your father did?"

The boy knew. "Well, I like little girls as well as I like boys, and you know that wine-rooms are bad places for little girls. This little girl and her mother, they are suffering just as you and your father are suffering; all because he broke the law."

The Judge sent for the girl, and he introduced

the two children. He drew the girl on to tell what "trouble" the violation of the law had caused her and her mother. The Judge explained why she should not hate, but be sorry for the man, since he was only thoughtless, as she was, and was in trouble, too.

"Here is his son, Paul, who has come to ask that his father may be allowed to come home for Christmas to see his family. His mother suffers as yours does; his sister has wept as you have wept. It is all, all trouble, and no one is worse than another. Now, what shall I do about letting Mr. Baker go home for Christmas?"

"Let him go," the girl said, and she and the boy joined in the plea. The Judge consented.

When Paul brought in his father to see the Judge, on the day after Christmas, the Judge sent the boy out of the room, then he praised the son to the father. It was a pity, he said, to bring up that boy in such a business.

"Judge," the man said, "you are right. I've been thinking it all over in jail, and I've made up my mind to get rid of this business and go back to the mountains where I came from."

The Judge did not send Baker back to jail; he suspended sentence, as his law authorized him to do, and the man did sell out and go back to the mountains. Now, when they come to town, he and his boy always call on the Judge, their "best friend."

"You see," the Judge says, "Baker wasn't a bad man. He did a bad thing, and that bad thing made a little girl bad. But what made him do the bad thing? To make his business good; to increase his profits. But there was the Law and the power of the State to compel him to restrict his enterprise within limits where it wouldn't hurt anybody else. That's where the System broke down; that's where it breaks down all the time. Why?"

Baker told him why. He said that he broke the law because the bosses told him he might. He contributed to their campaign funds, paid blackmail, and furnished "stuffers" to vote, so they told him he was "protected." "Then you came along, Judge, and you sent me up. I don't blame you. I blamed them, and I went to them for their protection. They said they couldn't handle you. They said they didn't mean I could break juvenile laws, but they didn't tell me that. I paid them, and they couldn't deliver the goods. That's why I blame them."

Baker blamed the bosses, and so did the other saloon-keepers. So did the people of Denver; most of us blame the political bosses. The

Judge himself blamed them for a long while, and he ought to have known better. One of his first political services was to help Governor Thomas destroy the power of Boss Thomas J. Mahoney, famous in Denver politics. And they did destroy Mahoney's power. But that made no difference. Only the man was down and out; the boss lived. Who was the boss of the political boss? For whom was blackmail collected from the saloon-keepers in return for which they were permitted to break the law, sell liquor to boys, and keep wine-rooms where girls might be ruined? The parties? For whom did the parties work? The parties worked for the big business interests of Denver and Colorado, as the Judge found out.

You hear in Denver that "the trouble with Ben Lindsey is that he 'butts into' everything." He does and he must. His critics mean that Judge Lindsey might solve the problem of the children, if, for their sake, he would not interfere with other evils. Many good men and women adopt that policy. Temperance reformers, to get their prohibition laws through, trade votes with the railroads; and charities and churches, colleges and all sorts of benevolent and reform groups, to say nothing of businesses, professions, and interests generally — we, all of us, are standing in with Evil, in the hope of destroying the particular little evils against which we are fighting. Lindsey won't. This is the institutional idea; this is the fallacy which makes men sacrifice civilization — for no less is at stake — for their church, their party, or their grocery store. If Lindsey should make this common, almost universal, mistake he might build up his Juvenile Court, they tell him, into a national, yes, an international institution, and send his name reverberating down through the ages. But Ben Lindsey won't do it; and he won't because he sees that he can't.

He can't for two reasons. One, as he soon learned, is that the problem of the children isn't a separate problem. Ben Lindsey discovered that bad children are made bad by the conditions which men create. And he went after some of those conditions, and when it was found that his legislation gave him power over adults that hurt children, as well as over the children, the leading citizens of Denver were incensed. Why? His authority over saloon and other vice interests loosened the hold the machines had over the vicious elements of society, and menaced the election frauds on which the business and political system of the state was built. And Lindsey saw, and he was told (though not in these words) that the big men of his state would prefer to see children hurt than business. So they fought him, and when he beat them, as we have seen, with the help of the men, women, and children of the city, they declared that he "had too much work to do," and that therefore they would take away from his Court jurisdiction over adults who contributed to the delinquency of children. In other words, they are indeed willing to let him do what he can for the kids after the harm is done, but he must not undermine the vice of the city, however much it may injure youth, the foundation of "prosperity."

Thus the first reason why he can't let all the other evils go to correct the one he is after, was his discovery that our apparently separate evils are all tied up together; they are all one evil; they are a System, as he calls it, of Evil.

The second reason is that Lindsey is so constituted that he must attack any wrong with which he comes in personal contact. We have seen how, accidentally, the County Judge drifted into the case of the children. That was characteristic. When he was a young lawyer he was beaten in a damage suit against the street railway by a "fixed" jury. Inquiring into the matter, he learned that jury-fixing was a common practice, and he attacked that practice. He drew a bill to enable a majority of jurors to render a verdict. The company offered his firm an annual retainer, but Lindsey declared that it was a bribe and refused it. "This was my first sight of the grand System," he says, "but I didn't recognize it as such. I've learned since that this is the way the interests get their first hold on promising or troublesome young lawyers." Lindsey put his bill through. Challenged as unconstitutional, it was first upheld, then thrown out by the Supreme Court of Colorado; "which gave me my first sight of the Supreme Court as a part of the System," he says.

His practice developed along probate lines, and he found the laws obscure and unfair. He revised them, and his revision, enacted, has been highly praised by the law journals. Indeed, his knowledge of probate law was one of the justifications for putting so young a man on the county bench. Lindsey is the author of the present election laws of his state. Everybody was complaining of the old laws, but nothing was done about them till Lindsey went to work and got them changed. I could go on for a page with practical reforms taken up by this man, all of them suggested by his accidental, personal contact with evils, and all having nothing to do with children. If Judge Lindsey had never heard of the problem of the children he would have been known as a man doing a man's work for men.

But the incident in his career which will show this best is his exposure of the County Commissioners. That also was begun by accident.

At the close of the Juvenile Court one Saturday afternoon, the Judge picked up idly from the clerk's desk a paper, which, as he talked, he glanced at. "To 1,000 sheets paper, $280." It was a bill, and the price interested the Judge. He asked the clerk about it. The clerk hadn't seen the bill. He "guessed" it was there by mistake; bills didn't come to him; "must have been meant for the clerk of the County Board." Lindsey sent the clerk to "see Mr. Smith, of the Smith-Brooks Publishing Company (which furnished the paper), and ask if the bill was correct." The clerk brought the answer that his (Smith's) "damned boy had taken the bill to the wrong place, and the price was none of our business." The Judge sent to the County Clerk for other bills charged to the County Court.

"I was amazed at the charges," he says. "Six letter files at $6 apiece; these cost me personally twenty-eight and thirty cents apiece. Paper which was charged for at the rate of $48 a thousand I could get for $6. I spent the night on those bills, and the next (Sunday) morning I took expert advice. I found that the County was paying several hundred per cent. too much for all supplies to my Court."

As with the children and as wit the Police Board, the Judge wished to give the County Commissioners a hearing, so he wrote them a letter containing the facts. "I thought probably they didn't know about these overcharges. I didn't want to misjudge them, and I wanted to examine into the situation with them privately and personally. I believe if they had come up with the truth, I'd have been satisfied if they had promised to cut it out."

The Judge received no reply to his letter. He sent another, and still no response; that is to say, none that was direct. There was an indirect response, however, which interested the Judge profoundly. Both the Police and the County Boards of Denver were bi-partisan, but the fighting line in the politics of the city was a machine, not a party line, and the Police and the County Boards were at odds. The County Board had appointed Lindsey a judge. When he went after the Police Board, Frank Adams, the president, unable to believe in honesty and sincerity, had looked around for an explanation of "Lindsey's enmity" to him; and the theory he fixed upon was that Lindsey, out of gratitude to the County Board for his job, was "hurting the party" to help Frank Bishop, the president of the County Board, who was a candidate for the nomination for Governor of Colorado. So now, when Ben "got after Frank Bishop's Board," he puzzled Frank Adams and all the other men in Denver who, to account for the conduct of others, read their own souls.

"What does Ben mean? Is he an ingrate? You go ask him what the hell he means." This was said by Commissioner Watts to the Judge's clerk, whom the Board had also "given his job." Cass Harrington called; the attorney to the County Board, this man had resigned to be "of counsel" to the Colorado Fuel & Iron Company. Others called, many prominent men. "This stealing," the Judge says, "had friends, political and business friends, and they were powerful men, all of them." He saw that he would also need friends, so the Judge paid some visits. He called on some other judges; he told them the facts, and he asked them to move with him for an investigation. They wouldn't.

"Why, Judge," said one of them, "you have your hands full now. You are doing more than two or three men can do. You oughtn't to want to know about this. I don't. That would make me responsible, and I don't want to have anything

to do with it. Go to the District-attorney.
. . . Well, then, that means that you know
what politics is in this town. My advice to you
is, let the whole thing alone."

This from a judge! And other officials took
the same view or a similar view: "You can't do
anything"; or "The County Board appointed
you; I believe in sticking by your friends"; or
"It will ruin you, Judge"; or "It will spoil your
work for the children."

The Judge went on investigating, and the
evidence he discovered and the things his
"friends" told him to stop him, showed him that
this County graft was well known, and that it
was but a small part of a system of graft. For
example, business men were in on the deals;
each commissioner had merchants for graft-
partners. And besides, the County Board was
a board of tax revision; it had remitted the taxes
of public service corporations, and it could "hurt"
or "help" property-holders generally. But the
Judge got help. Some of the early commissioners
"snitched" to the Judge; they didn't snitch like
the boys, "on the square" — they "squealed" to
save themselves, and the others squealed on the
squealers to get even. Oh, he got the facts! He
appointed a committee to investigate, and the
committee reported the facts — to the Judge.

A concerted effort was made to have the Judge suppress his report. Many respectable friends of the grafters went to the front for graft. They pretended to represent "business," the "party," "the fair fame of Denver," etc. They used the names of United States Senators Patterson and Teller. They were panic-stricken. As for the Judge, he was awed at the show of influence. "And," he says, "I was really in doubt lest I might be doing a great harm to accomplish a little good." But he was reassured. He sounded the United States Senators, and both Mr. Patterson and Mr. Teller sent back word to "go ahead and show up the grafters regardless of party." That was the first encouragement the Judge got. Finally, three of the County Commissioners called, and their pleadings decided him. They also prayed in the name of "the party," the "credit of business," Denver, gratitude, their families; but — there was no word about stopping the stealing! The Judge published the report in the Democratic newspaper, the *News.*

The County Board had to act; and it began with an investigation of its own — a farce, of course. "One thing I learned from it, however," the Judge says, "and that was that many men of business are cowards. The same experts who had told me that the commissioners were thieves, went on the stand and perjured themselves." And their perjury was all in vain. District-attorney Lindsley had to act. Lindsley is the man who got his office when Lindsey wanted it, and the Judge urged him now to do what he, himself, had thought of doing: use the power of the public prosecutor to prosecute public criminals and clean up the city. Lindsley wouldn't; he was in the gang, and other gangsters said he didn't dare. He proposed that the Judge meet with a committee of the party leaders and discuss what should be done. The Judge refused. And the newspapers made demands. So Lindsley had to make a show of action. He called on the Judge and talked about doing his duty. He has a peculiar whine, Lindsley has, and in that whining way he protested to the Judge that while he didn't believe the commissioners could be convicted, he would do his duty. Judge Lindsey happened to go down to the Democratic Club right after this talk, and he found Lindsley there drinking with one of the accused commissioners. And the information that this District-attorney drew was under a statute which limited the penalty to $300 fine and removal from office.

The newspapers, principally Senator Patterson's, forced this case to trial. District-attorney Lindsley refused to appear in it himself; he appointed a deputy, George Allan Smith, who, the Judge says, was faithful. (And evidently he was, for he was forced to resign after the trial.) No local judge cared to sit on the case, so a judge of the Pueblo district (controlled by the Colorado Fuel & Iron Company) was called in. For the grafters appeared Charles J. Hughes, a leading attorney for the corrupt corporations of Colorado (since elected a United States Senator). The story of the trial is a story of "jury work," stolen papers, conspiracies and plots, and an attempt to brand Judge Lindsey as "an ingrate" (to the System), a "reformer," and a "grand-stand player." (How they do hate to have a man serve and appeal to the people!) Nobody expected anything but a verdict of acquittal, and then Judge Lindsey was to have been put on trial.

But the jury convicted those grafters. How it happened I couldn't learn. Somebody blundered, I heard. The jurors apologized; the District-attorney apologized; the very judge apologized. Judge Voorheis delivered from the bench to those prisoners at the bar a speech which was eulogistic of them. He spoke of their standing and usefulness as Christian gentlemen and good citizens. He said they were victims of an evil System. He regretted that he had to impose any punishment, but he must; so he gave the smallest penalty provided by the law: "Ten dollars and costs!"

The learned judge was right: there is a System, and the penalties that System imposed upon Judge Lindsey were not light. His sentence was destruction. Knowing that money couldn't prostitute him, women were tried. The janitor of the County Court House wouldn't clean Lindsey's court-room and so neglected his closet that the Board of Health had to interfere. He was cut on the street by other officials and, to avoid hearing himself called insulting names, had to stay away from his club. His party council allowed the convicted County Commissioners to name their successors and to reject from the platform a plank declaring for honesty in office.

This persecution continued for a year or two and, it must be confessed, the Judge was aggravating. He not only refused to surrender; he went right on fearlessly supporting in public every good reform measure and movement that anybody proposed. For example, a convention, called for by the so-called Rush Amendment to the State Constitution, drew for Denver a good, new, home-rule charter. The big business interests "had to" beat it, however, because it gave the people a vote on all franchise grants and permitted municipal ownership. The only way to beat it was to have the ballot-boxes stuffed. Yet, when some inexperienced young men organized a League for Honest Elections, this County Judge came down off the bench to help the league. And, as usual, his speech was no mere perfunctory address on the sacredness of the ballot-box; he named names, and he named not merely the despised agents who did the dirty work; Judge Lindsey called the roll of the officials who employed and protected the ballot-box stuffers! The people, already aroused, became so inflamed that finally their rulers had to elect a pretty good charter themselves.

Do you see the situation? Do you see Ben Lindsey doing his duty, all of it, not only as a judge of children, but as County Judge, and not only as a judge on the bench, but as a man on the bench and off it? and fighting all the while for his life; cheerfully, without malice, but without fear? Paul Thieman in the Denver *Post* once called Ben Lindsey "the first citizen of Colorado," and declared that, not the mines and the mills, not the railroads, the farms, and the banks, but Ben Lindsey's work was "the greatest thing the state has produced." And from the point of view of the history of man, this is true. It looks absurd from a shop window, but Paul Thieman was seeing things through the eyes of a little boy he mentions, who, sitting silent one day watching the Judge deal out justice, suddenly rushed up and kissed him on the cheek. "I love you!" the child said.

The test came at the elections of 1904. The Judge had to run then, and he sought the office. "I had to," he says apologetically; "my work was only just begun." His enemies meant to defeat him. Who were his enemies? There was Frank Adams and his Police Board, whose co-partnership with vice and crime he had exposed and disturbed; they were still in office and powerful in his party. Then there were the County Commissioners whom he had driven to trial for grafting; they controlled the County Board, and the party machinery. These two groups with all their followers hated the just Judge, of course, and they proposed to beat him openly for the nomination. But wiser counsels prevailed. Other, cooler enemies, passed the word to beat him quietly. Lindsey was "popular" with the women and children, the leaders said, and — women vote in Colorado. The big leaders advised caution, and the scheme was to make him decline the nomination himself. They proposed to nominate as his associate on the County Bench a man who was "going to knock out all this kid business." They expected the

Judge to revolt, and he did; he said he would "denounce his fellow-candidate from the stump." This was the excuse the Democrats wanted, and they decided to drop the Judge.

But a hitch occurred. There was a row in the Republican party, and the dominant state leader, to affront the Denver boss, William G. Evans, nominated Judge Lindsey on the Republican ticket. This put the Democrats in an awkward attitude. They demanded that Lindsey be loyal to his own party and decline the Republican nomination. He refused. They offered him a better associate judge, if he would run only on the Democratic ticket. But the Judge knew that they meant to knife him, so he accepted their associate, but declared he would accept any and all nominations from all parties. And he did. And his party decided again not to nominate him. This was three days before the convention, but that was time enough for the Judge.

He went to the people. He published an open letter in the Denver *Post*. The newsboys, all friends of the Judge, cried it as news, and not only that, they sent kids as couriers to raise the gangs. Men took the letter home, and mothers turned out. But the children were before them. They poured out into the streets and, collected and organized by the newsboys, marched up and down the main streets, yelling for Lindsey. By the time the procession had reached the Democratic Club, the cries of the children had developed into a song which they sang as they marched and countermarched and halted before the club:

"Who, which, when?
Wish we was men,
So we could vote for our little Ben."

And they kept it up all that night and all the next day. It was most embarrassing to the politicians. "Little sons of ——!" exclaimed a leader in the club, "they are doing more than anybody else to beat us." But the answer was that cry from the street, "Who, which, when?" All day long, everywhere, the boys kept at it. And then the mothers of the city held a mass-meeting at the Women's Club. And then there was a mass-meeting of men, women, and children in the Opera House.

Ben Lindsey was nominated, "amid howls and curses" — and on his own terms, on his own party ticket, and all other tickets, excepting only that of the Socialists. Nominated by the people, he was elected by their unanimous vote; but that didn't settle it.

The Judge believed that the election of two County Judges was unconstitutional; if it was, the Mayor of the city would have to choose between him and his colleague. The Mayor, Robert Speer, was a Democrat and the leader of Lindsey's party. The Judge asked him whom he would choose. This Democratic Mayor said he would have to consult with William G. Evans, the Republican boss, before he could answer, and he did see Mr. Evans and the answer was that there would be no choice; the spring election was legal and would stand. But if it should not be held legal, then, the Mayor made plain, Judge Lindsey would not be the Judge.

"That's enough for me," said Lindsey. "I fight." And he went forth to fight. He went to the editors of Senator Patterson's two papers, the *News* and the *Times*, and to the Denver *Post*. They sounded the alarm, and they kept it up, too. Paul Thieman rehearsed the whole story of the kid's Judge as a serial. The people began to be interested, but they were too late; the conventions of both parties met and adjourned without nominating the Judge, and "Bill" Evans left for New York.

Mayor Speer, the Democrat, was in charge of this business for both parties, but he could not control the younger Republicans. They made such a fuss that the older leaders consented to recall the convention. It was to nominate Lindsey, of course, but this "matter of course" was so insisted upon by the System's organ, the *Republican*, that Lindsey became suspicious. He inquired, and he heard the night before the convention that all this talk was part of the game to keep the young Republicans away from the convention; another man was to be nominated in the Judge's place.

Lindsey called up his friends among the delegates, and the young men wanted to give up. The caucus had been held; the slate was fixed; it was too late to make a fight. The Judge wouldn't hear of quitting, however, so, in their desperation, one of them suggested seeing David H. Moffatt. Mr. Moffatt is the leading banker and financier of Colorado, and to go to him was to appeal over the heads of all the political bosses and the apparent business bosses to the very head of the System. Moffatt was the man to go to, but Lindsey didn't know Moffatt.

"Well, you know Walter Cheesman; go to him."

Walter Cheesman was a religious man, very rich and benevolent and an active supporter of the Humane Society and of Lindsey's Juvenile Improvement Society. So the Judge knew Mr. Cheesman, but it was not because of his benevolence that those young men suggested seeing him. Walter Cheesman was president of the Denver Water Company, and therefore "had to" be part of the System which causes the corruption and the evils that, as a philanthropist, he "had to" contribute money to ameliorate.

The Judge went to see the philanthropist. He told Mr. Cheesman about the plot and the caucus.

"You, Mr. Cheesman, you know," he said, "what I have done in that office. You know I have slaved and worked and fought; that it has been often a hell on earth. You know, too, that I have saved the county very much money, in many ways; that I have tried to walk straight and do right; and that I have begun for the children a work that must not stop now."

"Judge," said Mr. Cheesman, "I am sorry, and I have just been talking to Mr. Field about your case."

Mr. Field? Mr. Field was the president of the Telephone Company, another privileged business. The Judge was seeing the System plainly.

"Mr. Field and I discussed the case, Judge," said Mr. Cheesman, "and we are very sorry, but we can do nothing. With us, politics is business and — business comes first. You might as well understand it. My advice to you is to let go the judgeship, and the Children's Court. Mr. Shattock will be nominated by the Republican convention; Mr. Johnson will be nominated by the Democratic convention. That's certain. And I want to give you one bit of advice. Don't you run independent. I know what I'm talking about. You can't be elected."

So that was the situation; that was the System. The Judge rose:

"I'm going to fight," he said, "and I'm going to fight till I'm licked good and hard."

He went back and he told his young men. There was no time to appeal to the voters, but it wasn't necessary. Those young men scoured the town; they filled the streets and the convention hall. The excitement was intense. Speer, the Democrat, wired to Evans, the Republican, that the Republicans were pulling away, and that if they did, the Democrats would have to quit, too. Evans wired his orders back, but Lindsey was nominated by the Republicans, and the Democrats had to nominate him. They had to nominate and run their whole County ticket over again, and (this is the funniest thing that I know in politics) the Democratic gang that had hatched this scheme to "lose Lindsey somehow in the mix-up" — these grafters, elected in the spring and settled at their graft, were defeated in the fall! Lindsey alone was reëlected. And the Supreme Court did declare the spring election void. The gang had beaten themselves. And the people — the women, the children, the honest men of Denver — they had saved Ben Lindsey.

RUDOLPH SPRECKELS: A BUSINESS REFORMER

IT IS important to know Rudolph Spreckels. He is a business man. He never has been anything but a business man. He did not go to college and, except for some interrupted private schooling and tutoring, all the education he ever had was in business. That was thorough and practical. It began when, as a boy, he sat, silent, listening to his father and older brothers talking business at home. And he caught the spirit of modern business. His boyish ambition, confessed to the amusement of the family, was to be a millionaire. That was all. He didn't mean to run a locomotive, find the North Pole, write a sonnet, or set the world on fire. He didn't dream even of the management of some great business. No, young Rudolph looked past the work to the end thereof; he was "for results." He wanted millions. And he succeeded; before he was twenty-six he was able to retire a millionaire, self-made.

Certain events in the business world called him back to life in a year or two, and — to get to the point — this rich young man of business went in for political reform in his city. That alone is important, but that doesn't half express Rudolph Spreckels's mind. He has said that he will devote the rest of his life — and, if need be, his fortune — to reform: general reform. For when he has "made good" in San Francisco, he proposes to try some other cities. New York attracts him; so do Chicago and Denver.

New York will arch its brows and smile; Chicago may laugh. But Rudolph Spreckels has tackled big men and big jobs; he never has failed; he is unlicked. He has "hate of hate, scorn of scorn." He doesn't care who laughs first. With his quizzical, winning smile, he says:

"I don't care who sneers in the beginning, or who doubts. I don't doubt. I fix my eyes on a purpose, and — I'm sure of the end."

It won't do to waive this man lightly aside. He has health and youth, will-power, and persistence, and ability. This young captain of industry is the kind of man that has done so much evil in this country. He was born and bred to the type that has built and robbed railroads, "made" and unmade states; corrupting business and courts and governments, but — accomplishing its end. When the goal of such a man is the creation of a monopoly of all the food or all the oil or all the steel in our world, we take him seriously — too late. I think that Rudolph Spreckels, capitalist, bank president, captain of industry, who, at thirty-five, has devoted his knowledge of men and business methods good and bad; his patient impatience; his talent for organization and his executive ability, to reform in the united cities of America — such a man is worth our study.

At any rate, he is the political ideal of the business world. All over the country I have heard business men say that what we want is some *good* business man who will apply *good* business methods to politics and government and give us a *good*, businesslike administration. The efficacy of this solution is dubious, but never mind. Here we have the business men's dream come true; here we have the business man "sacrificing his money and his still more valuable time" to the public service. How do business men receive the devotion of Rudolph Spreckels? Do they like and applaud and support him?

No. Business men do not like and applaud and support Mr. Spreckels. They denounce him and they oppose him and they oppose his reform. The leading business men of San Francisco hate and they vilify him, and they oppose his prosecution of criminals. They and their

From a photograph by Habenicht, San Francisco

RUDOLPH SPRECKELS

organs fight on the side of graft against this young business man who has gone in for politics. And not only the San Franciscans; the business men of the East, and especially of New York, have turned their newspapers against him. And Mr. Spreckels smiles; he expected all this. Why?

There was no doubt about the badness of politics in San Francisco. "Labour ruled there," and the business world has been "long" with pity for "poor old 'Frisco." Why then this opposition of the San Francisco business men to Mr. Spreckels? What do they say against him? Not very much. They attribute political ambition and, in the same breath, a business motive to his efforts for political reform; they say he wanted a street railway franchise and sought to "get in on" the United (Street) Railways of San Francisco. Patrick Calhoun offered him an interest in that company, and Spreckels declined it; and he has promised publicly that he will never own, directly or indirectly, a share in any public utility company and that he will take no office in the city government. Nothing has been produced from his business record against him. That must be well known, and since it was a record of "success," I expected to hear of sharp deals and queer turns; but, no, nothing of the sort. Mr. Spreckels must indeed be a good business man. You will hear, as I did, that "Spreckels got a lot of people into a railroad and then sold it out to the Santa Fé." That is true. Spreckels did that, but not Rudolph Spreckels. That was an act of his father, Claus Spreckels. Again, they asked me if I didn't know that the public utility system of San Diego was a Spreckels monopoly. I did, but I happened to know what many Californians seem not to know, that the Spreckels of San Diego is not Rudolph, but a brother of his and a personal enemy. Claus Spreckels is interesting; the whole Spreckels family may be well worth knowing, but most of them are in business or private life. Our subject is Rudolph Spreckels, the business reformer; not his family — except as "blood will tell."

The Spreckels family is an institution in California and, generally regarded as a unit, is not popular. The Spreckelses fight. They fight hard. But they don't fight together. They are not a unit. The family fights inside as well as out, and not all the members speak to one another. They differ among themselves in character, tastes, methods, purposes and, apparently, in morals. All they seem to have in common is a certain aggressive independence. They are in business what Labour would call "scabs." They work by themselves and each by himself.

They play with others, and the family "stands well" both downtown and up, but there is more fear than affection in their social and financial reception. They are a family of individuals, and individuality is offensive not alone to organized labour; organized capital hates it, too. And the Spreckelses are capitalists.

Claus Spreckels, the sugar magnate, was the head of the family. A German peasant, he came to this country when he was about eighteen years old, with two German thalers in his pocket. But he had the capitalist's instinct in his heart. After clerking one year in a grocery store, he bought the business — on credit; and he extended both. In a few years he sent home to the village next to his for the young girl who became the mother of his family.

The Spreckelses moved to California in 1856, opened a grocery store in San Francisco and — extended the business. Seeing that there was money in beer, Claus Spreckels built a brewery. Seeing that there was money in sugar, he built a refinery. There were other refineries; Claus Spreckels beat his competitors, but when the American Sugar Refining Company came along and, buying them up, offered to buy him out or, as Labour says of "scabs," "beat him up," he fought. And he fought not only in self-defence —

he took the offensive; he built an independent
refinery at Philadelphia and, carrying the war
thus into the enemy's own field, Claus Spreckels
compelled a division of the territory; the Pacific
Coast for his. Because of a personal affront
by the president of the Gas Company in San
Francisco, he started a rival concern and he
marked down the price of gas so low that it never
did get all the way back. And because he was
dependent in business on the Southern Pacific
Railroad monopoly, he did not "lie down"; he
helped build that competing line which became
a part of the Santa Fé system.

"He sold out," they say. Yes, he sold out,
but at his price, and he never "stood in"; he
never was "satisfied," "safe," "reasonable." And
that's why "they" are down on Claus Spreckels.
If he had been "satisfied" with his grocery-
store, he might have become a patient grocer. If
money was all he was after, he might have been
a rich brewer. If he had been "reasonable"
with the Sugar Trust, "fair" to the gas company
and had stood "in" with the railroad, he might
have become an "organized capitalist" and a
dummy director in these and in many other businesses. But he must dominate whatever he
took part in. Impatient, implacable, ruthless,
his "Dutch obstinacy" made him fight, and the

result was that Claus Spreckels was a captain of industry, retired, but victorious; not only rich, but an independent financial power. You hear that his methods were — those of big business. I don't know anything about them, nor do I care. It isn't the father that is trying to clean up San Francisco, it's the son.

And Rudolph Spreckels is the son of Claus; not only of his loins, but of his spirit. He was the eleventh or twelfth child; he couldn't recall which, off hand, and it does not matter, for now he is the first. This masterful father tried to dominate his masterful son, and they clinched. It was a long, bitter business fight and, in the course of it, Rudolph Spreckels discovered that there is such a thing as Organized Capital. He learned that a financial power like Claus Spreckels can close all the banks and shut off credit to his "scab" enemies. But Claus Spreckels learned some things, too — among them the character and resources of his own son.

"I never was beaten but once in my life," he is quoted as saying not long before his death, "and that was by my own boy."

This sounds like pride, and it was known in financial circles downtown that when the head of the Spreckels family went away, he left his affairs in the hands of Rudolph, his eleventh or twelfth child, the president of the First National Bank.

Rudolph is only thirty-five years old, but he began his career early. He was, like Roosevelt, an asthmatic child, and when the attacks were upon him he used to go off by himself on his pony, seeking relief "on the ranch" or in the woods. When he first disappeared in this sudden way, the family was alarmed, but as he continued to do it, no further protests were offered. Self-reliant by birth, this boyish practice developed that trait in him, and some power of reflection, too. For solitude is good for the mind. But Rudolph could not go regularly to school, and his progress seemed to be irregular and aimless.

When he was seventeen, his father walked into the library one day and bade him choose on the spot one of three courses: college; a trip around the world with his tutor; or business. Rudolph chose business on the spot. And, on the spot, the father directed him to go to Philadelphia and help his brother, Claus Augustus, run the independent refinery that was fighting the Trust. The boy went and, advanced rapidly from department to department, he learned early the principles of business and — the lack of them.

Young Rudolph saw machinery destroyed by

his father's employees. Sticks, stones, tools were thrown in among the parts, which were broken, of course. Watching, the boy caught the vandals and learned that they were bribed by agents of the Trust to do what they did!

He saw, in the morning, pans of sugar spoiled during the night. Staying up one night, the boy tried to find out who was to blame, but he saw no workman neglect his duty. Nevertheless, in the morning there was the same old trouble with the vacuum pans. Rudolph discharged the night superintendent, and, taking the place himself, filled it for four to, six months, and he did the work well or, at any rate, honestly. No more sugar was spoiled at night.

In the course of this fight, it became manifest that the Trust knew the secrets of their rivals' business. They seemed to have each day the exact condition of the independent's stock, orders and finances. There was a period of mystery till suspicion settled upon the chief accountant. Shadowing him, they saw him copy the figures and take them to a certain cigar-dealer, who carried them in the morning to the Trust.

Thus it was that before he was twenty years old, Rudolph Spreckels learned at first-hand that capital "throws bricks"; that it "destroys property" and "hurts business"; and that it bribes men, not alone in politics, but in business. This schooling did not make a cynic of him, however, nor a "crook." He fought these methods, and he beat them and the Trust.

At one great crisis in the fight, when his brother Gus was away sick, Rudolph carried through a coup which is remembered yet in the trade. The Spreckelses were overstocked with sugar; all their warehouses were filled; great purchases of raw were coming forward and, because the price was being cut every few days, the dealers were living from hand to mouth. One night Rudolph (age eighteen, remember) told his city and outside salesmen to meet him the next morning at seven o'clock. When they reported, he bade them wire all brokers that sugar was to be advanced 1-16th of a cent a pound. The older men were aghast. What if the Trust kept the price down?

"Never mind," said the boy. "Say we will fill immediate orders at the old price, but after that ——"

The orders came in with a rush. Rudolph watched the Trust. He knew that he had this advantage: he was in command in his refinery. In the Trust the principals were probably away from town or not yet up; subordinates were in command, and subordinates cannot take chances on losing their jobs. They would hardly dare take the initiative and keep prices down. So he reasoned, and he was right. The Trust followed Rudolph Spreckels's lead, and three times that day he advanced the price. And he sold out all his stock and all that he had in sight. The cutting of prices was resumed, but once again the boy beat the Trust by this same trick. And so, before he was twenty, Rudolph Spreckels measured himself with great captains of industry and — became sure of himself.

At any rate, he was bold enough to fight his father, and he knew what that meant. This quarrel, alluded to above, broke out during their struggle with the Trust. On one side were Gus and Rudolph; on the other, the father and his other sons. It was a general business row at first, but as it grew the Spreckels sugar plantations on the Hawaiian Islands became the bone of contention. A losing business, Rudolph visited them; he saw neglect, mismanagement, extravagance and stealing, and he declared that the plantations could be made to pay. He and Gus bought them; Rudolph took charge and, cutting out the graft and introducing method and discipline, was getting things on a paying basis, when a crisis occurred. They needed more time and money. The rest of the family wouldn't give them either. Very well, Gus and Rudolph would borrow of the banks. Their security was good, the plantations were sure payers, but the banks refused any "accommodation." The young men went from one bank to another till they realized that there was an understanding among these Organized Capitalists; the word had been passed not to let the two Spreckels boys have a cent. For a while they stared at ruin, but they hustled around and finally found a private capitalist who backed them; and they made good. They sold the plantation at a price which netted them a fortune each.

Rudolph thought he was through with business. Investing his money in real estate and gas stock, he retired to the country and, content with his rents and dividends, was neglecting his duty as a stockholder to develop a beautiful estate in Sonoma County, when bad news came. His father had started the gas war in San Francisco. It seemed that the gas works were blowing smoke in the old man's windows. He protested, in vain, and one noon at the Pacific Union Club he met the president, Joe Crockett.

"Look here, Joe," he said, "I've had enough of that smoke of yours. You'd better do something ——"

"The Club is no place to discuss business,"

said Crockett, and he turned on his heel and walked off.

Claus Spreckels was amazed, and angry. "I'll make you regret this!" he said, and in twenty-four hours he had organized the Independent Gas and Electric Company. Rudolph Spreckels knew that a fight with Claus Spreckels meant economy and able management for the old company. Gas was $1.25, and the Independent proposed to sell it at 75 cents. When Rudolph saw his stock drop from 85 to 60, he came to town to attend to his duties as a stockholder and — to learn what graft is in business; and what politics is in business; and what the relation of said business corruption is to political corruption.

Rudolph Spreckels made some swift, superficial inquiries about the gas company, and he heard that it had a big floating debt. There were other signs of neglect in the management, yes, and of inefficiency. The directors were all "leading citizens," "prominent business men," "veterans in finance." They were just the sort of men that business men would put upon a board of aldermen or supervisors to give good business government. Yet this young man found that these picked business directors were neglecting their duty to him as a stockholder, very much as his supervisors neglected their duty to him as a citizen and property holder. And that wasn't all: the company wasn't earning the dividends it was paying to him! Why? The price of gas was high enough; gas companies elsewhere earned big dividends at a much lower rate, and his father was proposing to reduce the price from $1.25 to 75 cents. Young Mr. Spreckels couldn't get answers to his questions from the officers and directors; they wouldn't listen to him. So he did as reformers do in politics; he appealed "to the people," and the people heard him gladly. In other words, the stockholders to whom he addressed a circular elected Rudolph Spreckels to the Board of Directors. Then he found out what the matter was.

Those respectable old business men on the board were dummy directors. They took orders like our dummy legislators, and, like these despised politicians, were organized by a boss who ran this business as our political bosses run cities and states, inefficiently and dishonestly. Mr. Spreckels sent to Chicago for a chief accountant; and he sent so far because he needed a man who would be free from local reverence for the standing of the officers and directors of the San Francisco Gas Company. He feared "pull" and "corruption." And the Chicago man came;

and he soon was keen on the scent. He became excited. He was on the track, he told Mr. Spreckels, of "something sensational."

"Go ahead and get it!" Mr. Spreckels ordered.

"But, no"; the accountant said it was so big that he must first have a talk with his Chicago chief about it. The Chicago chief came; there were a few days of mystery, then the accountant and his chief both left the coast together.

"I never got that something big," Mr. Spreckels says now, with a smile. He wasn't balked, however. He put other investigators to work and, though they found nothing "big," they did find something small, very small. Besides general confusion, mismanagement, unearned dividends and inefficiency, there was graft. The directors got gas, electric light, gas ranges, coke, and other supplies free. That was their price, perhaps. That was the way the boss, Joe Crockett, bribed them, but the business boss had another political method of control. He gave places to relatives and friends of the directors and other influential men. The pay-roll was "padded," like a city pay-roll, to make jobs for persons with pull.

How can business men despise politics so? How can they pretend to dread the inefficiency, the pulls and the graft of public ownership of

public utilities, when they know that this San
Francisco Gas Company is a typical example
of "private" or business management of this
class of business? And Mr. Spreckels didn't
find out for whom and for what Joe Crockett
wanted to run the company; but the rest of us
have. We learned in the life insurance and
railroad investigations what that "something
big" is.

Mr. Spreckels was busy. He reported to that
board of directors what he had discovered, and
he suggested that they cut out all this "dry rot"
— the financial term for corruption. There was
a scene. There was just such a howl at this
reform in business as there is in politics, and
more hypocrisy. Those old directors were in-
digant. To think that they, gentlemen, men
of business standing and years of experience,
were to be insulted and dictated to by a boy of
twenty-eight! He should learn that he couldn't
dominate them. They were having troubles
enough from one Spreckels already; they wouldn't
put up with another "in their midst."

But that boy of twenty-eight was, indeed, a
Spreckels. Independent, wilful, he was sure of
the end. He had the facts. He appealed again
to the stockholders, who, like him, had been
allowing themselves to be voted by "the party

in power." He reported to them the condition of things and, offering a ticket in opposition to the regular ticket, he won. Enough of Spreckels's directors were elected to give him control. He did not take the presidency. Because his father was fighting the company, he put up W. B. Bourn for president, but Rudolph was boss. And he cut off more than $300,000 of useless expenses (graft, politics, and inefficiency) in the first year!

It was while he was in control of the gas company that young Spreckels got his first insight into the government of the city. He found upon the padded pay-roll a man employed at $500 a month to collect the bills against the city for public lighting. Inquiring why, Mr. Spreckels was told that "this arrangement facilitated" the collections; that the collector was a politician, with a following and a pull; he could get the money without delay, and — besides — was "useful in many ways." Mr. Spreckels understood. He discharged the man.

"What was the result?" I asked Mr. Spreckels, when he told me of this incident.

"Some delay; that was all," he said.

One day an employee brought Mr. Spreckels the bill for gas furnished to the city gas inspector. This official had always ignored his bills and the

company had never cut off *his* gas.   What would
Mr. Spreckels do about it ?

"Treat him like anybody else," was the answer.

When Mr. Spreckels told me of these incidents,
I explained to him that such things happened in
most cities; that this was part of what business
men called political blackmail; that business
men, especially those in public service corporations, commonly submitted to and excused this
corruption on the ground that, to protect the
interests of their business and stockholders, they
"had to."   They were "held up."

"What do you say to that, Mr. Spreckels ?"

"I say that you don't have to be blackmailed,
even if you are in the public service business.
A little backbone is all that is needed — unless
you want things you shouldn't have."

"And that is true even as against a Labour
government ?"

Mr. Spreckels smiled.   He knew that the
"Labour" government was no more "labour"
than the Republican party was "republican"
and the Democratic party "democratic."   He
knew that the boss and the leaders of the Labour
party, and the officials of the Labour administration, were willing to sell out their followers
and the city to capital.   And this he knew at
first-hand.   Soon after he and the Labour boss

came into power, Spreckels in the San Francisco Gas Company and Ruef in San Francisco, they met. Mr. Spreckels has told under oath the story of that meeting. He says:

"Ruef was brought into my office by Mr. Charles Sutro and introduced and left there, and he stated to me that he thought he had legal ability and could be of service to the corporation 'otherwise.' He suggested that he be employed as counsel for the company."

To have the political representative of Labour offer to represent a "hated capitalistic" corporation shocked Mr. Spreckels, the capitalist, no more than it did citizens or the workingmen themselves. That was old and, as newspaper men understand, it is news, not evil, that stirs men. Mr. Spreckels declined Ruef's offer, but let it pass without a protest. When, however, a little later, the boss came back and proposed to him to use Organized Labour as a "capitalistic club" in the interest of a capitalist, Mr. Spreckels was aroused. That was news. Mr. Spreckels has recounted this experience also under oath:

"Mr. Ruef called on me at the time of the issuing of the city bonds," Mr. Spreckels's affidavit reads, "and he asked me to get up a syndicate for the purpose of taking them over. He said it could be guaranteed that the bonds would be

sold to my syndicate. I asked him how he
could possibly guarantee such a thing when it
(the bond issue) was open to public bidding.
Ruef said that was easy. They could *call a
strike on the street-car system of San Francisco*,
and with every street-car line tied up, he would
like to see the capitalists or bankers, other than
the (inside) syndicate, that would bid."

That was the incident which fixed the determined mind of Rudolph Spreckels upon political
reform. His present enemies — business men,
who cannot conceive of a business man taking
part in public affairs except for a business motive
— date Mr. Spreckels's interest in his city from
1906, when, they say, he failed to get a certain
street railway franchise that he wanted. But
this bond issue experience was two years before
that, in 1904, and from his interview with Ruef
that day, he went straight to a luncheon where
to several men of his acquaintance (who remember) he told the story and declared he was going
to employ detectives, investigate the government
and present evidence to convict the men that ran
the city and Labour. He talked to others about
it. Professor Loeb, the biologist, recalls that
Mr. Spreckels talked of his plan to him on an
overland train in September, 1904. So there
are witnesses for those who doubt, but I happen

to know from conversations with Older and Heney in Washington, before the franchise matter came up, that Spreckels was the man who was to back their investigation in San Francisco.

The franchise matter is, however, a most important incident in the development of the public character, interest, and ideas of Rudolph Spreckels; and, likewise, in the history of the corruption and reformation of the city. Brown Bros., bankers, of New York, managed the consolidation of the San Francisco street railways. These had been held separately by the Southern Pacific crowd and by other groups of capitalists. As the earnings increased, the fare had to be reduced, higher dividends paid, or the stock watered, and, of course, the stock had been watered. The consolidation meant more watering, and the result was a capitalization amounting to several times the cost of construction.

This over-capitalized consolidation was taken over by Mr. Patrick Calhoun, of New York, Cleveland, St. Louis, and Pittsburg. And genial San Francisco merchants, in conversation with me, sympathized with this very charming gentleman, "because," they said, "he really was cheated by our Mr. Huntington." But Mr. Calhoun has left everywhere the reputation of a very astute financier; he probably knew what he was about; he knew how he could make San Francisco pay dividends on his watered stock. At any rate, he added about one-third more water.

His scheme was to take out the old cables and put in the overhead trolley. He knew how people object to that system, but in an easygoing community like San Francisco and with a "Labour" government, anything should go. He was so sure of success that he recommended his stock to his friends and to the bankers who direct the investments of widows and orphans. Moreover, he filled solid with cement some of the cable conduits, which might have served for the underground wires. Mr. Calhoun was sure of himself and of San Francisco.

But one day, while the scheme was fresh, Rudolph Spreckels was invited by Charles Page, an attorney, to join with some other property owners on Pacific Avenue to consider the proposed overhead trolley. He went to the meeting and he heard them decide to oppose the change — as to Pacific Avenue. A petition to the supervisors had been drawn to that effect. Mr. Spreckels remonstrated. He said that he, too, objected to overhead wires, but he thought it wasn't right to fight for their own street in the interest of their property alone.

"I don't want an overhead trolley in front of

my property," he said, "but I suppose that other people don't want it in front of their property, either. Certainly the city's supervisors should treat all streets alike, and we shouldn't ask them to favour us particularly."

He moved that they oppose the overhead trolley on the whole Sutter Street (cable) system. That was agreed to; the old petition was torn up and a new one drawn. Solicitors were engaged to get signatures, and with 75 per cent. of the property-owners' names upon it, the paper was presented to the Board of Supervisors. And the supervisors refused the grant. But this was the old, so-called Phelan Board, which held over into the Schmitz administration. In 1905, when "Labour" came into complete control, the outlook for Mr. Calhoun and his street railways was better. It was known that the "Labour" supervisors would sell out to "Capital." And it was supposed that, of course, Capital would sell out to Capital.

The United Railways Company tried to "get" Rudolph Spreckels. I mean that Patrick Calhoun offered Rudolph Spreckels a bribe. Let me hasten to add that business men may not call it bribery; such as Mr. Calhoun would call his proposition to Mr. Spreckels "business"; and it was "business." But one of the evidences that have gone to persuade me that the ethics of American politics is higher than the ethics of business, is that this typical piece of "business" would be called bribery and corruption in politics, even by the low-down politicians themselves. They might take the bribe, but they would take it knowing that it was a bribe.

The company tried "reason" first. Arthur Holland, the then president of the United Railways, and Chapman, the general manager, called upon Mr. Spreckels. He had become the head and front of the opposition, and they asked him to withdraw. His reply was that he had read all the published arguments of the company against underground trolleys. There was nothing in them, he said, and he asked if they had any others. They said no, that the engineering impossibilities were all they had to offer. There were some sixteen deep depressions on the proposed lines, and in the rainy season these could not be drained.

"That, then, is your only reason?" Mr. Spreckels asked.

That was all, they said.

"There is no other?" Mr. Spreckels made sure. "You don't mind the difference in cost?"

Not at all; they were sure.

"Very well," Mr. Spreckels said. "Then I

have a solution. I will put drains on the present (cable) conduits, and keep them dry. I will keep them so dry that you will yourselves admit that they are dry. But, if I do that, I shall expect you to install the underground trolley in those conduits."

They refused this proposition, and Mr. Spreckels told them why.

"You haven't given me your real reason, and I will continue to fight."

Then came Mr. Patrick Calhoun talking "business." There were three meetings. The first was a general, pleasant chat at the Bohemian Club between Messrs. Calhoun, R. B. Hale, James D. Phelan, Rufus B. Jennings, and others. They couldn't get very far without Mr. Spreckels, so he was sent for, and Mr. Calhoun soon saw that Spreckels was the man. He was keen, firm, amiable, but not to be charmed or fooled. Evidently Patrick Calhoun made up his mind then to "get" Spreckels, for, after the meeting, he asked for a second meeting with him alone.

They met at the Canadian Bank and went to a private room in the Mercantile Club upstairs. After some preliminaries, Calhoun offered to modify his overhead trolley plans to this extent: he would except Pacific Avenue. That was the street on which Spreckels lived. Mr. Calhoun would leave the cable there for the present, at least, and, if he ever did apply electricity to that line, would use the underground conduit. Mr. Spreckels understood the proposition perfectly, as his reply showed. He said that no concession to him or to his street could break his allegiance to the other property owners. Mr. Calhoun went away disappointed. But he tried again.

The third meeting was again in the Canadian Bank building, and Mr. Calhoun had a witness present, his brother-in-law and manager. Mr. Spreckels had none, so I must be careful. Mr. Spreckels says that Mr. Calhoun explained that he couldn't put in conduits all over the city. But he could put in some, and he told where. Also, however, he would tunnel the Powell Street hill and make Powell and Sutter the most valuable transfer-point in the city.

"Is that because I own property at that point?" Mr. Spreckels asked.

"Why, no," Calhoun answered. "Are you interested? I didn't know that."

Besides this offer, Mr. Calhoun bid to remove street-cars altogether from Pacific Avenue and take the parallel street, Broadway. That would make Mr. Spreckels's street more attractive, and as for the convenience, Mr. Spreckels and his friends used automobiles and carriages. And

Mr. Calhoun went on to tell Mr. Spreckels in a very flattering way that he was the kind of man he wished to have with him, and he suggested that Mr. Spreckels take a stock interest in the United Railways. Mr. Spreckels put the whole business aside with a reference to "people that didn't live on Pacific Avenue and did not ride in automobiles and carriages." He was quiet about it, but he understood it. He was being offered personal inducements to betray the other property owners with whom he had associated himself and of whom he was the leader; the price held out to him was expected to bribe him over to the side of the United Railways.

"Did you understand this to be bribery?" I asked Mr. Spreckels.

"Of course it was bribery," he answered. "Bribes aren't always offered in cash, and corruption isn't confined to politics. Anything that tempts any man from what he thinks to be his duty, is corruption."

Mr. Spreckels resisted the temptation easily. He told Calhoun, as he told Calhoun's predecessors, that he would fight, and he went out and organized a company to build and operate an underground trolley line in Bush Street. That is the offence charged up to him by his fellow-capitalists now. At the time he proposed his scheme it was not regarded as bad. On the contrary, it was spoken of as public-spirited. It was perfectly understood then that Rudolph Spreckels sought only to prove on Bush Street that the underground trolley was feasible. He expected to incur no loss; he must make the road pay to prove his point. But there was to be "no big money in it," either. One of the terms stated in the papers and to be fixed in the franchise grant from the city, was an agreement that the city was to take over the plant at cost plus interest, at any time it pleased after the demonstration had been made. The scheme was conceived neither as a self-sacrifice nor as selfish; it was only a weapon made for a particular fight, the fight for the city beautiful as against Patrick Calhoun and dividends on the watered stock of the street railway company.

But the earthquake knocked that weapon out of Rudolph Spreckels's hand. The articles of incorporation were filed a day or two before the disaster of April 18, 1906, and Rudolph Spreckels, invited by Mayor Schmitz to join the Committee of Fifty that was to rehabilitate San Francisco and govern it, at last, as it should be governed, by its best citizens in its own best interest, as a community of men and women — Mr. Spreckels left his company in the air and devoted himself

to this bigger, finer task. And he was absorbed
for a while. It was an inspiring spectacle, that
of those fifty leading men leading a whole city
of men and women in the work for the common
good. But Spreckels was the first to see that the
grafters smelt the graft and that the fifty, reduced
to forty, caught the smell, whiffed, and dashed
all together — low politicians, high financiers,
and dignified attorneys — for the graft. Herrin
was on hand; Harriman came flying to the rescue
and — to get his rails farther into the city. Calhoun came out to get, while the city was down,
the franchise held up before, but "arranged for,"
and — he got it. But Rudolph Spreckels saw
now that the fight wasn't with Mr. Calhoun; and
neither was it with Schmitz and Ruef. It was
with some sort of a big, general condition. So
he went back to the big, general war he had
planned with Heney and Burns — before the
earthquake; before that franchise for Calhoun
came up — his plan as outlined years before to
his friends at lunch, the day Ruef offered to lend
him Organized Labour to knock out Organized
Capital and seize a bond issue. Rudolph
Spreckels went on with his plan for such an
investigation and fight of the corruption in San
Francisco as he had made and won in San Francisco gas.

That's Rudolph Spreckels's story, in brief. Can you see the man? Stress has been laid upon his youth and his self-reliance, his fearless readiness to fight. But there is an amiability about the man that is very winning. He is hard, hard as youth, both in conflict and in his judgments of men. "Are you with me?" he asked a friend, and when the friend began to "explain," Spreckels cut him short: "Then you're against me. That's all I wanted to know." And his friend didn't like that; none of the men that know him do; Spreckels is so cold-blooded in opposition. But he is reasonable, most generous, and even charming as an ally. When Heney's friends learned that he was "with Spreckels," they warned him.

"Look out, Frank! You want to run yourself and all your own undertakings. So does Spreckels, and Spreckels will run this prosecution of yours. He must dominate." "I know," said one banker; "I've gone into business schemes with him, but I never do now any more unless I'm willing to have him be the whole show. It's safe to let him — he is a master manager; but I found out that if anybody opposed him, he would bust the scheme, you, and himself rather than not have his own way."

So Heney expected to have trouble with

Spreckels, and the two have clashed sharply, as only two such men can. But Spreckels, aggressive though he is, and positive, is not quick-tempered like Heney. He is serene and, when Heney storms, he waits. Heney is just and — he has humour. So Spreckels smiles till Heney laughs. Then, whoever is right wins, and whoever is wrong doesn't care, for there isn't a petty trait in either of these men. If they ever fall out, it will be because they ought to, for the big difference between them is fundamental.

Heney is a democrat; Spreckels is an aristocrat, and an autocrat. Both of them have been too active all their lives to have thought out their philosophies to the definiteness of policy, and they should be able to go far together before they split. For they both are, and probably long will be, fighting what both of them detest, a rotten plutocracy, founded on class hate. But, by and by, when they come to build up where they have torn down, either Heney or Spreckels will go asunder or Spreckels will go on learning what Heney knows by heart.

I say "go on" learning because I think I never have seen a man learn so fast as Mr. Spreckels has. That is why I believe in him. Since the first time I met the man, I have never doubted his integrity; nor the singleness of his unselfish purpose; nor his capacity to do great deeds. All the stated objections of his fellow-business men to this business man in politics are silly and all their real objections are nothing but the symptoms of the corruption of the commercial mind and its class-conscious folly. The trouble with Mr. Spreckels is that he *is*, like his critics, a business man and that his scheme for political reform is a business scheme.

He believes that all men are divided into two classes: good men and bad men. Anybody who has thought about actual life knows that there is something in the plea of railroad and public utility men, that they "have to" be bad; that there are certain businesses which no man can "succeed" at and be honest. But Mr. Spreckels has that great fault of the self-made man; he has learned not from the experience of others, but only from his own, and what he doesn't know isn't known. He is unacquainted with the literature and the history of politics and government; he has no economic enlightenment at all. He is truly a practical man, and his practical experience is exceptional. He knows that he, as a gas magnate, did not bribe anybody and that he didn't "have to." If you call his attention to the salient fact that he didn't make a "success" of gas; that he didn't "finance" the company, but only managed it in the interest of the stockholders, he smiles.

"That is all any public utility man should be allowed to do," he says.

So Mr. Spreckels proposes to put the bad men of San Francisco in jail. But what then? What is to prevent the generation of other bad men?

There is where Mr Spreckels thinks his scheme excels all others. He knows it won't suffice to have Heney "put away" the few "bad men" Burns can catch. He knows that eternal vigilance is the price of good government. So he proposes, after this prosecution is over, to establish a permanent bureau, a staff composed of an expert accountant, to keep watch of the city's books, contracts, etc.; a detective to shadow forever the men in public office; and an attorney to receive, order, complete, and present the evidence in court. This has been done before, but never mind; it has never been done as Rudolph Spreckels is proving that he means to do it. There may be some objection to spying, but Mr. Spreckels says such a watch is the common, every-day practice in banks and in other business. So let that pass.

But what is to prevent Mr. Spreckels's accountant from "selling out"; his detective from

"standing in"; his attorney from "taking perfectly proper fees" from other clients? The
vigilance of Mr. Spreckels. He will watch his
watchers. So it comes down, finally, to the
character of Mr. Spreckels. That happens to
be about as sound a foundation as any one
man can furnish, but it is a one-man scheme.
It isn't democratic. The democratic theory is
founded on the expectation that self-government,
by its very abuses, will tend gradually to develop
in all men such a concern for the common good
that human nature will become intelligent and
considerate of others. That sounds almost Christian, and it isn't business. In business the old
autocratic practice prevails; one man is boss,
and he runs everything and everybody.

That is why business men's reform movements
seek to abolish or subordinate the board of aldermen and to concentrate all power in the mayor.
They want a good, responsible king. And if
they would only elect men who would be king,
they might be satisfied, but the "good" business
man they choose is usually of the sort that looks
up to "big" business men; he has the prejudice
of his class against the political boss, but when
he discovers that this low-down politician is the
mouthpiece of the high-up business men, he takes
orders as well as the ordinary heeler. "Better,"

says ex-Boss Buckley, of San Francisco, who tried him out.

Business men ought to elect a "big" business man mayor. Rudolph Spreckels is the very type. He wouldn't look up to anyone and no politician, no matter whom he represented, could get Mayor Spreckels to "take programme," as they say in the West. But big business men "despise politics" and scorn office-holding; they are too proud, or something, to "appeal to the people," and they have a class aversion to publicity. Mr. Spreckels, possessed of the virtues, has some of the faults of his class. He, too, despises politics; he told me he never had voted in his life; and he promises, with pride, not to take office. It is sometimes a duty to take office; it is as ridiculous for a citizen in a republic to boast that he won't as it would be to announce with pride that he will not go to the front in time of war. As for the fine instinct of your sensitive gentlemen for privacy, criminals have that. And as for rendering an account to the people, somebody has to; and Mr. Spreckels lets Heney issue the statements of the prosecution to the public.

Now I have shown, I think, why business men should be for Rudolph Spreckels. Why haven't I shown why real democrats should be against him? There are two good reasons: one is that while he has some of the faults of his kind, he hasn't all; he lacks those that are dangerous. The other is that he is getting over those that he has. His original idea was to let whosoever would nominate and elect whomsoever they pleased. But politics is interesting, and I noticed that Mr. Spreckels could not keep his hands off. He regretted it, but he had to help run the board of aldermen after the members confessed; and he had to help name a mayor when Schmitz was convicted. And in doing these things, he had to consider the wishes of the public, as he wanted to. Well, this was politics, and it was amusing to observe that Mr. Spreckels showed a native talent for the game. He says he won't, but he will play it, as he should.

And he will be boss. He thinks not, of course; he hates the word. We all do. But he will have the power. Since he is back of the prosecution, and will be back of his vigilantes, men do, and they will continue to come to him for — advice. His advice may be good, and he may be, therefore, a good boss. But a boss he is and a boss he must be. But his scheme, like the whole idea of the San Francisco prosecution, is extra-legal and unsafe.

Mr. Spreckels now, like any other boss, is working through agents: Heney, Langdon, etc.

They are doing well; they may do better; but they may do something that Mr. Spreckels would not have done. Mr. Langdon may become jealous of his prerogatives; the mayor may adopt a policy that is repugnant to Mr. Spreckels, and yet not criminal. Mr. Spreckels will see then that he can't, and that he shouldn't, carry out his ideas, no matter how good they are, except in a legal office where he has himself the power and is, in his own person, responsible to the other citizens of the city, who should be free to elect or defeat him.

That means going to the people, yes, but Mr. Spreckels has learned something about the people. When I first met and heard him talk about "business," I said:

"But, Mr. Spreckels, business won't help you. You'll find, if you go far enough into this political corruption, that business graft is at the bottom of it. And when you touch that, your own class, the business men of San Francisco, will go back on you."

He smiled; he knew all that. But what he didn't know, and what I saw him find out when his own class did go back on him, was that the people, yes, even Labour, would listen. Organized Labour, led by the same kind of selfish grafters that lead Organized Capital, held off like its capitalistic twin, but the rank and file were reasonable and capable of some little self-sacrifice. And Mr. Spreckels's personal experiences were private, with a few men. He won't address a crowd, but Heney does and he sees that Heney rarely fails to get a response from his juries and from "the masses" generally. Well, the masses decide in this country and their decisions are good, and the reason they are good is not because the people are better than their "betters," but because they are disinterested. They are not in on any graft, so they can be fair.

But the best hope of Spreckels lies in this rare trait: he has mental as well as moral integrity. He has class prejudices, but they take a peculiar form. A capitalist, he can see the beam in the eye of capital as clearly as he can the mote in the eye of labour; and the only sense of class that he shows is in his real scorn for the workingman's brick and the politician's petty blackmail. He would let them go to get the big, real deviltry of his own class, which is the source of our corruption, political, business, and labour, too. And he did.

Mr. Spreckels was fair. He gave his own class a chance. He passed the word in business circles that he was going after grafters; that he

knew business men were held up; he argued
that they couldn't like to be held up and, therefore would undoubtedly be glad to help expose
and destroy the whole blackmail system. He
invited the business men of San Francisco to
turn state's witnesses and help him "get" the
politicians. But no business man accepted his
hospitality. They all "stood pat"; some of
them went on being "held up" by the politicians
who — did accept Mr. Spreckels's invitation. For
he sent it to them also.

And when they turned state's witnesses, there
was clamour downtown. A strike was impending,
the car-men's strike, and Spreckels himself has
suffered from labour's tyranny. "Everybody"
wanted the unions smashed and Patrick Calhoun
promised to smash them. No matter. A whole
lot of leading business men, the very leaders of
the city, were indicted for bribery or corruption
and Calhoun was among them. Spreckels "went
back on his class." That's what was said, and he
was "cut"; his family was punished; his bank
suffered a (rich depositors') run. Spreckels was
unmoved; he was getting publicity, but he took
it. He called at his bank; lunched at "the"
Club; and he appeared constantly in court.
He was following the evidence.

This is all that is necessary. Let such a man

as this — honest, fearless, young and open-eyed — let Rudolph Spreckels but follow the facts; they will teach him the truth, and, no matter what the truth may be, he will tackle it; and he will tackle it right or — quit.

"And Spreckels can't quit," Heney says. "I don't say he won't; he can't."

W. S. U'REN, THE LAWGIVER

OREGON has more fundamental legislation than any other state in the Union excepting only Oklahoma, and Oklahoma is new. Oregon is not new; it is and it long has been corrupt, yet it has enacted laws which enable its people to govern themselves when they want to. How did this happen? How did this state of graft get all her tools for democracy? And, since it has them, why don't her people use them more? The answer to these questions lies buried deep in the character and in the story of W. S. U'Ren (accent the last syllable), the lawgiver.

They call this man the Father of the Initiative and Referendum in Oregon, but that title isn't big enough. U'Ren has fathered other Oregon laws, and his own state isn't the limit of his influence. The Dakotas have some similar legislation. Meeting on a Western train one day a politician who seemed to know all about things there, I inquired into the origin of the Dakota laws.

"There's a fellow over in Oregon," he answered — "funny name — he tipped us off and steered us; sent drafts of bills and pamphlets containing arguments. I can't recall his name."

"U'Ren?"

"That's it; that's the man."

They are getting good laws in the State of Washington, also. I asked in Seattle where they came from. Very few knew, but those that did said: "U'Ren of Oregon."

The first time I heard this name was in Rhode Island. Ex-Governor Garvin, the advocate of democratic legislation for that law-bound state, knew about U'Ren. After that I used to come upon his influence in many states and cities where men were tinkering with the sacred constitutional machinery that won't let democracy go. But my last encounter with the mysterious ubiquity of this singular man's influence was amusing. Spreckels, Heney, and the other fighters for San Francisco thought of going to the people on a certain proposition and, seeing thus the uses of the referendum, wanted it. I suggested writing to U'Ren. They never had heard of him, but they wrote, and he came. And he heard them out on their need of the referendum.

"But I think," said U'Ren, "that you have it in your city charter." Everybody looked incredulous. "Where is the book?" U'Ren asked. "I think I can find it. I certainly had

WILLIAM S. U'REN

some correspondence with the makers of that charter; I think I drafted a section — yes, here it is. [He read it to himself.] It isn't mine — not very clear — but [handing back the book] good enough for your purpose, you see."

William Simon U'Ren, the lawgiver, was born January 10, 1859, at Lancaster, Wisconsin. His father is a blacksmith, and his father's seven brothers were blacksmiths; their father was a blacksmith, and their father's father, and his father, and his. As far as the family can trace from Cornwall, England, back into Holland, they see an unbroken line of blacksmiths. And preachers. Five of U'Ren's seven uncles preached and, among their ancestors, other blacksmiths preached. And William U'Ren himself is both a blacksmith and a preacher in a way; in a very essential way.

"Blacksmithing is my trade," he says. "And it has always given colour to my view of things. For example, when I was very young, I saw some of the evils in the conditions of life, and I wanted to fix them. I couldn't. There were no tools. We had tools to do almost anything with in the shop, beautiful tools, wonderful. And so in other trades, arts and professions; in everything but government. In government, the common trade of all men and the basis of all social

life, men worked still with old tools, with old
laws, with constitutions and charters which
hindered more than they helped. Men suffered
from this. There were lawyers enough; many
of our ablest men were lawyers. Why didn't
some of them invent legislative implements to
help the people govern themselves? Why had
we no tool makers for democracy?"

U'Ren is a very quiet man. He never would
strike one as a blacksmith. He never would
strike one at all. Slight of figure, silent in motion,
he speaks softly, evenly, as he walks; and they
call him, therefore, the "pussy cat."

"You see," he purred now, "I saw it all in
terms of the mechanic."

But he feels it all in the terms of religion.
His mother, also Cornish, also of the class that
labours hard, was also religious — a Methodist.
She taught her children from the Bible. Je-
hovah, Moses, and Jesus were the ideals of this
humble family, and, for some reason, Moses
caught the imagination of her oldest boy, William.
He always wanted to hear about Moses, the
lawgiver, and when he could read for himself, Ex-
odus and Numbers were the books he loved best.
And just as some boys want to be Napoleon, so
young U'Ren dreamed that when he grew up
he would be like Moses, the giver of laws that

should lead the people out of Darkness into the land of Promise. But, of course, the Biblical hero-worship, taught him first by that pious woman, his good mother, made it a religious influence, as it still is, for when U'Ren, the blacksmith, is fashioning his legislative tools he works not alone with the affection of the true mechanic, but with the devotion of a faith that his laws will indeed deliver the people from bondage.

All his life William U'Ren had heard of liberty. His father's father lived in Cornwall on land leased for ninety-nine years; his mother's father on land leased for "three lives." That's why his father emigrated at seventeen, and his mother at ten, to the "land of the free." And one of William's first recollections of "American liberty" is of our war against slavery. His mother told stories of "poor little black children sold away from their mothers," and his father pointed out the power of the "slave interest." He realized the Power of Evil, that father did.

A strong, independent spirit, he wanted to work for himself. He was an expert mechanic. The son tells how once when they got a job together, he boasted of his father's skill, and the next time a piece of work came along calling for a master workman, the elder U'Ren was put to it. He did it to a turn "in one heat." So he

was in demand as "a hand," but he had a head
and he "hated a boss." He wouldn't stick to
a good job, no matter how good it was. He
must "move on," seeking liberty — freedom to
do his own work in his own way. He couldn't.
The best pay for a blacksmith was in big organizations like the copper mines of Lake Superior.
He tried farming. He led his family West,
from Wisconsin to Nebraska; over into Colorado; back to Wisconsin; down again to Wyo-
ming and Colorado. It was no use. Father
and sons, they all worked as only border farmers
work; they couldn't earn enough ahead to buy
their liberty; or, if they got a start, something set
them back.

U'Ren visualized one tragic day out of this life
for me. His father had taken up a homestead in
Nebraska, and they had made a farm of it. William
remembers halting, on his way to town one morning, to look back from a hill over the rich, yellow
level of their crops spread out under the sun.
When he came home that afternoon, he stopped,
stunned, on that same hill-top. The sun still
shone, but the homestead, the whole country,
was bare and brown. The boy understood then
what one of the plagues of Egypt was. The
grasshoppers had passed, a cyclone of them.
and in four hours the U'Rens were ruined.

"I was brought up in the fear of the poor,"
U'Ren says, "the terrible fear of poverty." But
not in hate; at least, not in the hatred of men.
"Things make men do bad things," he says.
He does not believe in bad men and good men,
and, as we shall see, he deals placidly with both
kinds. "Conditions are to blame for all evil,"
he pleads patiently, "conditions that can be
changed." His father, who pointed out conditions to him, taught him also to fight. But he
was to fight for justice, not for hate.

Since the family moved about so much, William
seemed always to be "the new boy" at school.
The others picked on him. He was still a child,
quick-tempered, but not aggressive. And the
first time he was tempted to fight, when he was
seven years old, he took his mother's counsel
that only

> "Dogs delight to bark and bite;
> It is their nature to."

William didn't fight. But when, not long
after that, at Nevadaville, Colorado, Davie
Radcliffe called Willie U'Ren a liar, Willie con-
sulted his father. The father reflected a moment,
then said in a way the boy never forgot:

"Never hunt a fight, boy, but never run from
one; never suffer wrong or injustice."

The next day Willie U'Ren hunted the fight

he had avoided. He found Davie; Davie didn't care to fight then. But another boy accommodated Willie. Johnnie Badger, the fighter of the school, licked Willie that day; and the next; and the next. Willie came back for his daily licking till his father happened to hear of it.

"What's the matter, William?" he asked. "Can't you lick that boy?"

"Not yet," said William, "but I will some day."

The father took his boy in hand, taught him how to use his fists and — Willie went to school and licked Johnnie Badger. "And then," U'Ren says, "we became good friends."

A salient trait of U'Ren, the man, is his perfect self-possession. His father developed that in him. One day William was sent to a neighbour's for a set of double-trees for a wagon. He hitched a trace to it and, letting his horse drag it home, lost one of the clevis pins. His father rebuked him sharply, and William flew into one of his violent but infrequent passions. His father was silent. He didn't want to break the boy's spirit; he waited till William "felt bad." They were haying together then, and at one of the pauses to rest the father talked quietly about self-control. One must learn to govern one's self, he said, and he concluded: "If *you* don't, William, *you* might *kill*."

No one who meets W. S. U'Ren now could believe that he ever had a temper. It took time, but the character-building done for the boy both by his parents and by himself was good work well done. And his mental development was still more interesting. Though his father's discontent kept the conditions of their life critically before him, there was no understanding of causes. The family read "Greeley's Paper," and both father and son followed politics. But the first definite sense of the economic problems underlying politics came to William himself when he was hardly thirteen. The farmers in the Nebraska district where his father had his homestead, needing a school, met to devise ways of making the absentee land-owners pay for it.

"It seemed to me, as a boy," U'Ren says now, "that something was wrong in this. If it was right for those non-voting landholders to own the land, it was wrong to tax them for the school they did not use. Or, if it was right to tax them, it was wrong for them to hold the land they did not use. I puzzled over this, but I could not put my finger on the injustice I felt lurking somewhere."

He never spoke of this. He was a solitary soul, as his sports show. He didn't dance, nor even play much. He liked to hunt and think, to work

and think, to read and — dream. While he
learned his trade, and learned to love it, and
while he worked the farm and took pride in his
straight rows of corn, his ambition ran off to
politics. But not to the game. Congress was
his goal. That was where the lawgivers gathered.
To fit himself to make laws, he must study law
and, in Denver, he entered an office as a student,
but not with the idea of making law his career.
One of the firm, Merrick A. Rogers, encouraged
U'Ren there. "Money-getting isn't a very high
object, not for a life," he used to say. And despite his terror of poverty, U'Ren has always
regarded the practice of his profession as a secon-
dary consideration. He is a legislator.

Politics comes first with U'Ren. He makes
his living with his left hand; his right is for the
state. And that such citizenship can be effective
is demonstrated by this remarkable fact: The
Father of the Initiative and Referendum, the first
legislator of Oregon, has held office but once in
his career. He has done what he has done as a
citizen in politics.

His first experience of the game was in Denver
when he was a law student. The Presidential
campaign of 1880 was on and U'Ren had just
come of age. The Republican party needed the
help of all good men and true, and first-voters

were invited to work. U'Ren volunteered. He offered his services with the enthusiasm of youth and the fervour of that secret inspiration of Moses. And the leaders welcomed the boy. They put him to work. They directed him to aid in colonizing voters in a doubtful ward!

U'Ren was stunned. He did not know such things were done. He was horrified, but fascinated. He said nothing; he didn't do the work, but he hung about watching it done. The dreamer was allowed to see the inside. There were anti-Chinese riots in the town. The mob marched through the streets crying "The Chinese must go!" and threatening to kill them. U'Ren became excited. Here was oppression of the weak. At his request, he was appointed a deputy to "protect the poor Chinamen," and he served in all earnestness till an insider explained to him that the mob was organized and the riots were faked — to get the good citizens out to the polls to vote for "law and order and the Republican party."

The elders forget how young people feel when they first discover that the world isn't what schools and grown-ups have taught them. It would be better to teach the truth; then the new citizens would be prepared for the fray. As it is, the sudden shock carries away not only the "illusions," but more often the character of youth. Not so with U'Ren, however. His dream of Congress vanished, but his hope of inventing laws to make such evils less easy and profitable — that stayed. Indeed, this was the time when the dominant idea of his life took its first definite form.

"As I watched this fraud, and saw that it was the means by which the other evils were maintained, I felt clearly that a modicum of the thought and ingenuity which had been devoted to machinery, if given to government, would make this a pleasant world to live in. That men were all right at bottom, I was convinced, for I noticed that we young men were honest and capable of some unselfish service. It was the older men that were 'bad.'"

Sickness befell U'Ren, a long, lingering, weakening illness, that took all the sand out of him. He was admitted to the bar, and practised long enough to see the trickery and the injustice of the Law. He edited a newspaper at Tin Cup, a mining town, but he saw that that business had its frauds, too, and that the editor is no freer than his father, the blacksmith, was. So he quit, and began just such a wandering life as his father had led. In pursuit of liberty and health, he moved about from Denver to Iowa, back to

Colorado, on to California, the Hawaiian Islands, and Oregon, and back, getting better and worse till 1889-90, when something happened; something for which these wander-years and his whole life and his father's had prepared him.

He read "Progress and Poverty." It is wonderful how many of the men who are working for political reform got their inspiration from Henry George. "I am for men," George said, and he made men. No matter what the world may decide to do about his single tax, some day it will have to acknowledge that Henry George brought into the service of man more men of more different kinds than any other man of his day. U'Ren is not an orthodox single-taxer to-day; U'Ren cannot be classified economically at all; he thinks for himself. He read other books then; he reads other books now. Open-minded in the period when, as he says, "the hard conditions and selfish interests of life are ossifying most men," he never has been able to close up his mind. He is wide open to any truth from any source.

The way he started on his career as a legislator shows this. One day toward the end of his wander-years, as he was changing from the train to the boat on the Oakland (California) mole, somebody thrust into his hand a leaflet on

the "initiative." There was nothing about the
"referendum," and U'Ren had never heard of
either. But he had noticed that all the political
evils of all the cities and states, where he had
idly watched men defeat themselves, culminated
in the betrayal of the people by their representatives. And this leaflet showed how the people
themselves, outside of and over the heads of their
elected representatives, might initiate and pass
laws. Here was a tool for democracy; here was
a means to achieve the reforms Henry George
indicated. U'Ren determined then and there
to hammer this leaflet into a bill and pass it —
somewhere.

U'Ren didn't care where. The need of it
was universal in the United States. He thought
how useful it would be in Denver, in Iowa, in
Wisconsin; it was needed right there in California.
But he happened to be going to Oregon and —
that's how U'Ren came to be the lawgiver "of
Oregon."

The initiative — as a tool, remember; as a
means to an end; as a first political step toward
changing our economic conditions — this idea
gave purpose to his life. His health improved.
He went to Portland and, mousing around for
books and men, came upon E. W. Bingham.

"Ed. Bingham," U'Ren says, "was a lawmaker. He had the most wonderful constructive talent for law-building that I ever encountered."

Bingham was working with an Australian Ballot League. He was secretary, and he taught U'Ren to be secretary of things. "Never be president," he said. "Never be conspicuous. Get a president and a committee; and let them go to the front. The worker must work behind them, out of sight. Be secretary."

U'Ren has always been secretary; clerical, impersonal, but busy, like Bingham. He has given credit for all his work to other men. The first time I met him, he talked of leagues and committees of leading citizens — bankers, railroad men, corporation attorneys, corrupt politicians — whom he named. But I noticed that while the members of U'Ren's several committees knew something about their own work, they seldom knew anything about that of the other committees of which U'Ren was secretary; and when it came to precise information, they all would say, "You must see our secretary, a Mr. U'Ren, for that." A Mr. U'Ren was the one man in Oregon who knew all about all this legislation.

Well, Bingham had drawn the Australian ballot law for his league, and he talked it over, section by section, with U'Ren, who thus got from an expert his first lesson in law-building. The next thing was to pass it. U'Ren asked why they didn't get the platform committee of the Republican Convention to endorse the bill. Bingham laughed, and so did a senator who was present, but the dreamer "rushed in where angels feared to tread." You will hear to-day in Oregon that U'Ren is "the smoothest lobbyist" in the state, and he is. He is calm, conciliating, persistent; and he fits his argument to his man. He talked politics to that platform committee; he gave, not his reasons for wanting the Australian ballot, but arguments which appealed to these party politicians. And they listened. Then Bingham appeared. Unlike U'Ren, Bingham was aggressive. He came into the committee room with fire in his eye, bulldozing, begging, reasoning, and threatening. They could put off U'Ren; Bingham hung on like a bulldog, and in the end, they got his bill endorsed by the Republicans. Then they went to the Democratic Convention and there also they won. And the Legislature, thus pledged, adopted Bingham's Australian ballot.

Started thus first in the public service, U'Ren had still to make his living. About that time he fell in with an interesting group of people, the Luellings of Milwaukee (Oregon), orchardists and nurserymen. Seth developed the well-known cherries, "Bing" and the "Black Republican," which latter the South re-named the "Luelling." Seth and his wife, and Alfred Luelling, were live-minded people, and they gathered about them other active brains. They thought, and they read; they had lectures and they recited from the English poets. Lacking orthodox teachers, they guided themselves through studies ranging from economics to spiritualism. Unafraid of any new idea, they gave a welcome and a hearing to any apostle of any ism. U'Ren was well received among them. He was taken into partnership in the business. When that failed in the panic of 1893, there was a quarrel, and bitter feelings which endure to this day, but U'Ren says that his health, his heart, and his mind all were better for this life among these people.

It was here that he heard first of the referendum. They were all members of the Farmers' Alliance, and Alfred Luelling brought to a meeting one night J. W. Sullivan's book on direct legislation in Switzerland. It contained the whole set of tools of which, hitherto, U'Ren had heard of but one, the initiative. This would enable the people to make laws; the referendum would enable them to stop legislation initiated

by their legislators. U'Ren was enthusiastic;
the whole alliance was. With these tools, the
people could really govern themselves. And
that is what these people wanted; they were
Populists.

We' of the East despised the "Pops"; but
their movement was to the reform movement
of to-day what the "extreme" Abolitionists of
New England were to the great movement that
produced Lincoln and the Republican party.
U'Ren became a Populist. But that party was
to him — what the Republican party is to him
now; what any party must be to any man who has
in mind the good, not of an organization, but of
a people—a means to an end, an instrument, a
political tool. The "Pops" were sincere people
who wanted to change things for the better.
There was a use for them, and U'Ren, who saw
it, joined them and soon was secretary of the
Populist State Committee.

And when, as secretary of the Populists, he
had worked the initiative and referendum plank
into their platform, he went forth as secretary
of a Direct Legislation League to the conventions of the other parties. And he lobbied
initiative and referendum planks into the plat-
forms of all of them, excepting only the Prohibi-
tionists, who, like the Socialists, "won't play"

with anybody else. Having the parties pledged, he set about making them keep their promises. He lighted a fire behind them.

U'Ren went to the people. They were ready for him. The year was 1893. Discontent was widespread. Agitation had taken the form of a demand that the Legislature to be elected in 1894 should call a constitutional convention to rectify all evils, and U'Ren was one of the many workers who went about pledging candidates. But he and the Luellings concentrated on the "I. & R.," as they called the initiative and referendum. As secretary of the Direct Legislation League he got up a folder stating simply the democratic principle underlying the initiative and referendum and the results to be expected from it. Direct legislation was an acknowledgment of the right of the people to govern themselves and a device to enable them to do so. The "I. & R." would put it in the power of the voters to start or stop any legislation, just like a boss. In other words, it would make the people boss; the legislators would have to represent the voters who elected them, not railroads and not any other "interest." Nobody could object (openly) to this; at least, nobody would out there in that Western state where the failures of democracy were ascribed, not as in the East, to the people, but to the business and political interests that actually are to blame.

Everybody worked. The women sewed the folders; two-thirds of the houses in Milwaukee were thus engaged that winter (1893-94); they prepared 50,000 folders in English and 18,000 in German; and the alliances and labour unions saw that the voters got and read them. The effect was such that when the politicians pleaded ignorance of the initiative and referendum, U'Ren could answer: "The people know about them." And that was true. After the election, these same workers, men and women, circulated a petition which, with 14,000 signatures, was presented to the Legislature.

Now, that is as far as a reform movement usually goes. U'Ren went further. Knowing that the representatives elected by the people are organized in the Legislature to represent somebody else, U'Ren went to Salem as a lobbyist, a lobbyist for the people, and he talked to every member of that Legislature. He saw the chicanery, fraud, and the politics of it all, but he wrung from a clear majority promises to keep their pledge.

"And we lost," he told me quietly. "We lost by one vote in the House and in the Senate also — by one vote."

"Fooled?" I asked.

"Fooled," said U'Ren. "It was done in the Senate by a wink, a wink from Joe Simon" (president of the Senate and boss of Portland).

"You understood. How did you feel?"

"We were angry," U'Ren answered. "I completely lost my self-control and I said and did things that were wrong. And when I saw my mistake, I remembered what my father used to say about self-control, and I tied a string on my finger to remind me. That device of the children worked with me. I think I never afterward completely lost my temper."

The act which U'Ren calls his mistake was to go out from that Legislature to punish the members who had broken their pledges; and that is what I can't help believing must be done. But U'Ren is one of those very, very few men that believe, after these 2,000 years, in the Christian spirit as a *practical* force.

"Alfred Luelling first questioned the wisdom," he said, "of punishing faithless legislators. We talked it over and I thought a lot about it. And I decided that he was right. After that, we never again punished men. Of course, we voted against a delinquent, if the parties gave us a choice; but our policy was to publish, not a man's delinquencies, but his promises."

Coming from a practical politician, this is a

most important tip for reformers. And U'Ren is a practical politician. He learned something from that Legislature. Watching it as, when a boy, he watched Denver politics, open-eyed, he saw what he saw, and his mind, never taught to blink the facts, took in what his ears and eyes perceived. When he came home, he organized his county, and he organized it well. The "dreamer" became the boss of his (Clackamas) county, but he was not a selfish boss. This was his chance to realize his young dream of Congress. The Populists wanted him to go, but he knew now what Congress was, and "What could I have done against the combine that ran it?" he asked. "I could do nothing but protest at Washington," he added. "In Oregon I could get the initiative and referendum through."

So he ran for the assembly and was elected. This was in 1896. Bryan was running for President, and Oregon was a Free Silver state. Even Republicans like Senator Mitchell were for silver; they were called "Silver Republicans" just as in the East we had "Gold Democrats." The Populists elected thirteen assemblymen, the Democrats three, the Republicans forty-four; in the senate the Populists had three votes, the Democrats three, the Republicans twenty-four. And this is important because that Legislature never was organized; it was the famous hold-up session, a scandal yet in Oregon. And U'Ren was one of the managers of that hold-up. Oh, he had learned a lot of politics!

The demand for a constitutional convention was waning. Leaders like U'Ren realized that a convention might not be so amenable to public opinion as the Legislature, so he was for the initiative and referendum by legislative amendment. That would require the passage of the resolution through two legislatures in succession and then a vote by the people. This way looked long, but U'Ren, as a boy, had proven on Johnnie Badger that he was built to fight till he won. And he had a plan. He had seen in the last session how a delegation such as the "Pops" had now could be used to play politics with, and U'Ren had made up his mind to play politics — for the people. He began right after election.

Oregon at the time was in that primitive stage of corruption where personalities still played a part and any cash briber had a chance for high office. The railroads ruled, but the dominant road, the Southern Pacific, was a foreign corporation. Its bosses might have gone to the United States Senate from Oregon if they had lived there, but they were elected by California, so Oregon was open to its own rich men. And

many of them sought the "honour." They
paid out great sums trying to get it. The politicians told me that these bankers, editors and
business men were "played for suckers" year
after year; and any Oregonian will tell you with
a laugh the names of the victims of this long-
drawn-out comedy.

U'Ren understood this. In 1897 Senator
Mitchel was to be reëlected; U'Ren had no
doubt of that, and he called on him to trade
"Pop" votes for his help on the initiative and
referendum. Politician as he was, Mitchell
talked favourably in August, not at all in November, and just before the session, "went back on"
the measure entirely. He told U'Ren why.

"I've got three "Pop" votes that nobody can
get away," he said.

"Are you sure?" asked U'Ren, who could
hardly believe that the Populists, so new and so
enthusiastic, would surrender so soon to "the
conditions that make men bad."

Mitchell was sure; he advised U'Ren not to
introduce the bill. "My people won't stand
for it," the Senator said.

Mitchell had made one other shift of position.
A Silver Republican all through the Oregon
campaign (which ended in the June election),
he came out after it for McKinley and gold.

Some of his lieutenants left him, among them
Jonathan Bourne, Jr., a man we must know.
He is now a United States Senator from
Oregon. You have heard of black sheep? Well,
Jonathan Bourne was the black ram of a rich
old New England family. After a wild time at
Harvard University and a wilder time "about
town," he went West and had the wildest time
of all. I think U'Ren will not charge him up
to conditions; I've heard him say that Bourne
was improved by age. Bourne learned his game
from Mitchell, who learned his from Quay in
Pennsylvania, whence Mitchell came (after a
change of name). And the lesson of the Quay
school of politics was not to organize like Tammany for the year around, but to "let her rip"
till just before a campaign, then make a new
"combine."

When Mitchell made his gold "combine,"
Bourne made his new silver "combine" and —
U'Ren joined Bourne. Mitchell didn't have
the three Pop votes. U'Ren found that his delegation was solid, and ready to trade. All they
wanted was (1) the initiative and referendum,
(2) a good registration law (Ed. Bingham's),
and (3) Pop judges and clerks of elections.
Bourne wanted to be Speaker. He was willing
to swing his delegation to the Pop bills in return

for their votes for his speakership. This settled
the House; they looked to the Senate. The
President, Joe Simon, was the man who beat the
constitutional convention with a wink. No
matter. U'Ren wasn't punishing men. He
called on Simon. He knew Simon wanted to go
to the United States Senate. Simon didn't say
so. No. Simon's conversation suggested that
President Corbett of the First National Bank
would make a good Senator, but the politicians
understood that Corbett was "only Simon's
rich sucker." And so it turned out, for when,
later, Simon did control a legislature for Corbett,
Simon, not Corbett, was elected to the United
States Senate. But U'Ren wasn't interested in
senatorships. He believed that Simon would go
into a strong combine to beat Mitchell. And he
was right. Since the terms — U'Ren's "fool"
legislation and Bourne's speakership — were satisfactory, Simon delivered the Senate.

Does it begin to appear now how U'Ren got
his good laws in the bad state of Oregon? Do
you begin to understand why it was that "leading
citizens" and "corrupt politicians," the very men
who are against reform elsewhere, "passed all
these reform measures ascribed to U'Ren?" Most
of these men didn't know what they were doing,
and they didn't care. They wanted something

for themselves; U'Ren wanted something for the
people. On that basis, William U'Ren went
into every political deal that he could get into.

And that he was a factor to be reckoned with,
he proved right away. Quick, quiet, industrious,
he had his "combine" organized before Mitchell
woke up. The Simon-Bourne-Pop crowd captured the temporary organization of the House.
This they did by a snap. They weren't ready
to elect a United States Senator, and since the
election must be held, by law, on the second
Tuesday after the permanent organization was
effected, their play was to put off the election of
a Speaker. U'Ren himself made that play.
There was a contest over one seat in the House.
U'Ren was on the committee and he controlled
three of the five votes. He wouldn't report.
The minority, seeing the game, rushed back and,
reporting a row in the committee, caused a row
in the House. And a mad scene it was. The
Mitchell men rose in a rage and, all on their feet,
were crying "Fraud!" and demanding "Action."
When U'Ren arrived, his side, uninformed and
without a leader, was in a state of confusion.
They greeted him with a cheer and he took the
floor. Quietly, with great courtesy and unexpected ability, he met the attack. Everybody
else was excited. U'Ren alone was cool and, as

man after man arose to accuse him, he, with the papers they wanted in his pocket, answered with reason and with tact. And his self-possession soon possessed the House. "It is wonderful!" a woman spectator exclaimed. "Whenever that man speaks, you can feel a sense of quiet settle upon the whole House." Little known in the state and known to the politicians as "the dreamer," U'Ren's debate that night made him a reputation. The recollection of everybody present was vivid ten years afterward, when I inquired, but when I mentioned it to U'Ren, he smiled; he never fools himself.

"It is easy to make a reputation as a parliamentarian," he said, "when you have the chairman on your side."

He won out; that is what he recalls. He beat permanent organization that Monday night, and thus put off the senatorial vote for two weeks. And then followed, not two weeks, but a session, of bribery, drunkenness, hate, and deadlock. Men were bought, sold, and bought back again. Both sides used money fiercely; and since there was no appropriation bill, the members got from the state no salary, no mileage, nothing; they had to have money. Well, they got it. Bourne set up a private house, somewhat like the "House of Mirth" at Albany, N. Y., where he "kept" men·on his side. Mitchell ran the price of votes up to thousands of dollars, and he and his lieutenant, Charlie Fulton (later a United States Senator from Oregon), paid out the money in cash. The Pops caught them at it.

Johnson Smith, assistant warden of the Penitentiary, then a Pop assemblyman, proposed to go to Mitchell and take some of his money for evidence.

"Go ahead," said U'Ren. "We'll vouch for your purpose in doing it."

So Smith got from Mitchell and Fulton $1,500 as for himself, and $250 as for the go-between. The next day, when the Mitchell men were trying to gather a quorum, Smith stood outside in the lobby. Rushing up to him, Fulton ordered him to his seat. Smith laughed.

"Why! Aren't you going in?" said Fulton. And when Smith said he wasn't, Fulton flew into a rage. "Didn't you take our money and promise to go in?"

"Yes," said Smith, "I took your money. You were so damn fresh and free with it, I thought I'd take a piece. But it's you that's sold, not me."

There was more to this dialogue, but the sequel will interest the people of the United States who want to know about their United States Senators.

Governor (now U. S. Senator) Chamberlain of Oregon made an affidavit for Francis J. Heney to send to President Roosevelt, deposing and swearing that when Smith was under consideration for appointment to the penitentiary, Fulton protested on the ground, not that Smith had taken Mitchell's money, but that, having taken it, he had not stayed bought! Charles W. Fulton is fundamentally corrupt.

"No," says U'Ren. "That was in war time, and we mustn't judge men in the heat of battle by the standards of cold blood." But U'Ren is excusing the bribery of 1897; the Senator's protest to Governor Chamberlain was in 1903 — in cold blood. But never mind Fulton. How about U'Ren? That deadlock, which he helped to manage, lasted to the end. Nothing was accomplished; no Senator was elected, no legislation passed, and everybody concerned was under suspicion. U'Ren himself had charges to answer. He was accused of taking money from Bourne, and calling together the Pop committee, he admitted that he had borrowed $80. He had to, he pleaded. He had opened a law office in Oregon City, but a "country lawyer" in politics earns very little, and since there was no appropriation bill, he got no pay as an assemblyman. He earned none, he admitted, and he abided by that. For when the next Legislature voted full salaries and mileage to its predecessor, U'Ren and one other member, George Ogle, sent back their warrants. So he never did get any money for that time and, to exist, he had to borrow from Bourne. But the $80 was a loan, not a bribe; he has long since paid it back and, since he suggested the whole deal, the money did not affect his conduct. His committee exonerated U'Ren, but the transaction hurt him, and so did some letters of his which, published later, showed how he traded with the powers of evil; as he did — and as he went on doing — deliberately, in cold blood, as George Ogle knows.

George Ogle, farmer and Populist, is notoriously honest. He was U'Ren's best friend, and when in the fall of 1898 Ogle's mother died, he asked U'Ren to deliver the funeral address. The next day Ogle mounted his horse and rode back to town with U'Ren. It was a cold ride in the rain through slush, but they had a warm talk, those two. U'Ren had run for the Senate that summer against George C. Brownell, the Senator from Clackamas who, as chairman on the committee on railroads, had represented for years the corrupt system of Oregon in the Senate. He beat U'Ren, who turned right around and made a deal with him. U'Ren promised to help elect Brownell to any office he might choose to run for next time, if the Senator would work in good faith for the initiative and referendum. Ogle knew this because he was one of the "Pops" U'Ren had asked to join in his bargain. And Ogle had been thinking it over ever since, and now, out there in the mud and sleet of that country road, he asked U'Ren what the fight was to cost him, U'Ren.

U'Ren understood, and he answered, "I am going to get the initiative and referendum in Oregon," he said, "if it costs me my soul. I'll do nothing selfish, dishonest, or dishonourable, but I'll trade off parties, offices, bills — anything for that."

Ogle objected. "Good things are not worth that price," he said.

They were both thinking of Brownell, of course, and U'Ren said he had to deal with the men in office. "We can't choose our human instruments," he argued, "and we can't change political methods till we have passed some legal tools to do it with." And he recalled a story Ogle had told him once of a cattleman who discharged a cowboy because he returned from a search for some cattle with an explanation of his failure to find them. "I want my cattle, not your excuses," the cattleman said, and "that," said U'Ren, "is what the people say to us." It was the old question whether the end justifies the means.

They quarrelled over it, those two good friends. It was a quiet quarrel and it is being made up now, but they parted then for many years, Ogle returning to his farm, U'Ren to the lobby at Salem.

And U'Ren used the lobbyist's means to attain his end. He and Frank Williams watched their "friends" and made new ones. Brownell was true; also he was clever. He didn't pretend to believe in the "crank" measure. "I've got to vote for it," he would say to his "practical" colleagues. "My district is chock-full of 'Pops' and I have to placate them. And what does the initiative and referendum amount to anyway? It's got to go through two sessions. Pass it now and we can beat it next time." But Brownell's best service was in trading. Once, for example, Williams, one of Lincoln's old secret-service men, learned that two Senators were quarrelling over an appropriation for a normal school. U'Ren arranged through Brownell to get appropriations for both. Two normal schools for two "I. & R." votes! And it was either at this session or the next that U'Ren and his friends connived at what he calls a "vicious gerrymander."

"We helped through measures we didn't believe in," U'Ren says in his plain way, "to get help for our measures from members who didn't believe in them. That's corruption, yes; that's a kind of corruption, but our measures were to make corruption impossible in the end."

The "I. & R." passed in 1899, 44 to 8 in the House, 22 to 6 in the Senate. And U'Ren went on working. The moment the session closed, the Direct Legislation League (W. S. U'Ren, secretary) set about making it impossible for Brownell's friends to "beat it next time." U'Ren instructed the voters. The propaganda was systematic, thorough, complete, and the politicians knew it. And the politicians knew now that U'Ren's word was good, and his support worth having. So in 1901, when the measure came up for second passage, U'Ren, from the lobby and after more dickering, saw it go through unanimously. And at the next general election (1902) the people approved it, 11 to 1.

Thus it was, then, that the people of Oregon achieved actual sovereignty over their corrupted state — by the methods of corruption. What good has it done them? They have the power to change their constitution at will; to make laws and to veto acts of their Legislature, but laws and machinery are of no use to a people unless

there are leaders to apply them. The referendum
which U'Ren found in the charter of San Francisco was a dead letter; Heney didn't even know
it was there. And Heney's exposure of Oregon
came two years after U'Ren had his "I. & R."
In brief, to repeat the question raised at the beginning of our story, Why don't the people of
Oregon use their power to change the system?

The answer is, as before, "W. S. U'Ren."
He knows the "I. & R." is nothing but a tool;
that it is worth while only as it can be used to
change the "conditions that make men do bad
things"; and he means to use it. Indeed, he
proposed, when he got it, to proceed at once to
economic reforms. But wiser heads counselled
that, until the new instrument had been tempered
by custom, it would be better to use the "I. &
R." only to get other new tools. So the Direct
Legislation League gave way to a Direct Primary
League, and W. S. U'Ren, secretary, drew a bill
for the people to initiate that should enable them
to make their own nominations for office and thus
knock out the party machines. While this was
doing, a railroad planned a referendum to delay
a state road which the Chamber of Commerce
wanted, and the Chamber, in alarm, threatened
an initiative for a maximum rate bill. That
settled the railroad, pleased the business men

and showed *them* the use of the new tool. And when, in July, 1903, a circuit court declared the "I. & R." unconstitutional, there was backing for the tool. U'Ren was able to get Senator Mitchell, Brownell, and eight other political and influential corporation attorneys to appear before the Supreme Court, to defend the "I. & R.," which was sweepingly upheld.

The Direct Primary Bill was passed by the people in June, 1904, 56,000 to 16,000. A local option liquor bill was passed by initiative at the same time, and in November several counties and many precincts went "dry." U'Ren had nothing to do with this last, but he did have very much to do with another important enactment — the choice of United States Senators by direct vote of the people.

This radical reform was achieved without secrecy, but yet without much public discussion. It was a bomb planted deep in the Direct Primary Bill, and U'Ren planted it — with the help of Mitchell, Brownell, Bourne and two or three editors of newspapers. The idea occurred to U'Ren to write into the Primary bill a clause: that candidates for nomination for the Legislature "*may*" pledge themselves to vote for or against the people's choice for United States Senators, "regardless of personal or party preference." Mitchell helped to draw the clause, now famous as Statement No. 1, which legislators might sign, and he expected to be and, if Heney hadn't caught him grafting, he would have been elected on it without having to bribe legislators. U'Ren would have helped him. As it happened, Mulkey (for a short term of six weeks) and Bourne were the first Senators elected under the amazing law which hardly anybody but U'Ren realized beforehand the full effect of.

That Jonathan Bourne, Jr., should have been the first product of the popular election of Senators has been used to disparage this whole Oregon movement, but Bourne had backed all these reforms with work and money, and U'Ren says he is sincerely for them. But U'Ren tried to get another man to run, and turned to Bourne only when he was convinced that, to establish Statement No. 1 as a custom in Oregon, the first candidate must be a man rich enough to fight fire with fire if the legislators should be bribed to go back on their pledges. So, you see, U'Ren was still thinking only of the tool, and he won again. For the knowledge of Bourne's resources and character (and, also, a warning from the back country that the men with guns would come to Salem if their Legislature broke its pledge) did have its effect. The Legislature confirmed

Bourne without bribery and with only four votes against him.

The Direct Primary Law settled, a People's Power League was organized (W. S. U'Ren, secretary) to use the people's power, but U'Ren still stuck to tool making. Other reformers used the "I. &. R." for particular reforms. The Anti-Saloon League passed a local option bill; the State Grange enacted two franchise tax acts, which the Legislature had failed on; and U'Ren's league put through a constitutional amendment to cut out the state printer's graft. On the other hand, a graft bill to sell the state a toll road, another for woman's suffrage, and a liquor dealers' amendment to the local option bill were all beaten by referendum. But U'Ren and the League worked hardest for and passed, by initiative, bills extending the "I. & R." to cities and towns, and giving municipalities complete home rule — more tools. And so — next year, initiative bills were passed to let the people discharge any public officer of the state and choose his successor by a special election (this is the famous "recall"); a corrupt practice act; to make the people's choice of United States Senators mandatory; and, deepest reaching of all, proportional representation. All tools. There were referendum petitions out, also; two against ap-

propriations, one to make passes for public officials compulsory, another to beat a sheriff's graft.
But U'Ren was still after the tools.

But will this tool-making never be over?
"Yes," said U'Ren; and he added very definitely,
"Reform begins in 1910." And one proposition
in the list for 1908 showed what we may expect.
This was a bill "to exempt from taxation factory
buildings and machinery; homes and home im-
provements, but not the lots nor the farms."
Quietly worded though this was, the reform involved
is economic, and economic reforms are, as we
have seen, what U'Ren is after. And he will get
them, he and the people of Oregon. I believe
that that state will appear before long as the
leader of reform in the United States, and if it is,
W. S. U'Ren will rank in history as the greatest
lawgiver of his day and country.

But what about the man? What about reforms got as he has got his? It must be remembered, before passing judgment, that Oregon
was in that stage of corruption where the methods
were loose, crude and spontaneous. Perhaps
the condition I mean can best be brought home
by citing an agreement *written* by Harvey W.
Scott, the really great editor of that really great
newspaper, the *Oregonian* (and of its afternoon
edition, the *Telegram*), one night in 1903. There

was a contest on for United States Senator.
Scott had hopes. Bourne had had them, but he
had nothing left but a small minority of legislators. These he owned, however; they had cost
him $25,000. Scott wanted Bourne's legislators,
so on the last night of the session he wrote the
agreement printed below, and Wm. M. Ladd,
the leading banker of Portland, *wired* it (hence
the verbal errors) to Salem. Here it is:

"In case I receive Jonathan Bourne, Jr.'s,
support for United States Senator at the joint
session of the Legislature to-night, I hereby agree
to use the full power of the *Morning Oregonian*
and the *Evening Telegram* to defeat John H.
Mitchell at the next senatorial election, and elect
Jonathan Bourne, Jr., in his place.

"I further agree that if I receive the support
of Jonathan Bourne, Jr., for United States Senate
in the joint session of the Legislature to-night,
that if elected I will turn all the Federal patronage
over to Jonathan Bourne, Jr.

" I hereby further agree in lieu [view] of receiving the support of Jonathan Bourne to-night at
the joint session of the Legislature, that whether
elected or not, I will pay to Jonathan Bourne
$25,000 in United States gold coin."

Scott didn't get his senatorship; Brownell
threw it to Fulton, but that is neither here nor

there. Other contracts like this are in the
the safe-deposit vaults of Portland, and they
illustrate the state of corruption W. S. U'Ren
worked his reforms through. And all U'Ren
did was to trade, dicker, and connive. I've told
the worst of it — yes, practically all of it; and it
may not be considered as very bad; certainly it
never was selfish; but it was corruption. So I ask:

"Isn't U'Ren only *our* damned rascal?"

I put the question to U'Ren himself one day.
I was at his home, a small cottage on a point
of land that looks up the Willamettte River to the
famous Falls. One afternoon, when the country
lawyer was telling me his story, the "wrong as
well as the right of it," and we were in the midst
of one of his deals, his wife looked into the parlour
and asked him if he wouldn't get her some wood.
He rose and we went out to the wood-shed; and,
as he chopped, I said:

"How well off, are you, U'Ren?"

He rested his axe to answer: "I think," he said,
"that I am one of the richest men in Oregon."

"How is that? Have you made money?"

"My earnings average about $1,800 a year.
But that isn't what I mean. I haven't any
money, but I haven't any wants either, not for
myself."

"What about your conscience?" I persisted.

"What have those compromises with corruption cost you?"

"Nothing," he said. "I never have done a dishonest or a dishonourable thing."

"No, but you have made bargains with the devil to get him to pass your laws. You remember Moses? He also broke the covenants of the Lord, and you know what happened to him. He was taken up where he could see the Land of Promise, but he wasn't allowed to go over into it. Why won't it be so with you? You may have saved the people of Oregon, but haven't you lost your own soul? Won't you go to hell?"

He was looking down while I spoke, and he didn't see that I was speaking half in fun. Evidently he considered the prospect seriously, for after a moment, he looked up steadily at me, and in even tones answered out of his deliberation.

"Well," he said, "I would *go* to hell for the people of Oregon!"

THE END

INDEX

AMERICANA LIBRARY

The City: The Hope of Democracy
By Frederic C. Howe
With a new introduction by Otis A. Pease

Bourbon Democracy of the Middle West, 1865-1896
By Horace Samuel Merrill
With a new introduction by the author

*The Deflation of American Ideals: An Ethical Guide
for New Dealers*
By Edgar Kemler
With a new introduction by Otis L. Graham, Jr.

Borah of Idaho
By Claudius O. Johnson
With a new introduction by the author

The Fight for Conservation
By Gifford Pinchot
With a new introduction by Gerald D. Nash

Upbuilders
By Lincoln Steffens
With a new introduction by Earl Pomeroy

The Progressive Movement
By Benjamin Parke De Witt
With a new introduction by Arthur Mann

*Coxey's Army: A Study of the
Industrial Army Movement of 1894*
By Donald L. McMurry
With a new introduction by John D. Hicks

Jack London and His Times: An Unconventional Biography
By Joan London
With a new introduction by the author